ET 31506

**Neutralizing
Inmate Violence**

Series on Massachusetts Youth Correction Reforms

Center for Criminal Justice
Harvard Law School

- Reforming Juvenile Corrections: The Massachusetts Experience by Lloyd E. Ohlin, Robert B. Coates and Alden D. Miller

- A Theory of Social Reform: Correctional Change Processes in Two States by Alden D. Miller, Lloyd E. Ohlin and Robert B. Coates

- Diversity in a Youth Correctional System: Handling Delinquents in Massachusetts by Robert B. Coates, Alden D. Miller and Lloyd E. Ohlin

- Designing Correctional Organizations for Youths: Dilemmas of Subcultural Development by Craig A. McEwen

- Neutralizing Inmate Violence: Juvenile Offenders in Institutions by Barry C. Feld

Neutralizing Inmate Violence

Juvenile Offenders in Institutions

Barry C. Feld
University of Minnesota

Center for Criminal Justice
Harvard Law School

Ballinger Publishing Company • Cambridge, Massachusetts
A Subsidiary of J.B. Lippincott Company

 This book is printed on recycled paper.

Prepared under grant numbers 72-NI-99-00096, 73-NI-99-00556, and 74-NI-99-0176 in the National Institute of Law Enforcement and Criminal Justice, grant numbers 76-JN-99-0003 and 76-JJ-99-0452 in the National Institute of Juvenile Justice and Delinquency Prevention, both in the Law Enforcement Assistance Administration, U.S. Department of Justice, and under grant numbers 71-35X-905A1, 71-35X-905A0, 73C-060,231, 74C-084,2332, and 75C-047,2391 in the Massachusetts Committee on Criminal Justice, and with help from the Center for Criminal Justice using funds from Ford Foundation grant 690-0122. Points of view or opinions stated are those of the authors and do not necessarily represent the official position of the U.S. Department of Justice, the Massachusetts Committee on Criminal Justice, or the Ford Foundation.

Copyright © 1977 by Ballinger Publishing Company. All rights reserved. No part of this publication may be reproduced, stored in a retrieval system, or transmitted in any form or by any means, electronic mechanical photocopy, recording or otherwise, without the prior written consent of the publisher.

International Standard Book Number: 0-88410-790-6

Library of Congress Catalog Card Number: 77-21389

Printed in the United States of America

Library of Congress Cataloging in Publication Data

Feld, Barry C
  Neutralizing inmate violence.

  (Series on Massachusetts youth correction reforms)
  Bibliography: p.
  Includes index.
   1. Juvenile delinquency—Massachusetts. 2. Juvenile corrections—Massachusetts. 3. Subculture. 4. Prison violence—Massachusetts. I. Title. II. Series.
HV9105.M4F44   365',42'09744   77-21389
ISBN 0-88410-790-6

To Patricia, Effie, and a dream . . .

Contents

List of Figures and Tables	ix
Foreword	xi
Preface	xv
Author's Note	xxv

Chapter 1
Subcultural Violence, the Institutions,
and the Inmates — 1

The Institutional Setting	5
The Research Design	18
Background Characteristics of Cottage Inmates and Staff	23
Summary	38

Chapter 2
Organizational Structure and Program
Characteristics of the Cottages — 39

Staff Ideology and Goals	42
Cottage Programs and Social Control Strategies	59
Summary	88

viii Contents

Chapter 3
The Inmate Subcultures   91

Theories of Subculture Formation	91
Inmate Perceptions of Cottage Purpose	95
Problems of Adjustment and Motives for Exploitation	102
Inmate Cooperation with Inmates or Staff: Opportunities to Resolve Problems of Adjustment	107
Inmate Perceptions of Staff	107
Inmate Perceptions of Other Inmates	114
Inmate Adaptations	116
Solidarity	123
Summary of Inmate Perceptions and Subcultural Adaptations	126

Chapter 4
Social Structure of the Inmate Subculture   131

Violence and Aggression	131
Informing	138
Other Indicators of Subcultural Normative Orientation	143
The Inmate Subcultures: Discussion and Conclusions	163

Chapter 5
The Presenting Culture: The Influence of Sex and Race on Subcultural Adaptation   171

Sex-Linked Differences	172
Race-Linked Differences	180

Chapter 6
Outcome and Conclusions: Institutional Treatment and the Differences It Makes   189

Appendix	207
Notes	213
Bibliography	229
Index	237
About the Author	241

List of Figures and Tables

FIGURES

2-1	Correctional Typology	41
2-2	Cottage Position within the Organizational Typology	56

TABLES

1-1	Mean Age of Cottage Residents and Percentage Over Age 16	25
1-2	Percentage of Black Inmates	25
1-3	Mean Age of First Contact with Juvenile Court	27
1-4	Offenses for which Inmates Are Presently Committed	28
1-5	Seriousness of Inmates' Current Offenses	29
1-6	Prior Institutional Experience	31
1-7	Cottage Staff Characteristics	35
1-8	Cottage Population and Staff-Inmate Ratio	37
2-1	Selected Indicators of Staff Ideology and Goals	44
3-1	Inmate Perceptions of Cottage Goals	98
3-2	Coded Interview Response: "What do you think this place is supposed to do for you?"	100
3-3	Coded Interview Response: "What's the toughest part of being here?"	103
3-4	Inmate Perceptions of Staff	109
3-5	Inmate Contacts with Staff	112
3-6	Inmate Perceptions of Other Inmates	115
3-7	Inmate Adaptations	118

3-8	Coded Inmate Response: "What do you have to do to get a parole or a weekend?"	121
3-9	Inmate Solidarity	125
4-1	Inmate Views on Informing	140
4-2	Inmate Subculture Orientation	144
4-3	Inmate Leadership Characteristics	149
6-1	Deviant and Conventional Orientation	190
6-2	Inmate Self-Concept	192
6-3	Percentage of Inmates Recidivating	195
A-1	Correlation Matrix: Respect for Authority	212

Foreword

During the seven-year period from 1969 to 1976, some of the most sweeping reforms in youth corrections in the United States took place in Massachusetts. The state's Department of Youth Services became a highly visible national symbol of a new approach to juvenile corrections through its repudiation of training schools and its advocacy of community-based services. Over the same period the study of these reforms by the Center for Criminal Justice, Harvard Law School, generated a detailed and extensive body of data about the processes of change and their impact. The five books that make up this series are based on that data. In a time of increasing concern about the extent and seriousness of youth crime, this work is of special importance. The books are intended not only to constitute a comprehensive case study but also to explore significant issues of theory and policy and to present an analytic record of experience that will serve as a useful guide to other states that seek to improve the effectiveness of their youth corrections system. More broadly, these books provide important insights into the process and problems of effecting change in human service agencies.

*   *   *

Traditional public training schools have been the focus of criticism for several decades, with attacks coming from three major sources. First, critics have argued that these institutions are partly responsible for high rates of recidivism because of their criminalizing effects on the young people who emerge from them. A second source of criticism has come from proponents of treatment ideologies. They argue that counseling and therapy should replace traditional custodial care, and that youthful offenders should be dealt with at home and in their communities. A third challenge to training schools has come from advocates of the civil rights of children, and has focused on due process, the "right to treatment," and the "right to be left alone." These challenges have put strains on the correctional systems in many states and have raised important questions about whether programs can help young people and still meet a community's demand for protection.

These questions were confronted during a period of crisis, reform, and reaction in Massachusetts correctional policy that made the state a unique site for observation and evaluation. It was at the beginning of this period that the Harvard Center for Criminal Justice inaugurated its study of the reform process. A brief review of the events surrounding the Massachusetts reforms will allow for a better perspective on the scope of this project.

* * *

A series of crises in youth correctional services in Massachusetts was followed in 1969 by the resignation of the long-time Director of Youth Services who had strongly supported the use of traditional training schools. Recidivism rates for youth ranged from 40 to 70 percent, and investigations of the system, with accompanying newspaper coverage of its dramatic shortcomings, led civic and professional groups and the public to support reforms.

When Francis Sargent became Governor in 1969, he expressed his strong support for reforming youth services. In the fall of that year he appointed a new commissioner, Dr. Jerome Miller, to head a reorganized Department of Youth Services. Miller took charge with a mandate from the legislative and executive branches of state government and from liberal reform groups to develop new programs, although the scope of the mandate was broad and undefined.

For the first two years Miller sought to create a humanized and therapeutic climate within the existing institutions. Visible symbols of the old system such as dress and haircut requirements were abandoned. This raised a storm of protest from old-line staff who resented such attacks on their absolute control. Miller's order not to strike a youth brought similar outcries. In the early months Miller's efforts were hampered by financial limitations and the tradition-minded bureaucracy he inherited. Nonetheless, by the spring of 1971 Miller and his new planning unit had prepared a reform plan which focused on decentralized, community-based treatment centers—both residential and non-residential.

These moves were met with resistance from the adherents of the old philosophy. Many of them were close to influential legislators and community leaders in the small towns close to the training schools. And they had relationships with judges, probation officers, and public officials, many of whom shared their views about the proper function of the training schools. During his first two years, Miller was faced with two legislative investigations of his reforms.

Meanwhile, Miller decided that therapeutic communities could not be run successfully in the existing institutions, particularly in view of the resistance from old guard personnel. In the most dramatic stage of the reform process, he moved to close the old training schools, to establish a network of decentralized community-based services, and virtually to end locked facilities for youth. He took steps to establish a structure more closely tied to community life: regionalization of services; new court liaisons; diagnostic and referral policies; individual case decisions; the monitoring of services increasingly purchased from private agencies; and staff development programs to reassign, retrain, or discharge former personnel.

Suddenly in January 1973, after three hectic years of change, Miller resigned to become the new director of Family and Children's Services in Illinois. He believed that administrators initiating major reforms invariably become expendable because the hostility which focuses on them creates a barrier to completing the process of reforms and that a new commissioner could best finish the job. When Miller left, financial and personnel problems had not yet been resolved, and a new system of residential and non-residential services had not yet fully replaced the old.

Under Miller's successors as Commissioner, Joseph Leavey and John Calhoun, the Department has consolidated the new network of community-based programs and resolved many of its administrative problems. It has had to contend, however, with a sizable amount of public counter-reaction, including strong pressure to increase the availability of secure facilities to the courts.

Massachusetts has demonstrated that radical changes in official ideology and programs can be achieved over a comparatively short period of time, but the traditional training school system that existed in Massachusetts is still the dominant pattern throughout the country. In light of this situation, it is clear that the Massachusetts reforms, and the political and organizational upheavals that accompanied them, have presented to policy makers and scholars a rich opportunity to study a crucial issue in human services and to learn something as well about complex change in process.

The Center for Criminal Justice at Harvard Law School has taken advantage of this opportunity for the past seven years. This project was undertaken shortly after the Center was established. One of our principal goals in creating the Center was to engage in major empirical projects that would provide data and analytical insights to guide policy makers in the administration of criminal justice. The work reflected in this series of books has been the largest by far of our projects. Under the leadership of Professor Lloyd Ohlin a remarkable group of scholars—the authors of the books in this series—have combined their varied backgrounds and skills to make a major advance in knowledge and theory in a field that has traditionally been dominated by fads, fashions, and untested dogma. This collaborative effort by Ohlin, Miller, Coates, Feld, and McEwen had the benefit of the work of a fine supporting staff and profited from the advisory and critical roles played by other staff members of the Center, our Criminal Justice Fellows and visiting Research Fellows.

Only time tells which intellectual undertakings have a major impact on the development of social institutions. I can only record my sense that this volume—and the others in the series—reflect a rare convergence of a fascinating and significant set of social changes with the tireless, objective and imaginative efforts of a unique group of scholars.

James Vorenberg
Harvard Law School

Preface

This project began in the winter of 1969–70 in anticipation of major reforms in the Massachusetts youth correctional system. From a personal standpoint it represented a fresh opportunity to study two important correctional problems previously explored to some degree in two separate projects: the process and impact of significant changes in correctional policy and the relationship between the organizational structure of correctional programs and peer group subcultures among inmates. An earlier opportunity to study the first issue, change in correctional organizations, occurred from 1953 to 1956 when I directed a study at the University of Chicago of a major change in the Wisconsin prison probation and parole system as a consequence of transfer of corrections to the welfare system. This project, supported by the Russell Sage Foundation, was carried out with the assistance of Donnel M. Pappenfort and Herman Piven and, in the final year, Donald R. Cressey. It yielded many insights into problems of organizational change and the internal dynamics of prison life which have found reflection at various points in the present study. Extensive use has been made of the Wisconsin data to test the generalizability of new theoretical perspectives developed in the analysis of the Massachusetts data and reported most fully in the second book in the series, Miller *et al.*, *A Theory of Social Reform*.

An earlier opportunity to undertake a comparative analysis of the second issue, relating to the effect of organizational differences on peer group subcultures and inmate response to program intervention, occurred from 1957 to 1960 when I codirected with Richard A. Cloward at Columbia University a study of a public and private training school for boys in New York State. The results of this project were never fully developed but generated theoretical insights which were incorporated into our book on *Delinquency and Opportunity* (1960), and into the program of Mobilization for Youth project on the Lower East Side of Manhattan. The Massachusetts data has provided an excellent opportunity to explore much more intensively the sources of subcultural variation, and the books by Feld and McEwen report the results of this objective. In addition, more probing study of inmate response to programs was possible through the analysis of cohort data reported in the volume by Coates *et al.*

Initial explorations in 1969 utilizing staff and fellows of the Center for Criminal Justice led to intensive participant observation and formal interviewing of Department of Youth Services staff and youth in the summer of 1970. The direction of the total project crystallized when I was joined by my associates Alden Miller, late in 1970, and Robert Coates, in 1971. Barry Feld, who had been one of the observer-interviewers in 1970, directed a subculture study in selected institutional cottages in the summer of 1971. This type of study was extended to the community-based programs of the deinstitutionalized system by Craig McEwen in the summer of 1973. Barbara Stolz, who participated in the subculture study of the summer of 1971, began in 1972 a doctoral study of the state-level political process external to DYS. This study was complemented by a parallel dissertation analysis of organizational and political process in the central office of DYS by Arlette Klein.

In approaching the project as a whole, Miller, Coates and I developed a general conceptual framework, an observation guide which was employed throughout most of the study, and a system-oriented strategy of program evaluation. While we worked closely as a team, sharing most decisions in a collegial fashion, there was some specialization in terms of principal interest. I was particularly interested in the construction of a case analysis of the entire reform effort and its relevance to broader trends of correctional policy. Miller was especially interested in the system-wide analysis of the process of change, with an emphasis on the effectiveness of interest group tactics. Coates was particularly concerned with issues of program evaluation in the context of active change, and in the conceptualization of community-based corrections.

During the course of the Harvard study, seventeen separate data-gathering efforts took place, focusing on recidivism, program dynamics, the relations between youth and correctional staff in various settings, and the politics of the reform and counter-reform movements. These components of the overall study are shown in the accompanying diagram in relation to the major historical events of the reform. They combine variously in the present series to form the perspectives from which the authors of the five books viewed the day-to-day reform process in the Massachusetts youth correctional system and in other systems that faced similar upheavals. Each book has important implications for the study, promotion, or restraint of change in other social service settings as well. As briefly summarized here, they range from the most comprehensive perspective to the most particular.

Reforming Juvenile Corrections: The Massachusetts Experience (Ohlin, Coates & Miller) provides a description and analysis of the entire Massachusetts youth correctional reform process and a comparative assessment of the effectiveness of successive correctional policies. The presentation sets the analysis in the context of ideological conflicts about youth in trouble. We discuss successive phases of the reform process and the conditions leading to it, using an analytical structure that guides narrative development and critical discussion while employing data from all seventeen components of the Harvard study. We thus seek to explain from a broad policy perspective not only why and how the changes occurred but what effects they had on youth, staff, and other involved groups.

The series proceeds to a more detailed analysis of the process of change. *A Theory of Social Reform: Correctional Change Processes in Two States* (Miller, Ohlin & Coates) draws extensively on classic sociological literature while using the events in Massachusetts and the earlier correctional reform movement in Wisconsin to develop a conceptual model that identifies key interest group constellations, their critical characteristics and interrelationships, and the dimensions of their impact upon correctional systems. Conclusions based on an analysis of largely qualitative data are tested in the development of a mathematical simulation. The book addresses policy issues centering on ways to promote or hinder reform.

The diversity of programs developed during the reform years offered a natural laboratory for the testing of policy. As some five hundred youths moved through the complex network of Massachusetts correctional programs, including non-residential programs, foster care, forestry, group homes, boarding schools, secure programs, and adult jails, the research staff followed and documented their progress. In *Diversity in a Youth Correctional System: Handling Delinquents in Massachuestts* (Coates, Miller & Ohlin), both the short-run and long-run impact of such program sequences become

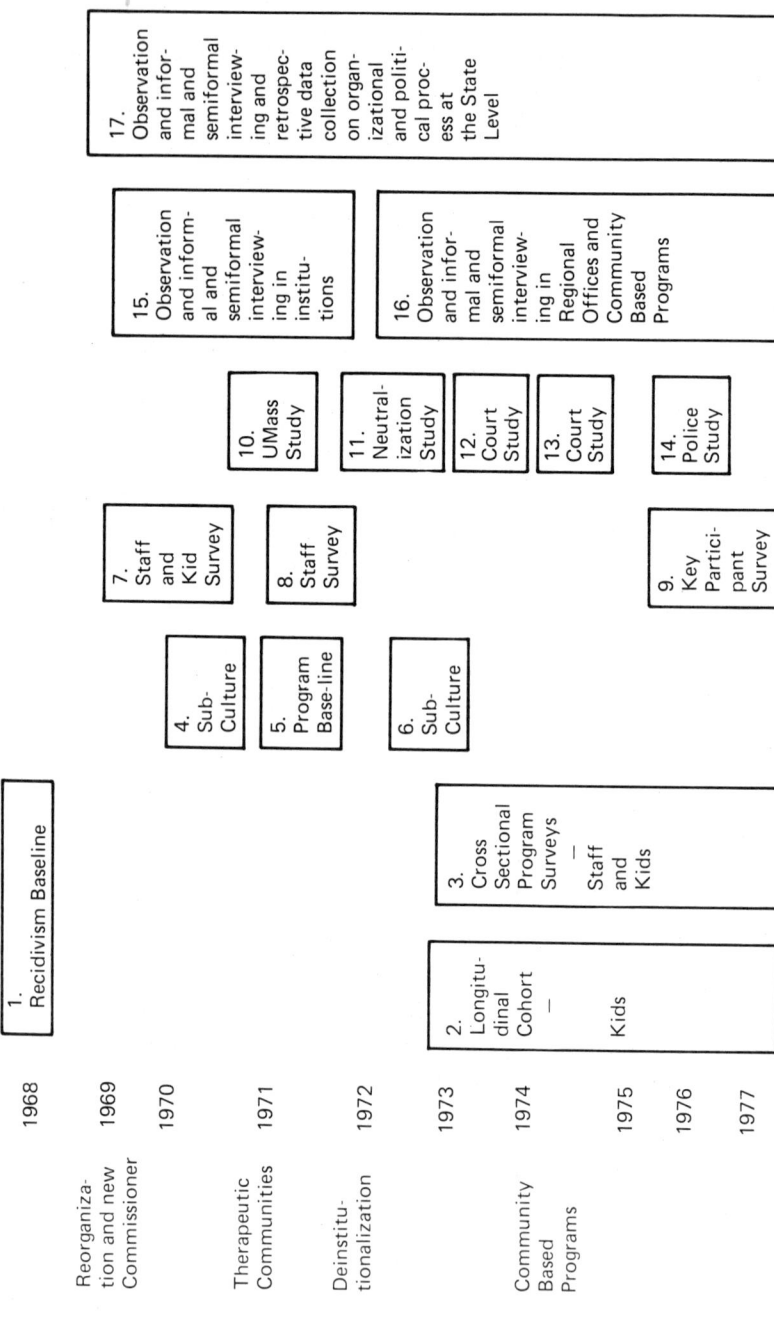

Components of the Study

1. *Recidivism Baseline:* A study of official records of youth paroled before the reforms to provide a comparison baseline for recidivism of youth passing through the new programs.
2. *Longitudinal Youth Cohort:* Repeated interviewing of youth at different points in their progress through the system from intake to return to the community, along with official records checks of recidivism for comparison with the recidivism baseline.
3. *Cross-Sectional Program Surveys, Staff and Youth:* Interviews to further characterize programs through which youth in the cohort had to pass.
4. *Subculture, 1971:* Interviewing and participant observation in selected programs before the closing of the institutions.
5. *Program Baseline:* Interviewing in institutions immediately prior to the closing.
6. *Subculture, 1973:* Interviewing and participant observation in selected programs after the closing of the institutions.
7. *Staff and Youth Survey:* Interviewing in institutions during the first year after reorganization.
8. *Staff Survey:* Informal interviews of remaining staff in the institutions after most of them had already closed.
9. *Key Participant Survey:* Interviews of staff throughout the reform system after consolidation of the reforms.
10. *University of Massachusetts Study:* Interviews and observation at the University of Massachusetts conference used to place youth taken from the closing institutions.
11. *Neutralization Study:* Interviews with participants and observation of the process of setting up group homes in specific communities, during which attempts were made to neutralize community resistance.
12. *Court Study, 1973:* Interviews and observation to assess the interface between the courts and the Department of Youth Services.
13. *Court Study, 1974:* Continuation of Court Study of 1973.
14. *Police Study:* Interviews, questionnaires, and observation to assess the interface between the police and potential DYS youth.
15. *Observation and Informal and Semiformal Interviewing in Institutions:* Monitoring of the day-to-day process.
16. *Observation and Informal and Semiformal Interviewing in Regional Offices and Community-Based Programs:* Monitoring of the day-to-day process.
17. *Observation and Informal and Semiformal Interviewing and Retrospective Data Collection of Organization and Political Processes at the State Level:* Monitoring of the day-to-day process.

clearly visible through quantitative analysis of longitudinal data characterized by approximately 2,500 variables. By synthesizing and cross-testing various theoretical perspectives on the youth correctional process, we were able to focus important policy issues concerning the quality of life within programs and the extent and quality of linkages to the community, all of which vitally affect the youths' future relationship to society.

A detailed look at the problems of both innovative and more traditional youth program settings is provided in *Designing Correctional Organizations for Youths: Dilemmas of Subcultural Development* (McEwen). Using participant observation and survey methods the author contrasts ten institutional program settings for youth with thirteen others that were part of a community-based system developed to replace the training school system. In calling upon a range of settings unusual in previous subcultural research, McEwen presents a detailed analysis of day-to-day interaction patterns that reflect different policies of community contact, egalitarianism, youth participation in decision-making, degree of supervision, and selection of youth with special background characteristics. These policies and patterns of interaction are then related to outcomes in youth subcultural beliefs, youth behavior, and the relations between youth and staff.

The final volume in the series, *Neutralizing Inmate Violence: Juvenile Offenders in Institutions* (Feld), focuses on a subset of ten program settings for youth, ranged across a custody-treatment continuum within the confines of training school institutions. In this more intensive look at a traditional group of institutions, also used for other comparative purposes in the preceding volume by McEwen, participant observation and survey methods are combined to examine in closer perspective the connection between the official correctional organization and inmate subcultures. The study explores ways of creating diverse patterns of official programs and subcultural responses within the confines of the same institution. Feld focuses sharply on policy issues concerning organizational means for the control of violence in institutional settings and contributes to more general theory of complex organizations.

The series thus offers an opportunity to examine a broad range of theoretical and practical concerns, the interrelationships of which are virtually impossible to perceive in a less comprehensive study. The project was originally designed to do this and was supplemented by special studies as new issues and problems developed in the reform process.

Since the Massachusetts study focused on controversial issues, every effort was made to encompass as wide a range of perspectives on these issues as possible. The theoretical structure of the project was designed to articulate the different interests that coalesced into support or criticism of various reform measures or their consequences. This led us to search out persons holding widely divergent views and, where necessary, to undertake special studies of some groups like judges and police to make sure their perspectives were adequately represented. Our own research staff was composed in such a way as to assure sympathetic understanding of opposing points of view. In fact we encountered the common research experience of staff identification with their respondents, particularly in the course of participant observation. This required special attention to the problem of achieving a balanced assessment over-all by having a variety of interviewers collect data on the same topics.

It should be kept in mind that problems of change and policy implementation in youth corrections have much in common with problems in other human service organizations—adult corrections, mental health, retardation, and welfare social services. The theories and strategies of change, the methods of evaluating service systems and the development and implementation of new policies represent forms of knowledge and insight of equal utility and transferability to these other types of service organizations.

A large number of people have been involved in this study between its inception and the completion of the manuscripts in this series. In addition to Ohlin, Miller, Coates, Feld, McEwen, Stolz, and Klein, whose roles were described above, there has been a large field staff ranging at times up to twenty people. It is not possible to fully state our indebtedness to the dedication and enterprise the field staff displayed or to acknowledge fully their contribution. Here we can only list their names:

Nathaniel Ackerman
Henry J. Albach IV
Wendy S. Allen
Mark E. Ashburn
Ira M. Baline
William Bazzy
Bonnie B. Boswell
Judith H. Caldwell
Robert Chilvers
Roy Cramer
Diane C. Engster
Finn-Aage Engster
John R. Faith

Elizabeth Farrell
Robert Fitzgerald
John H. Fleming
Gail Garinger
David D. Garwood
Paula A. Garwood
Geoffrey Ginis
Preston B. Grandin
John Greenthal
Nancy Hall
Elinor C. Halprin
Kenneth Hausman
William Hill

Albert R. Johnson	Fern Selesnick
Stewart W. Kemp	James R. Shea
David R. King	Carol Sherman
Gwen Kinkaid	Shelley Stahl
Neil Koslowe	Mary Strohschein
Cheryl A. La Fleur	Kip R. Sullivan
Thomas Manley	Hollis Sutherland
Jacqueline Miller	Arthur R. Swann
Andrea Mintz	Blue Tabor
Mary Morton	Eva Teichner
Fern Nesson	Christian S. Schley
Susan Nyman	Jane E. Tewksbury
Gail A. Page	John Troubh
Linda Perle	Helene Whittaker
Clifford Robinson	Elizabeth Williams
Wendell P. Russell, Jr.	Anne Yates
Kurt L. Schmoke	Alma Young

Judith Auerbach and Jan Schreiber joined the project during the final year and a half as editors. Though special acknowledgement is included in the author's note to the individual volumes which they edited, the wealth of experience and professionally sound judgment they brought to the overall project proved of enormous help in identifying and clarifying the special contributions of each of the books and the series as an articulated whole. Marion Coates did most of the computer programming after 1971 and brought to this task great patience and perseverance in setting up and checking out complicated forms of data processing. An expert consulting team from the firm of Peat, Marwick, Mitchell and Co., led by Robert Nielson, undertook the very difficult task of a comparative cost analysis of the old and new correctional programs.

Secretaries who worked on the project included Christine Conniff, Deborah Cooper, Lorna Dumapias, James Franklin, Kathleen T. Gardner, Nancy Le Massena, Nancy J. March, Darnney L. Proudfoot, and Lucille Young.

Throughout the course of the project we received support and useful suggestions from Center staff members and directors of other projects at the Center. Most of all, however, we are deeply indebted to Professor James Vorenberg, Director of the Center. From the beginning Jim provided constant encouragement, criticism, and professional judgment, especially when trouble-shooting was needed in periods of crisis. Rosanne Kumins, Administrative Assistant of the Center, could always be counted on for help in moving the project along through innumerable hazards, but she also managed our budgets and accounts despite the exasperating complexities of coordinating funds from different sources. I am personally grateful to Harvard Law School Dean Albert M. Sacks for his encouragement and generous grants of research leave so that I might remain deeply involved in the research effort.

Special assistance was provided by staff of the funding agencies, especially James Howell of the Office of Juvenile Justice and Delinquency Prevention, Law Enforcement Assistance Administration, U.S. Department of Justice, and Robert Cole and Karen Joerg of the Massachusetts Committee on Criminal Justice. The Massachusetts Office of the Commissioner of Probation, under the direction of Elliot Sands, Commissioner, Joseph Foley, Assistant Commissioner, and Mark Santapio, in charge of the records, was of great help in securing data on recidivism.

Obviously, the study could not have been done at all without the generous cooperation of the staff and youth of the Massachusetts Department of Youth Services throughout the project with the constant support of Commissioner Jerome Miller, his successor Commissioner Joseph Leavey, and finally the present Commissioner John Calhoun.

Funding for the project came from several sources. The project was begun using the Center's own funds from its original Ford Foundation grant. Beginning in 1971 the project was funded in large part by the Massachusetts Committee on Criminal Justice, and aided by matching funds from the Center's Ford Foundation grant. In 1972 additional funds were granted by the National Institute of Law Enforcement and Criminal Justice, Law Enforcement Assistance Administration, U.S. Department of Justice. This support was later taken over by the Office of Juvenile Justice and Delinquency Prevention, when that office was founded and eventually became the principal source of funds for the project as a whole in its final two years.

Lloyd E. Ohlin
Harvard Law School

Author's Note

This research could not have been completed without the help, assistance, encouragement, and cooperation of many different people and organizations. This study was funded by the Commonwealth of Massachusetts Governor's Committee on Law Enforcement and the Administration of Criminal Justice Project Number 75–35X–905A1, for whose support and assistance I am grateful.

The research was conducted under the auspices of the Center for the Advancement of Criminal Justice of the Harvard Law School. More than simply research support, the Center provided a congenial, intellectually alive, and stimulating setting in which to work and grow. This is attributable in no small part to its Director, Professor James Vorenberg, who constantly encouraged and challenged new ideas. I owe a very special debt to the Center's Director of Research, Lloyd E. Ohlin. He has been a warm and generous friend whose patience, understanding, and encouragement through the many stages of the research contributed immeasurably to the undertaking. He provided a sounding-board for the testing of new ideas, and his advice, counsel and suggestions helped to eliminate many stumbling blocks and to clarify and resolve many difficulties. I am also grateful for the intellectual comradeship I shared with Drs. Alden D. Miller and Robert Coates, directors of other research projects at the Center. During the period I was at the Center, we shared the excitement and frustration of the changes taking place within the Department of Youth Services. I am particularly indebted to Alden, for his invaluable methodological assistance throughout the project from design through analysis. I also had the good fortune to be assisted by four outstanding, conscientious research assistants: John Greenthal, Kip Sullivan, Ken Hausman, and Barbara Stolz. Their dedication to a summer job was a researcher's joy, and their many long hours in the field produced a richness of data that is seldom matched.

I am also indebted to many people throughout the Massachusetts Department of Youth Services for providing us access and sharing their world with us. I am very grateful to Commissioner Jerome G. Miller for allowing us to examine the processes of change he initiated. His willingness to subject himself to the critical analysis of independent evaluation without restrictions afforded us a rare research opportunity. I also appreciate the generous assistance provided by the executives of the various institutions. They helped us identify the cottages we wanted to study, facilitated our entry there, and explained our role to the staff. At the Lyman School for Boys, this was Frank Ordway and Rev. Robert Brown. At the Lancaster Industrial School for Girls, this was Claire Donovan. At the Shirley Industrial School for Boys, this was Paul Dickhaut. I owe a special debt to Paul. He unselfishly shared his knowledge of institutional life with me, intuitively knowing what sociologists only rarely discover. I am indebted to the directors of the cottages that we studied who eased the way for us and assisted us on numerous occasions: Peter Mahoney; Rene Vadnais; Joe Vescey; John Ribeiro; Alexandra Vozick; George Costello; and David Simon. I also appreciate the assistance and cooperation that we received from all of the staff members and personnel in the cottages. Their patience with our persistent questioning and their willingness to explain the obvious for our benefit greatly enhanced our research experience.

I must also acknowledge my debt to the residents with whom we came in contact. We were interlopers in their "home away from home," intruding in their lives. They assisted us generously and completely, aiding our understanding of their circumstances even when it could have been to their own detriment. If this study has any effect, I would hope that it might make the living experiences better for their brothers and sisters, wherever they may be.

I am also indebted to the University of Minnesota Law School which facilitated the completion of this book. The Law School Alumni Association research fellowships afforded the opportunity to write and revise this manuscript over several summers. Nanci Smith provided outstanding secretarial assistance through several drafts of this manuscript, and her cheerful patience through many modifications and revisions is appreciated. I received many constructive comments, criticisms, and suggestions for improving the manuscript from Professors John Clark, Donald Cressey, and David Ward although, of course, the remaining deficiencies are my own responsibility. Judith Auerbach at the Harvard Law School Center for Advancement of Criminal Justice provided essential editorial assistance in bringing order out of chaos.

Finally, I must thank my wife Patricia for her unselfish acceptance of this "jealous mistress" during the several years of this project. Her tolerance and patience with my distracted preoccupation; her support, assistance, and involvement in the research from its inception has been a constant source of strength, for which I am grateful.

Barry C. Feld
August 1977

✳ *Chapter 1*

Subcultural Violence, the Institutions, and the Inmates

Over the past decade or more, efforts to treat delinquent and criminal offenders in institutional settings have been under attack from a variety of sources. Serious questions have been raised about the fundamental assumptions of rehabilitation and whether adequate knowledge exists to achieve human change on any systematic basis. In the face of rising crime rates, some critics of rehabilitation contend that the deterrent, incapacitative, or retributive goals of social control should take precedence over rehabilitative aims. This study, in examining juvenile inmate subcultures and the way they are influenced by the organizational structure of correctional institutions, has important implications for correctional policy.

The control of violence in institutional settings is a salient goal of any correctional reform policy. Policymakers, media, and the public all debate without resolution the issues of secure care and the causes of violent behavior in secure settings. Many systems are not moving toward community-based care as a serious alternative to institutional life in part because of the prevalence of aggression within their traditional settings: it has become difficult for practitioners as well as the public to conceptualize the possibility of a correctional setting without violence. And those systems that are attempting community-based treatment must still cope with the problem of secure care for some of their charges.

An examination of the ways in which organizations, staff, and inmates interact and affect each other can produce a better understanding of the process of violence in correctional settings and the alternatives to such institutionalized aggression. This study examines these issues from the perspective of juvenile inmate subcultures. It looks at the characteristics of a number of youth correctional programs in their institutional settings to discover how the formal organization influences the qualities of the informal inmate system.

Inmate subcultures emerge within the confines of correctional institutions. The particular characteristics of a subculture reflect both the structural features of the formal organization and the personal characteristics of the subculture population. In juvenile institutions the development and characteristics of subcultures reflect adolescent peer-group relationships, the social background of delinquents, the tendency of people in extended contact with one another to elaborate a social structure, and the need to develop a collective response to shared problems. Inmate group characteristics include the emergence of norms and values that regulate group activities and individual behavior, the distribution of inmate roles and status according to the subculture's values, and the socialization of new inmates into the group [1].

One characteristic feature that pervades most studies of prison cultures is their "oppositional" quality—the hostility and antagonism between inmates and staff—subsumed in an "inmate code." It is generally recognized that the antagonism of the informal inmate group toward correctional organizations may prevent the attainment of formal organizational goals, including efforts at treatment.

Two alternative explanations are offered to account for the oppositional content of the inmate code and social system. Commonly referred to as the "indigenous-origins" model and the "direct-importation" model, they attribute the organization and content of the inmate culture to different sources and social processes. The indigenous-origins model provides a functionalist explanation that relates the values and roles of the subculture to inmates' responses to problems of adjustment posed by the deprivations and pains of imprisonment. The formal organization of the prison is seen as shaping the informal inmate social system.

A competing interpretation attributes the normative order of the prison to the values—especially the criminal values—held by the inmates prior to incarceration [2]. According to this theory, the characteristics of the inmate population determine the nature of the subculture, and in a prison population an oppositional, criminal value system predominates. The principal difference between these two interpretations hinges on whether the inmate culture is seen as a response to the conditions of imprisonment or merely as an extension of previously held values.

The more recent studies of subcultures and their development have tended to adopt polar positions, attributing the characteristics of the inmate social system almost exclusively to either those factors within penal institutions that create negative subcultures or those outside factors that bring negative subcultures into the correctional setting. A more fruitful approach to this problem may well be a combined analysis—an attempt to discover the way in which external social roles and previous experiences mediate inmate perceptions of institutionally posed problems of adjustment and limit or prepare the individual and the collectivity to respond to them. Variations in organizational goals and intervention strategies will produce differences in the informal inmate social system as it responds to the institutional environment and the situationally posed problems of adjustment. However, although the inmate subcultures are malleable and responsive to organizational manipulation, the pre-institutional experiences of the inmates influence the types of adaptations that arise in response to the formal organizational structure.

Inmates with comparable background characteristics and pre-institutional experiences will thus develop varying subcultures when confronted with different organizational structures and treatment strategies. On the other hand, inmates with differences in salient background characteristics such as sex or race may respond differently to objectively similar organizational settings as a reflection of their pre-institutional experiences. A full understanding of variations in inmate subcultures requires an examination of both of these sets of factors.

A number of studies of inmate subculture frequently note the prevalence of violence within the subculture and the function of violence as a basis for stratification and role differentiation [3]. While violence is most obvious in the form of direct physical aggression, it can also be manifest through verbal aggression or psychological intimidation reinforced by the threat of more direct action. The threat or use of force may be used to create or reestablish relationships of domination and submission, and it is in this interactional context that prison violence acquires salience.

Many of the maxims of the inmate code can be seen as ways of regulating or reducing the levels of violence and exploitation among inmates. Similarly, many of the argot roles described in the subculture literature differentiate inmates on the basis of their use of instrumental violence or their responses to its use by other inmates. Moreover, many of the deprivations relied upon in functional explanations of subculture formation can be resolved on an individual basis by the use of violence. Material deprivations can be relieved through violent exploitation or intimidation. Sexual satisfaction can be obtained through violent exploitation. Status, prestige, and the respect of other inmates, as well as self-esteem, can be gained in the course of violent interactions. Thus, while imprisonment may impose certain deprivations, violence within the subculture provides at least some inmates with a potential solution, albeit at the expense of other inmates.

Violence is a great unequalizer. Not all people can use it with equal success and, in the absence of effective controls, it provides its users with an almost unassailable competitive advantage. The efficiency and economy of violence as a mode of social control also means that a comparative handful of individuals willing to use force can dominate a much larger, albeit less aggressive, group.

Using a functionalist framework, this study proceeds from the hypothesis that organizational features bear heavily on the prevalence of inmate violence. Organizational characteristics may determine both the quantity and quality of deprivations—that is, the motivations and incentives for some inmates to resort to aggression and the exploitation of others. Organizational features also influence the circumstances under which inmates may relatively freely carry out their threats to other inmates; the organization can offer the opportunity to use violence successfully to relieve deprivations.

Organizational features appear in this way to be linked to an inmate's incentive to resort to violence, and they also provide a conducive environment in which to carry out violent activities. Inmate violence, in turn, greatly influences many other aspects of subculture organization. Differences in inmate violence and the corresponding subcultural differences appear to be related to organizational features that either reduce the physical or psychological incentives of inmates to resort to violence, the circumstances under which they can use it successfully, or both. Our organizational analysis focuses on the structural features, intervention strategies, social-control practices, and the nature of staff-inmate relations that appear to reduce or exacerbate the levels of violence within the inmate social system.

The prevalence of inmate violence also reflects the characteristics of the incarcerated. Many inmates in prisons and juvenile correctional facilities are drawn from subcultures or social classes in which the use of violence is widespread. To a considerable degree, therefore, resorting to violence within institutional subcultures may reflect influences of cultural importation. Emphases on toughness, physical integrity, and manliness reflect some of the values of the culture of violence from which many inmates are drawn, as well as the values contained in the inmate code [4]. The extent to which prior social experiences prepare inmates to cope with the violence within the prison subculture may determine the nature of their institutional adaptations and their responses to the problems posed by incarceration.

Understanding the processes of subculture formation is essential to the development of effective correctional programs. Since inmates typically spend the bulk of their time in the company of fellow inmates, modifying the roles, values, and orientations of the subculture becomes one of the critical tasks in bringing about inmate change [5]. If, as the cultural importation theorists hypothesize, modification of the organizational structure has only a minimal impact on the character of the inmate culture, then programs for inmate change are destined to fail. On the other hand, if the culture is amenable to organizational manipulation, then the forces of the informal social system can be mobilized to further the goals of the organization. This study, then, attempts to assess the extent to which the subculture is subject to organizational influences and modification, with corresponding short- and long-term changes in inmate attitudes and behavior.

Since only a comparative study would allow the identification of factors in the institutional environment that were related to differences in the inmate subculture, we selected ten cottages from the training school system of the Massachusetts Department of Youth Services, the ten together representing a wide variety of goals and treatment techniques. During the summer of 1971 the daily life in these cottages was shared by a team of participant observers, who extensively interviewed staff and inmates. Their interview and questionnaire material was supplemented by observation field reports, institutional records, court reports, and psychological evaluations, which allowed for a thorough synthesis of information from several kinds of souces [6].

THE INSTITUTIONAL SETTING

Prior to 1948, when a juvenile was adjudicated delinquent in Massachusetts the presiding judge made a disposition in terms of length of sentence and place of commitment among the state's various juvenile institutions. In 1948 the legislature removed sentencing discretion from the judges, created a quasijudicial Youth Service Board, and gave it the responsibility to classify, train, and supervise the adjudicated delinquents committed to it by the courts [7]. In 1952 the

Youth Service Board became the Division of Youth Services, an administratively autonomous agency of the Massachusetts Department of Education.

The director of the Division of Youth Services also served as the chairman of the Youth Service Board, and in this dual capacity was responsible for the daily operation of the division. With two additional deputy directors appointed by the governor, the board was responsible for making all decisions relating to the transfer, treatment, placement, parole, and discharge from custody of juveniles committed to the division.

Beginning in 1965 a number of agencies, including the Governor's Management Engineering Task Force (1965); the Massachusetts Attorney General's Advisory Committee on Juvenile Crime (1966); the Children's Bureau of the U.S. Department of Health, Education, and Welfare (1966); the Massachusetts Committee on Children and Youth (1967); and a special committee of the state senate (1967) issued increasingly critical reports and studies about the chairman of the Youth Service Board and his operation and administration. Augmented by a public controversy over the administration of the Bridgewater Institute for Juvenile Guidance, the exposure ended in the political ouster of the director of the Division of Youth Services in May 1969. This was followed by legislation prompting an administrative reorganization of the division into a department, and a nationwide search to find a commissioner for the newly created Department of Youth Services [8]. The various critical studies and the ensuing political controversy all provided a mandate for change in the organization and the operation of youth services in the state.

In the fall of 1969 Jerome G. Miller was appointed commissioner of the internally divided agency. He was charged with reforming the department administratively and introducing progressive treatment practices. Miller took office with several general goals. He hoped to have fewer and smaller institutions, primarily designed for youths who posed a special danger to the community or themselves. More immediately, he hoped to humanize the institutions and introduce an innovative treatment program modeled along the patterns of a "therapeutic community" [9]. Such a treatment setting called for participative involvement by staff and youth in an active resocialization community in which both groups could express their feelings openly and honestly.

To achieve these goals, one of Miller's first official acts was the closing of the Bridgewater Institute for Juvenile Guidance. Although purportedly a treatment facility, the institution had been used by staff in other institutions to warehouse chronically recalcitrant inmates, and it was the political controversy surrounding this institution that brought Miller into office. During the course of the next year and a half he attempted to close the other institutions as well.

As part of the effort to establish treatment programs, Miller brought in several consultants to help staff develop therapeutic communities within their institutions. Miller also tried to humanize conditions and vitiate the more custodial aspects of the system by centering programs and treatment within self-contained cottage units. He prohibited staff from striking or corporally punishing the residents, eliminated the mandatory short haircuts for boys, allowed them to wear their own clothes rather than state-issued uniforms, discontinued the practice of marching silently in double lines from one activity to the next, and in some institutions permitted the residents to carry their own cigarettes. In addition the period of confinement was reduced from about ten months to approximately four months. To the extent that these changes were implemented in the institutions, they helped to reduce the generally unpleasant custodial climate, but they also created a great deal of staff resentment against what was regarded as excessive permissiveness.

Beginning in June 1970 Miller began to make a number of fundamental structural changes. Institutional decentralization was intended to provide greater autonomy and independence for the cottages within each institution, thereby transforming each cottage into a small therapeutic community. To accomplish this goal, Miller had to modify the basic structure of the institutions, changing them from hierarchical bureaucracies into participative, problem-solving cottage groups.

The three major institutions had been traditional training schools with a multiple-department structure. The clinical, vocational, academic, and cottage-life programs were relatively autonomous, with minimal coordination or involvement of staff people in areas of the inmates' lives apart from their own specific functions. Miller's process of reorganization was intended to integrate and coordinate all of the programs at the cottage level. In order to involve all the staff members in an integrated treatment program, vocational, academic, clinical, and cottage program staff were assigned to cottages in mixed groups, and as a group were given primary responsibility for the residents of that cottage. Within each cottage a director assumed overall responsibility for developing the cottage programs, coordinating the staff activities, supervising the daily life of the residents, and conducting the cottage community meetings. Cottage community meetings involving all of the staff members and residents were introduced to increase communication and interaction between staff and residents. Under this plan, all of the staff and residents were to become active participants in a cottage-based problem-solving community, and numerous efforts were made to create a social climate conducive to this goal.

The process of decentralization was not easy. The community meetings and the changes in institutional focus placed the staff members under a great deal of stress. They were forced to rethink and change their ways of dealing with the committed youths. Staff had previously occupied well-defined, authoritative positions within a highly structured setting. They had had a variety of social-control techniques available to them for enforcing inmate obedience and conformity. By the summer of 1970 their roles were more diffuse, uncertain, and inconsistent. The staff had difficulty in interpreting Miller's directives, and their resistance was substantial. They were suddenly expected to tolerate a great deal more acting out, abusive language, and inmate recalcitrance under the new administration, and this created personal anxiety and a sense of loss of discipline and control.

Decentralization was also difficult for the institutionalized youths themselves. Although the previous system had been considerably more rigid and authoritarian, it had provided security and comfort in the predictability and certainty of staff and inmate role expectations. It was easier for many to conform to the institutional rules than to meet the new demands for personal growth and change; the loss of these supports placed more stress on the internal coping capacity of youthful inmates. Staff uncertainty about their own roles and inconsistency in treatment also contributed to the anxiety of the youths.

By the summer of 1971 the process of cottage decentralization provided an ideal subject for research. The various autonomous cottages, freed from institutional constraints, developed their own distinctive personalities, treatment techniques, and life-styles. Cottage staff experimented with a diverse range of traditional and innovative treatment alternatives that provided significant program variation for comparative purposes. Although many cottages continued to operate in much the same fashion that they had when part of the larger institution, several others took advantage of the opportunity to try new strategies and develop new programs. The result was that a number of cottages were pursuing markedly different goals and utilizing significantly different intervention strategies.

The subculture study presented here was fortuitous to the extent that it occurred during one of the relatively stable periods of the reform process under Commissioner Miller. The summer months of 1971 were a period of lull and consolidation before the next round of changes, during which the institutions would be closed altogether. The administrators of each school were concerned with institutional stability after the stresses of the preceding year; those at the cottage level were concerned with refining and "institutionalizing" the cottage treatment programs they had developed.

Six months after our field work was completed, Miller began to realize his goal of discontinuing large institutions. The Industrial School for Boys at Shirley and the Lyman School for Boys at Westboro closed in January 1972. The residents of the Industrial School for Girls at Lancaster were transferred to private agencies shortly thereafter. None of the cottage programs we studied exists today.

The Industrial School for Boys, Shirley, Massachusetts

The Industrial School for Boys was established by the Massachusetts legislature in 1908. Located thirty-five miles west of Boston, its physical plant was situated on the remains of a Shaker village that flourished in this rural section of the state during the middle part of the nineteenth century. Like most training schools, the Industrial School was a minimum-security facility, with no fences or barred windows, and absconding was quite easy.

The main administration building stood on a hill overlooking the half-dozen cottages that housed the resident population. It contained the administrative offices, an auditorium, gymnasium, swimming pool, tradeshops, classrooms, counseling rooms, two chapels, and the library. Nearby was a cafeteria-warehouse where the "open-school" boys and staff ate their meals. There was a scattering of one- and two-family homes occupied by various members of the institution staff. Some distance removed from the rest of the school was a large football and baseball playing field surrounded by a high fence topped with barbed-wire. The fence was a relic from an earlier day when more emphasis was placed on security and custody, and the playing field was one of the few areas outside the cottages where large numbers of boys congregated. With the exception of the screened and fenced discipline cottage, it was the only place in the institution with such security provisions.

Prior to Miller's changes in policy and program, the Industrial School was reserved for older boys who were sent to it for vocational training. Beginning in June 1970 Miller deemphasized vocational education, discontinued coercing boys to work, and shortened the period of commitment from an average of ten months to a minimum of three months, and an average of four. The introduction of therapeutic programs and afternoon community meetings in the cottages further disrupted prevailing practices. Vocational education staff complained that deemphasizing vocational training and shortening the period of confinement, and also the teaching day, prevented them from teaching a boy a trade.

Miller drastically changed the organizational structure as well. Between January 1970 and July 1971 the position of superintendent changed hands six times. Miller also removed several other ranking administrators in the institution who had formed the nucleus of staff opposition to his programs. While these changes and the ensuing staff confusion had a deleterious impact on the traditional programs, the weakening of the central administration threw the various cottages on their own resources, and strengthened the processes of institutional decentralization and autonomy taking place in the individual cottages.

Decentralization gave interested staff members the opportunity to experiment with new programs. One cadre of such staff members was drawn from the Student Tutor Education Program (STEP), a federally funded educational program with which the Department of Youth Services had contracted to provide an alternative to the traditional institutional academic program. Many of them eventually became core staff members and leaders in several of the treatment-oriented cottages. These young, innovative people had no commitment to the prevailing institutional mode of teaching or dealing with children, and their approach brought them into frequent conflict with long-time staff and administrators.

But the shift to cottage-based communities with inmate participation in group meetings had greatly increased the level of interstaff conflict, and alienated the more traditional members of the staff. The vocational instructors resisted the pressures on them to modify their traditional tradesmen role, leave their shops, and participate in the cottage-based programs; the cottage parents' schedules and jobs changed, with new duties added; and the clinicians and cottage directors tried to coordinate these conflicting groups and develop sound cottage treatment programs. Meanwhile, the employees' union objected to the changes in staff schedules and staff roles that accompanied cottage decentralization.

By late fall 1970 decentralization was evolving into a cottage-based program, but the superintendent needed help in organizing a clinical team. The clinical assistance he requested was not forthcoming because personnel were lacking and Miller was reluctant to strengthen institutional programs. Throughout the winter of 1971 interstaff conflict continued, polarizing "old" and "new" staff. An impending legislative investigation further deteriorated morale and programs.

The situation became critical when the staff became aware that Miller planned to close the institution within two months. There was a great deal of anxiety among staff and inmates, and the last weeks of February were marked by a number of serious incidents: fires in the dormitories, fights, assaults on staff members, and running away. As a result of a deliberate policy, the number of boys in the institution was declining and cottage populations were consolidated to aid supervision and control.

During this period a consultant provided one cottage's staff members with clinical training in therapeutic community processes and helped them develop an integrated staff-team and balanced cottage-based treatment program. In view of the Industrial School's announced closing, this cottage staff and boys moved to the Lyman School to ensure and continue their treatment operations there. This cottage became known as Shirley Cottage at Lyman and is one of the units in our study.

By March 1971 the clinical consultant was training a second staff team to run a therapeutic-community program. In April 1971 they were given a vacant cottage on the Shirley grounds. This cottage, which became known as "I Belong," was operated independently, with meals eaten in the cottage, programs centered in the cottage, and contact with the rest of the school minimized. It is also included in our sample.

In late March the decision to close the institution in the immediate future was rescinded—a result of political pressures and increasing court commitments. The remaining staff, demoralized and confused, continued to resist the therapeutic community program; the administrator placed increasing emphasis on basic security and custody, and less on treatment. He was replaced shortly thereafter by a former acting superintendent and long-time Shirley staff member who intended to run a "straight place" and introduce some order and structure into the system. The general thrust of his administration was to reprogram the facility and get staff back to work again.

In May 1971 the resolution of union grievances, which centered around Miller's structural changes and use of personnel outside their official civil service job classifications, forced a drastic change in the administrative structure of the school. The oppositional administrative personnel that Miller had removed returned to their former positions and duties. The cottage directors were removed because such a position did not correspond to existing civil service classifications.

Since Shirley was still legislatively and administratively structured as a vocational training school, the overall effect of resolving the union's grievances was an undoing of the decentralized cottage-based approach. Except for the independent cottages, the traditional multiple-department structure, with counselors, cottage parents, vocational and academic teachers segregated in their respective departments, was reestablished until the institution was finally closed.

By the time of our study, one cottage had transferred to another institution, two had been closed through consolidation, and another opened as an independent halfway house. The two remaining open-school cottages and the discipline cottage operated as a vocational training school, although many of the traditional programs were weakened by the organizational turmoil. The clinical program consisted of orientation, classification, and the handling of administrative details and paperwork of weekend furloughs and paroles. There were no group-treatment or individual counseling sessions, and the cottage meetings were held on an occasional and perfunctory basis. The academic education program (STEP) was weakened by a number of staff departures; some left DYS while others joined the independently run halfway houses. Apart from the trades essential to institutional life-support—like the cafeteria and the laundry, which had a few boys assigned to them—the vocational education programs ran on a sporadic basis, if at all.

Our study of the inmate subculture included three cottages at Shirley: Cottage 8, one of the two "traditional" open-school cottages; Cottage 9, an autonomous discipline cottage; and the independently operated halfway house known as "I Belong," located on the school grounds. We selected Cottage 9 and "I Belong" because we expected that they would closely approximate maximum-security custody and group treatment, and while each contained somewhat different populations, the gains in treatment variation outweighed any losses in comparability. We studied Cottage 8, one of the open-school cottages, as a representative of the traditional industrial school.

The Lyman School for Boys, Westboro, Massachusetts

The Lyman School for Boys, established in 1846 from private funds contributed by Colonel Theodore Lyman and supplemented by state appropriations, was the first public institution exclusively for juvenile offenders in the United States. It was located thirty miles west of Boston near the town of Westboro.

The school had eight cottages, several of which dated from 1886, although a number of newer ones were constructed in the 1930s. While the Shirley inmate population declined, many others were diverted to the cottages at Lyman. The institution housed several newer programs—a cottage for girls, and Shirley Cottage, transplanted from the Industrial School. In addition to the cottages, the facilities included an administration building, school building, auditorium, cafeteria, and various shop buildings widely scattered around the grounds. The school building was substantially larger than the one at the Industrial School at Shirley, and reflected differences in program emphasis between the two schools prior to Miller's arrival. Although both had academic and vocational programs, the Shirley Industrial School traditionally emphasized vocational training for older boys, whereas Lyman emphasized academic education for somewhat younger boys. With Miller's advent, however, both program distinctions and population differences soon disappeared.

Miller also initiated a process of institutional decentralization at Lyman that resulted in a modification of programs and structure. As a result of better administrative communication and a more leisurely pace, the process of change was not quite as divisive or destabilizing as at the Industrial School. Miller had introduced cottage-based programs at Shirley in July 1970, with relatively little planning. At Lyman, cottage-based programming did not begin until September, after nearly a month of preparation. Here, cottage teams of academic teachers, counselors, and cottage masters met together to develop a therapeutic community program, and to coordinate all the programs—educational, clinical, and cottage life—and to involve the residents in a group decision-making process. Nonetheless, implementing cottage-based treatment programs still generated substantial resistance from the academic and vocational teachers who opposed leaving their classrooms and shops to work in the cottages themselves, and confused other staff members who were uncertain of their role in a cottage-based treatment program.

The number of runaways increased shortly after the new program opened. Part of the blame was placed on the new program, especially by staff who saw it as too permissive and questioned its viability and merits. Some residents perceived it as unduly restrictive because their activities were confined to the cottages. The runaway situation became so critical that after several failures to stem the tide, the superintendent of Lyman was temporarily relieved by a former acting superintendent from Shirley.

The administrative change, coupled with increased cottage decentralization, was effective in reducing the runaway rate. Although there was still uncertainty about what a therapeutic program entailed and confusion because of the administrative changes, in general Lyman adapted more successfully than Shirley. Therapeutic communities did not flourish in all the cottages; but to varying degrees cottage directors coordinated teachers, counselors, and line staff in each cottage and involved them in community meetings with the boys. Staff people became somewhat less resistant to the cottage-based programs, although the vocational instructors were not integrated into the cottage system.

In order to strengthen the individual cottage programs and reduce the effects of institutional constraints, weekly meetings were held for the directors of the individual cottages to discuss and coordinate the operation of their programs. Outside clinical consultants were introduced to assist in the development of more effective treatment programs. The institutional stability and the developing therapeutic communities allowed the former superintendent of the institution to resume administrative control. At this time the cottage that was transplanted from the Industrial School took up residence at Lyman, with its cottage-based programs.

When our research staff arrived at Lyman in June 1971, six open-school cottages were in operation, in addition to the transplanted Shirley cottage, the Lyman disciplinary cottage, and the girls' cottage. We eliminated the disciplinary cottage from consideration because the short period of confinement precluded the development of a stable subculture. The girls' cottage was atypical in a number of respects because of its location in the middle of a boys' school. In selecting three out of the six open-school cottages at Lyman, our dual research constraints of inmate comparability and treatment variability eliminated those cottages to which the younger boys were sent, and those which presented specially selected populations of long-term placements and the like.

In order to establish comparability between the cottages we studied at Shirley and those at Lyman, we chose the cottages housing the oldest boys at Lyman—Elms, Westview, and Sunset. We selected the transplanted Shirley cottage because it contained older boys in a treatment setting, and its population was comparable to the other cottages.

Industrial School for Girls, Lancaster, Massachusetts

The Industrial School for Girls, located near the town of Lancaster, some thirty miles west of Boston, was established in 1855. It was also the first institution for girls in the nation to use the cottage plan. Lancaster was small, with six cottages, an administrative office building, a chapel-auditorium, and an academic and vocational school facility. The school hospital also served as a security unit for those girls who were sequestered in individual rooms. Since there was no cafeteria as at Lyman or Shirley, meals were prepared by the girls and eaten in each cottage.

Although the staff people were aware of the new DYS commissioner's goal of creating therapeutic communities, Miller did not begin institutional decentralization at Lancaster until considerably later than he did at the other institutions—in part to await the retirement of its longtime superintendent, and in part out of uncertainty about the form female institutional programming should assume. Occasional meetings were held during the summer of 1970, and were attended by representatives of the girls, the staff members from the DYS central office, and middle-management and cottage personnel from the institution. Although the Lancaster staff discounted the significance of these meetings, which had minimal impact on day-to-day operations, they resented the intrusion of "outsiders."

In September 1970 the superintendent, who had dominated the administration and program policies of the school for many years, retired, as did the assistant superintendent. The third-ranking member of the administrative hierarchy succeeded them, although she shared responsibility for running the institution with a Miller aide assigned to the institution to work on programming. The administrative succession occurred with less institutional disruption than at either Shirley or Lyman, perhaps because the administrator followed the normal lines of succession and acted in a caretaker capacity, rather than having come from outside with a mandate to implement changes. Because of the reports staff had received from other institutions, they were apprehensive about the impending changes and about therapeutic communities, although very few changes were actually taking place. Apart from the assignments of counselors to the individual cottages, there was very little movement toward decentralization.

This apprehension and uncertainty continued until January 1971, when Miller introduced a "change agent," a quasi-administrator acting as a clinical consultant. Prior to his arrival, the institution had been tightly controlled by the superintendent. Any deviation from established practice required administrative approval. The three departments—education, counseling, and cottage life—were run independently of each other, and the administrator was the focal point for all cross-department communication.

Decentralization at Lancaster entailed isolating the administrator from direct supervision, reducing departmental separation, and creating sources of leadership within each cottage to provide program direction [10]. The counselors, who had been isolated by the departmental structure, were now each assigned to one specific cottage and given general responsibility for developing a therapeutic cottage program. The change agent conducted training groups to strengthen their counseling skills and increase their responsibility so that decisions formerly referred to the administrator could now be made in the cottages. The counselors did not emerge, however, as "cottage directors"; in some cases they had neither the skills nor sophistication to accomplish the task, and even with decentralization it was difficult to reverse the effects of their prior bureaucratic isolation. As a result, whatever cottage subcultural differences that emerged at Lancaster reflected personal differences among the cottage matrons and staff rather than any major structural or programmatic differences.

The change agent also conducted once-a-week cottage community meetings for staff and girls, although these responsibilities were turned over to the counselors within a month. The cottage meeting helped to loosen up the cottage climate by giving the residents a mechanism for changing the way the cottage was run. A number of rules were relaxed, girls were locked in their rooms less frequently, and cigarettes became more plentiful. However, the inexperience of the group leaders sometimes allowed the girls to use the meetings to retaliate against the matrons they felt had mistreated them, which in turn alienated cottage staff from the treatment program.

Further decentralization occurred when the academic school day was shortened and the school teachers were assigned to the cottages. Although this was intended to increase interaction with other cottage staff and residents and to integrate them into the cottage-based program, the teachers remained isolated. Instead of cottage staff interacting with the teachers and residents, the cottage matrons required the girls to remain with the teachers while they retired to staff quarters. The teachers, with no clearly defined role in the cottage, sat with the other teachers and occasionally talked with some of the girls.

By the time of the subculture study in June 1971, decentralization was not as advanced as at Shirley and Lyman. There were differences among the cottages, but these reflected the personal style of the cottage matrons rather than substantive program differences. To a much greater extent than with the boys' facilities, the girls' programs still operated on an institutional basis rather than a cottage basis.

Six cottage programs were in operation at Lancaster, although several were obviously unsuited to our research purposes. There were three open-school cottages, a secure unit, an honor cottage, and a cottage of boys aged twelve and under [11]. We excluded the boys' cottage because it would not be comparable with any other cottage we studied. The girls in the secure facility were locked in their rooms most of the day, effectively preventing the development of a subculture. We excluded the honor cottage because of its selected population and unique program. Of the three open-school cottages, all the pregnant girls were assigned to the one closest to the school hospital, where they made up 10 to 25 percent of the population.

We studied the two other open-school cottages—Clara Barton and Putnam—which were similar in their population and operation. The girls were assigned to either of these two cottages on the basis of available space, without any deliberate classification scheme.

Regional Training Center, Topsfield, Massachusetts

The last unit we studied was a new one at Topsfield, twenty miles north of Boston. It offered a number of attractive research opportunities, although it contained a relatively selected population and had begun operation only a few months before our study. It was coeducational, thus providing an opportunity to examine the effect of sex-role socialization on subculture formation. It also represented a major effort by the Department of Youth Services to create a therapeutic milieu *ab initio*, and we were interested in assessing the effectiveness of such a commitment.

The Topsfield facility had been a novitiate with a large building and spacious grounds. Prior to Miller's appointment, an acting commissioner negotiated the purchase of the property to set up a new treatment unit when the local community's option to acquire the property lapsed. For several months after taking office, Miller was involved in a number of stormy meetings with the community concerning the intended uses of the facility. At various times he envisioned using the facility as an intensive treatment center for small groups of youths, as a drug treatment center for addicted youths, as a drug training center for institutional personnel, and as a regional office to provide consultative services to the surrounding towns in developing delinquency prevention programs. The planned uses of the facility changed as the department's perceived needs changed, although there was considerable organized community opposition to most of the proposals.

The Department of Youth Services finally decided to use Topsfield as a treatment facility for juveniles and as a staff training center for institutional personnel. A treatment staff was assembled to run the facility, and twelve children were selected as the nucleus of the treatment program. They were unable to take up residence at Topsfield until a number of renovations were completed and, in the interim, the children occupied a vacant cottage at the Industrial School and commuted to Topsfield. This treatment program was quickly terminated due to serious staff divisions and the difficulties of conducting a treatment program under these conditions.

In April 1971 a small coeducational treatment program was begun again, this time with two boys and two girls in residence at Topsfield. The treatment staff emphasized individual clinical treatment as well as a therapeutic community program. Throughout the summer, the number of youths in residence gradually increased, so that by July 1971 when our study began there were seven boys and nine girls in the program.

THE RESEARCH DESIGN

In order to establish that certain subcultural variations grew out of differences in the cottage social structure rather than out of differences in inmate characteristics, we had to find cottage population comparability. Ideally we would have utilized a fully controlled, random assignment of inmates to the various cottages, since otherwise it could not be clear how assignment or population biases might affect subcultural development. Because we were unable to formally eliminate the influence of "imported" background characteristics as an independent cause, the lack of random assignments obviously detracts from our thesis that subcultural variation is a product of social structure variation. In the absence of randomization, however, we used a research design most closely approximating Campbell and Stanley's "static-group comparison," a design that compares a group that has experienced experimental treatment with another group that has not, for the purpose of examining the effects of the experimental treatment [12]. Although we did not have a control group, with ten treatment units we had a sufficiently large number of experimental groups to analyze data comparatively and thus to identify significant differences in the effects of treatments on youths with comparable background characteristics [13].

This type of research design contains several methodological weaknesses. In contrast to the true experimental design using randomization and control groups, the static-group design does not provide a formal means of establishing that the experimental groups would have been similar in the absence of the treatment. The lack of initial population equivalence requires an analysis of population selection, since the differences between groups may be the result of differential population recruitment. If this were so, the groups could be different even without the effects of the experimental treatment. Campbell and Stanley have observed that matching the groups on the basis of background characteristics may be an ineffective or even misleading way to control for selection biases [14]. It is, however, the only means available for establishing any comparability between groups already in existence.

We also had to confront problems of population bias and self-selection. The former stems from the use of any classifying criteria at all in the assignment of an inmate to a cottage. The latter stems from the practice in some treatment cottages of accepting only inmates who volunteer for the program. Another problem of self-selection may stem from sample population mortality, which gives rise to differences between the various treatment groups due to differential dropout rates, rather than to any treatment effects. This was not as serious a problem, since the opportunity to drop out was relatively limited, and it was taken into consideration in the research design [15].

Despite the fact that matching on background characteristics could establish only a relatively weak comparability, we took these factors into consideration in our initial selection of cottages, matching the cottage populations as closely as possible on a number of dimensions, including: age, race, criminal histories, juvenile court appearances, prior commitments to institutions, and the like. In addition to analyzing the differences among cottages that derived from treatment, we also examined the potential impact of a number of background factors that might be related to differences among the cottages. In the last section of this chapter we will present data on cottage and inmate characteristics to establish the population similarity of the various cottage groups. To the extent that these cottages populations are comparable, we strengthen our thesis that the differences among cottage subcultures derive from organizational features rather than from population characteristics.

In addition to matching and comparing the cottage populations, we used several statistical techniques—controlling for the effect of background characteristics within and between cottages, and allowing for interaction effects between background characteristics and the cottage treatment-type—to discover any relationships between a particular background characteristic and other differences in the populations within a particular cottage or cottages. This analysis, described in the Appendix, further enables us to assert that the major differences we obtained between cottage subcultures were a function of organizational, not population, differences.

Data Collection

The administrators of the institutions and cottages facilitated our entry into individual cottages. They explained the research project to cottage staff members and, in most instances, that was sufficient to ensure their cooperation. Since we had been engaged in field work at the institutions for more than a year before beginning this study, our close personal relationships with many staff members helped to overcome resistance from other staff.

We used a somewhat different strategy to gain access to the social world of the residents. In the cottages with good staff-inmate relations, an introduction by a staff member, followed by a further explanation of the research role to the inmates, was sufficient. In those cottages where staff endorsement might have barred access, we gained entry by hanging around and repeatedly explaining our research role until we were accepted. As part of an earlier study, I had lived in a cottage with a group of inmates for an extended period of time, sleeping in the dormitory with them at night and participating extensively in the activities of the inmate subculture. This established credibility and enhanced my reputation among the inmates for trustworthiness and reliability. Ironically, it had the same effect with the staff. As a result of these experiences, I also developed close relationships with several inmate leaders who provided entry into the more oppositional inmate subcultures by vouching for our character.

The field work and data collection took place between May and September 1971. The principal researcher, assisted by four others, gathered data in the various cottage units located in four Department of Youth Services facilities. We spent five to six weeks in each cottage, administering questionnaires and interviews to the staff members and residents. The bulk of the time was devoted to participant observation, studying, and recording the ways in which the inmates related to each other and to staff. Other data were obtained from institutional records, court reports, and psychological evaluations.

Both staff and inmates completed questionnaires, with most items adapted from other studies of inmate subcultures or prisons. We used a closed-ended format to simplify later coding operations. The staff questionnaires were self-administered in order to allow the researchers more time to engage in participant observation and to administer questionnaires and interviews to the inmates. In six of the ten cottages, 100 percent of the staff returned the questionnaire; more than 90 percent did so in the remaining cottages.

Reading difficulties and limited vocabularies precluded a self-administered format for the inmates. Instead, the researcher read the questions to groups of three to five residents who marked their responses on an accompanying answer sheet. The researcher could observe individual responses (although the others in the groups could not) and in this way help with any individual difficulties. This approach yielded very complete returns—95 percent or more in every cottage.

The structured staff and inmate interviews consisted of a number of open-ended items designed to elicit information that could not be obtained from closed-ended questionnaires and also to provide cross-checks on questionnaire and observation data. The interviews were all conducted face-to-face in relative privacy. Unlike the inmate questionnaires, which were administered to small groups, only one inmate was interviewed at a time. Similarly, the staff interviews were conducted privately, although occasionally it was necessary to interview them while they were on duty. To fully capture the information, the responses were transcribed in the course of the interviews. This strategy provided accurate renditions of the statements without interrupting conversation.

The problems inherent in participant-observation can be particularly troublesome in the setting of a correctional facility. The divided nature of the social system makes it difficult to participate in the staff and inmate groups simultaneously. The inmates' distrust of and hostility to staff is a major impediment for an outside researcher. In addition the staff members in our study were suspicious of outsiders because of earlier critical reports and the threat to their jobs posed by the reforms and changes. We overcame these suspicions by maintaining a constant presence, which allowed us to stay in the background and minimized any disruptive effects of the research.

Two researchers were in residence in the institutions during all or part of the study, although it was made clear both to staff and residents that the researchers were not employees of the Department of Youth Services. The other researchers maintained a continual presence by spending ten hours a day or more in the institution, including many evenings and weekends, and varying their arrivals and departures. They were present during the major daily events, like the cottage community meetings, as well as at times when very few regular staff were on duty. With minor exceptions the long hours and sincere interest overcame any objections to our presence, and gained the cooperation and trust of most of the staff and residents, alike.

It is also difficult for a participant-observer to establish a field identity. We used the observation role that Gold describes as the "participant-as-observer" strategy:

> The participant-as-observer role ... tends to minimize problems of role-pretending.... Probably the most frequent use of this role is in community studies, where an observer develops relationships with informants through time, and where he is apt to spend more time and energy participating than observing. At times he observes formally, as in scheduled interview situations; and at other times he observes informally.... During the early stages of his stay in the community, informants may be somewhat uneasy about him in both formal and informal situations, but their uneasiness is likely to disappear when they learn to trust him, and he them [16].

Although we did not attempt to disguise our research role, we had found in the course of our prior field work that it was best to describe our work as "writing a book on juvenile corrections." This role definition was not ethically misleading, since it reminded people that we were outsiders and that our observations might be published. The role definition was useful because it explained our presence in the field and provided a rationale for our participation in daily activities as well as a justification for our constant questions.

Our observations were recorded with a wide range of behaviors—not just "bad" behavior—and people quickly accepted note-taking as part of our role, thus minimizing the inhibiting effect of our writing. Moreover, the people we observed were deeply involved in their daily activities and our practice of recording them quickly became secondary. We tried to capture all of the essential details of an incident in our field notes, including the event, its outcome, the participants, and any significant comments or statements.

A basic problem of social research on deviant groups is that of assessing the validity of the data: Are respondents behaving or answering truthfully? Are they casting themselves in the best possible light, or conceivably, in the worst possible light?

We are confident of the validity of our data. The researchers established very good working relationships with most of the people with whom they came in contact, and several people commented on the openness and honesty with which they and others were treating us. We received a great deal of information that was either sensitive or placed the informant in jeopardy, which also suggested its basic reliability. Because the researchers were present over extended periods of time, a potential strain was placed on those who might try to pretend or play a role. Furthermore, we were subjected to some "testing" by staff as well as inmates until it became apparent that we did not pose a threat [17]. On the basis of the previous year of field work, we had demonstrated our reliability to staff and inmates on numerous occasions; this, we believe, helped to minimize the motivation to deceive.

Finally, one of the advantages of a "triangulated" methodology is the internal and external validation it provides. Self-reported background data can be checked against official records, interview sociometric data can be cross-checked against questionnaire sociometric responses, and so forth. While inconsistent results may complicate the analysis, consistent results strengthen confidence in the data. As our subsequent analysis will indicate, the degree of internal consistency across a number of dimensions using a variety of measures justifies this confidence.

BACKGROUND CHARACTERISTICS OF COTTAGE INMATES AND STAFF

In order to be certain that the subcultural differences we will decribe later in the study were a product of organizational factors rather than of "imported" features, it was necessary to establish that the various treatment strategies were being applied to essentially similar inmate populations. We selected cottages to obtain comparable populations, and in this section we compare a number of inmate background characteristics among the various cottages to demonstrate their similarity. We also discuss staff characteristics to a lesser extent, since these differences are related to the treatment strategies used in the various settings.

We matched our inmate samples on the basis of age, race, age of contact with juvenile courts, criminal offense patterns, and prior institutional experience. Some differences among the cottage were apparent on these dimensions. In general, the two Lancaster cottages —Putnam and Clara Barton—and "I Belong" had somewhat younger and less sophisticated delinquents, but apart from this difference there did not appear to be any systematic biases in the sample. We further tested to determine whether the cottage variations were a product of population differences, and while there were some, they do not appear to be the source of the substantial subcultural differences we obtained.

Age of Inmates

It was important that the inmates in the sample be approximately the same age, since we would expect that older inmates, particularly those with more extensive legal involvements, would tend to be more criminally sophisticated and inured to institutions. A disproportionate concentration of older inmates in a particular cottage might pose special problems for staff and also reduce cottage comparability. Table 1-1 contains the mean age of residents in the different cottages, and the proportion aged sixteen or older and seventeen or older. By selecting the cottages to maximize age comparability, we obtained a reasonably close age approximation among the various cottages. With the exception of the Lancaster cottages and "I Belong," which had somewhat younger residents, the average age was 15.7 years. Thus, if inmate age is related to criminal sophistication or a negative inmate subculture, there is little basis for distinguishing between the treatment-oriented cottages and the custody-oriented cottages. We also examined the proportions of inmates aged sixteen or older, as well as those aged seventeen or older. Again, with the exception of the Lancaster cottages and "I Belong," there is fairly good comparability among the cottages on the basis of residents' age.

Race

In our analysis of the inmate subcultures, we found several important differences between black and white inmates, presumably related to racial differences in the larger society. Moreover, a disproportionate concentration of black residents in a cottage could pose a variety of problems for the almost exclusively white staff. Table 1-2 presents the proportion of black [18] inmates in each cottage. While there was some variation in the proportion of black inmates in the cottages, it does not appear to have been a source of bias. There was a somewhat larger proportion of black inmates in the custody-oriented cottages than in the treatment-oriented cottages, but these differences were slight. The lower proportion of black female inmates was much more striking. The factors that have led to a disproportionate overrepresentation of black males in correctional facilities do not appear to operate to nearly the same extent in the case of black females.

Age of First Contact with the Juvenile Court

The initial age of involvement with the juvenile justice system is a frequently used predictor of subsequent criminal involvements. As an indicator of this early involvement, we compared the inmates' age at the time of their first contact with the juvenile court. We used this indicator rather than their age of first arrest or first police contact because it was less ambiguous and more indicative of a need to formally intervene. Table 1-3 shows the average age of first contact with the juvenile courts for each of the cottages, and the proportion of residents with juvenile court contacts by the time they were twelve years of age.

Overall, the residents of the custody-oriented cottages had somewhat earlier juvenile court involvements, with a greater proportion

Table 1-1. Mean Age of Cottage Residents and Percentage Over Age 16

	Custody-Oriented Cottages					Treatment-Oriented Cottages			
	Group	Individual				Individual	Group		
	Cottage 9	Cottage 8	Elms	Westview	Lancaster (Female—Putnam and Clara Barton)[a]	Topsfield	Sunset	Shirley	"I Belong"
Mean cottage age (years)	15.7	16.3	15.6	15.6	14.9	16.2	15.5	16.3	14.2
Percentage aged 16 or older	63%	87%	58%	59%	29%	73%	53%	88%	25%
Percentage aged 17 or older	15%	47%	13%	24%	6%	47%	13%	38%	0%

[a]The two cottages for girls are grouped together throughout the tables (with the exception of Table 1–8), producing nine categories, although the total cottage sample was ten.

Table 1-2. Percentage of Black[a] Inmates

	Custody-Oriented Cottages				Treatment-Oriented Cottages			
	Group	Individual			Individual	Group		
	Cottage 9	Cottage 8	Elms	Westview	Lancaster (female)	Topsfield (co-ed)	Sunset	Shirley	"I Belong"
Percentage of black inmates	19%	27%	35%	21%	11%	32%	25%	19%	25%

[a]For reasons explained in note 18, below, Spanish-surnamed individuals are included in this category.

experiencing court intervention by the time they were twelve. On the average the boys in the custody-oriented cottages had their first juvenile court contacts perhaps a half a year earlier than did their counterparts in the treatment-oriented cottages. The pattern for the female inmates was similar. There was considerable internal variation within all of these cottages on this dimension, but it did not appear to be related to other background characteristics or intracottage subculture differences.

Criminal Offense Histories

We compared the criminal and juvenile offense histories of the inmates because inmate perspectives and roles within the subculture could be related to the type of offense. Table 1-4 contains the inmate's report of the offense or offenses for which he or she was committed to the Department of Youth Services, which we coded into seven offense categories. Wherever possible we cross-validated these self-reports against the institutional records. Since many of the inmates who were adjudicated delinquent had committed more than one offense, the offense totals may exceed 100 percent. In Table 1-5 we collapsed the offenses in Table 1-4 into three categories of seriousness, classifying offenses against the person or against property and person as highly serious; property offenses, automobile offenses, and drug offenses as moderately serious; and public misbehavior and juvenile status offenses as the least serious. In instances of multiple offenses the inmate was classified on the basis of the most serious offense.

In analyzing Tables 1-4 and 1-5 we see that the great preponderance of crimes committed by boys consist of property-related offenses like larceny, burglary, or automobile theft. Apart from property offenses, however, there appears to be some skew in the offense distributions, with the inmates in the custody-oriented cottages having somewhat more serious offenses and correspondingly fewer less-serious offenses. For the vast majority of females, juvenile status offenses were the primary bases of commitment. Both the male property pattern and the female status pattern are characteristic of institutionalized juvenile offenders [19]. Moreover, there did not appear to be intracottage differences on the basis of offense for which the inmates were committed.

Prior Institutional Experience

Recidivism is often used as an indicator of criminal commitment and a measure of the extent to which the inmate has been socialized into a deviant value system. Table 1-6 compares the proportion of

Table 1–3. Mean Age of First Contact with Juvenile Court

	Custody-Oriented Cottages				Treatment-Oriented Cottages			
	Group	Individual			Individual	Group		
	Cottage 9	Cottage 8	Elms	Westview	Lancaster (female)	Topsfield (co-ed)	Sunset	Shirley	"I Belong"
Age of first contact with juvenile court	12.6	13.2	12.7	13.1	13.1	14.1	12.5	13.8	12.4
Percentage with first contact by age 12	56%	40%	51%	41%	29%	13%	47%	19%	50%

28 Neutralizing Inmate Violence

Table 1-4. Offenses for which Inmates Are Presently Committed *(percentages)*

	Custody-Oriented Cottages					Treatment-Oriented Cottages			
	Group	Individual				Individual	Group		
Offenses	Cottage 9	Cottage 8	Elms	Westview	Lancaster (female)	Topsfield (co-ed)	Sunset	Shirley	"I Belong"
Person[a]	11%	13%	23%	17%	5%	0%	7%	6%	13%
Property and person[b]	15	20	13	14	5	0	13	13	13
Property[c]	22	27	23	24	13	20	40	25	25
Automobile offenses[d]	56	27	35	31	15	20	53	19	13
Drug-related offenses[e]	26	33	33	24	20	47	0	7	0
Public misbehavior[f]	7	13	10	17	8	7	13	0	13
Juvenile status offenses[g]	11	7	15	21	85	60	7	19	13

Note: Percentages may total more than 100 because inmates may have been committed for several offenses.
[a] Includes such offenses as assaults, rapes, manslaughter, or murder.
[b] Includes such offenses as armed or unarmed robbery, pursesnatching or picking pockets.
[c] Includes such offenses as burglary, breaking and entering, shoplifting, larceny, vandalism, and forgery.
[d] Includes such offenses as larceny of a motor vehicle, using without authority, driving without a license, or some other variation of stolen car.

Table 1-4. (Notes) continued

e Includes such offenses as possession of drugs, being under the influence of drugs, or possession of narcotics paraphernalia.
f Includes such offenses as disorderly conduct, loitering, and public drunkenness.
g Includes the juvenile status offenses of running away from home, truancy, and "stubborn child."

Table 1-5. Seriousness of Inmates' Current Offenses (percentages)

Seriousness	Custody-Oriented Cottages					Treatment-Oriented Cottages			
	Group	Individual				Individual	Group		
	Cottage 9	Cottage 8	Elms	Westview	Lancaster (female)	Topsfield (co-ed)	Sunset	Shirley	"I Belong"
High	24%	36%	35%	27%	9%	0%	23%	21%	29%
Moderate	68	43	60	54	34	60	77	57	43
Low	8	21	5	19	57	40	0	21	28

Note: Totals may not add to 100 due to rounding.

inmates in each cottage with prior institutional experience. Overall, about 10 percent more of the inmates in the custody-oriented cottages had prior institutional experiences than did the inmates in the treatment-oriented cottages. A somewhat smaller proportion of the female inmates had prior institutional contacts than did their male counterparts.

Inmate Classification and Cottage Population Selection

In addition to comparing inmate background characteristics, we should note the process by which residents were assigned to the various cottages and the extent to which these populations reflected selected groups. Of the cottages we studied, the staff of "I Belong" and Topsfield exercised the greatest amount of control over which inmates entered their programs. Since these were relatively new programs the staff had screened and selected the initial inmate populations. One "I Belong" staff member succinctly noted the implications that this had for the cottage population:

> Compared to kids in other parts of Shirley, they're better than average. They've been screened. They're what you might call the cream of the crop. They're easier to work with; more of a willingness to be helped. The kids are younger and usually first-time offenders. They have a better chance because they haven't been exposed [to institutional living]. They haven't picked up on the games these guys [in Shirley] can play—the way they stick together. . . .

As our comparison of background characteristics indicates, the "I Belong" boys were somewhat younger, physically smaller, less criminally mature, less institutionally sophisticated, and easier to treat in a relatively free and permissive environment. Because of these selection factors, "I Belong" was perhaps the least comparable cottage in our sample. While they shared a number of characteristics with the residents of other cottages, some real differences did exist.

Similarly, one of the Topsfield staff members described the effect that their selection processes had on the characteristics of their residents:

> Compared to other kids in the Youth Services, they're very intelligent, passive kids who take a lot more on themselves, rather than others. The kids we have are less hard-core, if you want to use that term, than at other institutions because of the different type of selecting we have. We tried to pick kids who were more verbal than the average kid. They're basically a little more of a family problem than the average kid.

Table 1-6. Prior Institutional Experience (percentage)

	Custody-Oriented Cottages				Treatment-Oriented Cottages			
	Group	Individual			Individual	Group		
	Cottage 9	Cottage 8	Elms	Westview	Lancaster (female)	Topsfield (co-ed)	Sunset	Shirley	"I Belong"
Percentage of inmates with prior institutional experience	92%	82%	90%	62%	60%	87%	73%	67%	50%

Despite these screenings the Topsfield population was not appreciably different from the groups in other settings. Topsfield was coeducational, however, and the presence of both boys and girls raises obvious problems of comparability with the sex-segregated cottages.

The Shirley cottage staff exercised less control over the inmates entering their program than did Topsfield or "I Belong." They recruited their population from inmates at the reception centers awaiting institutional assignment. While the staff encouraged these boys to volunteer, they were under considerable pressure from the DYS to take boys who posed exceptional problems. Consequently, although they tried to control admissions, the counterpressure to take the more difficult boys effectively vitiated population selection biases.

Among the custody-oriented cottages, the Cottage 9 staff exercised the least control over their inmate intake. Any boy who ran away or violated some other institutional rule could be transferred to Cottage 9, which provided a secure facility for the open school. As one staff member observed: "They're in here for infraction on top of infraction. They're in the institution for doing wrong, and here [in Cottage 9] for doing wrong within the institution. They're doubly wrong." Almost all the boys in Cottage 9 were there for running away from the institution, although of itself this did not particularly distinguish them from the boys remaining in the open school [20].

The Cottage 8 staff exercised very little control over which boys were assigned there. New arrivals at the Industrial School were sent by the administration to Cottage 5 or Cottage 8 on the basis of the space available.

At the Lyman School there was some degree of selectivity in assigning boys to Elms or Westview Cottages. Although both cottages emphasized vocational training, the work demands in Elms were fewer than those of the Westview cafeteria program. Moreover, the cottage director at Elms ran a more highly structured program, and older or more difficult Lyman offenders were assigned to him because he had "more control than the other masters over the boys." As he observed, "If I wasn't doing such a good job, all their [institutional administration's] problems wouldn't be coming down to me. They claim I can reach kids better; I know this. I hate to get the problems [i.e., problem inmates], but I can't pass them off, they've got to go somewhere." As a consequence, there was some tendency for the inmates at Elms to be somewhat older and tougher than in some of the other Lyman cottages. But since Elms also had the largest cottage population, there was considerable internal variation.

The cafeteria program—food preparation and service—dominated

Westview cottage life. Since this program was more demanding than most other assignments, the cafeteria director and Lyman administration tried to fill it with inmates who volunteered. Many boys volunteered as a means of combatting institutional boredom, but since the program had to be staffed regardless of inmate willingness, many boys were simply assigned to it. Accordingly there were no pronounced differences between the inmates of Westview and Elms.

Sunset cottage received the older residue after boys were assigned to Elms or to Westview cottages. Whatever biases this selection process introduced were not discernible in the data, and the boys in Sunset appeared similar to those in Westview and Elms.

The criteria for assignment to cottages at Lancaster were among the least discriminating. There was some tendency to assign more difficult girls to Putnam cottage, which was reputed to have a more disciplined and structured program. In practice, however, the availability of bedspace was the predominant basis of classification. Moreover, our aggregation of the Lancaster data for most analytical purposes vitiates any selection biases.

Observations on Inmate Background Characteristics

In order to determine whether the cottage subculture differences we obtained resulted from organizational treatment differences or from imported features of the inmate populations, we examined the influence of background characteristics on inmate attitudes and perspectives. It is possible that certain background factors influenced an inmates' assignments to a particular cottage, and that such population selection biases could explain cottage subculture variations even in the absence of treatment. We found that residents of the custody cottages came in contact with the juvenile courts somewhat earlier than their treatment cottage counterparts. Similarly, the inmates in the custody-oriented cottages may have committed somewhat more serious offenses than those in the treatment-oriented cottages. Furthermore, a slightly larger proportion of the inmates in the custody-oriented cottages had prior institutional exposure as compared to the inmates in the treatment-oriented cottages.

These three measures of criminal sophistication—age of first involvement with the juenile justice system, criminal offenses, and prior institutional experience—differentiate between the custody and treatment-oriented cottages. This, coupled with the fact that the custody cottage staff exercised less control over the inmates assigned to them leaves the possibility that "criminal sophistication" might somehow have affected both the initial cottage assignment and the differences in treatment outcomes. Our analysis did not reveal any significant relationships between these three variables, suggesting that their effects, if any, are independent. Moreover, our analysis of the effects of these variables individually within each cottage did not reveal significant differences among the inmates on these dimensions (see the Appendix). Within the same setting, none of these characteristics discriminated among inmates. Thus our analysis satisfied us that despite the presence of some cottage population differences, they were probably not the sources of the substantial cottage variation we found.

Cottage Staff Characteristics

There were much greater background differences among staff in the various cottages than there were among inmates. Many of the differences in personnel characteristics reflect the demands of the job or the sophistication of the treatment techniques being used. A therapeutic community treatment program requires relatively well-educated or well-trained personnel. Similarly, treatment settings may entail greater and more active involvement by staff in inmate activities, and this would place a premium on younger staff members.

Table 1-7 indicates the proportion of staff in each cottage who were under thirty years of age and over fifty; college graduates; female; and those employed by the DYS for less than one year or more than five years. As can be seen, the treatment cottages were staffed primarily by younger personnel, while the custody cottages were predominantly staffed by older people. The low proportion of older staff in Cottage 9 reflects the physical requirements of the job: the need to occasionally physically restrain an acting out youngster. There was also a strong relationship ($r = -.579$, $p < .001$) between staff age and higher education, with the younger staff members much more likely to hold college degrees.

Since the younger staff members were disproportionately concentrated in the treatment-oriented cottages, these cottages generally had more highly educated personnel. Lancaster had a greater balance among staff in terms of age and education. Those programs treating female inmates—Lancaster and Topsfield—also had the greatest proportion of women on their staffs.

The custody and treatment cottages can also be distinguished on the basis of staff members' tenure with the Department of Youth Services. Miller had been in office approximately eighteen months when we conducted this study. We expected significant differences in treatment philosophies between staff members recruited during Miller's regime and those who joined under the previous, more cus-

Table 1-7. Cottage Staff Characteristics

	Custody-Oriented Cottages					Treatment-Oriented Cottages			
	Group	Individual				Individual	Group		
	Cottage 9	Cottage 8	Elms	Westview	Lancaster (female)	Topsfield (co-ed)	Sunset	Shirley	"I Belong"
Percentage of staff members under 30 years of age	0	19	13	30	39	78	80	44	75
Percentage of staff members over 50 years of age	11	63	53	50	39	0	20	38	13
Percentage of staff members who are college graduates	11	13	20	30	50	67	40	43	75
Percentage of staff members with tenure with the Department of Youth Services:									
One year or less	33	27	0	0	29	78	60	13	75
Five years or more	33	67	60	50	43	0	0	19	13
Percentage of female staff members	0%	40%	13%	10%	79%	44%	0%	19%	38%

todial regime. Only about 15 percent of the custody-oriented staff had joined DYS within the preceding year, as compared to nearly 50 percent of the treatment-oriented staff, who again tended to be younger and better educated. About 55 percent of the custody-oriented staff had been with the department more than five years, as compared with only 11 percent of the treatment-oriented staff. This process of self-selection and selective recruitment, coupled with substantial cottage staff differences in age and education, helps to explain the profound differences in staff treatment orientations and practices in custody and treatment settings that emerged through the processes of institutional decentralization.

Cottage Population Size

There appears to be a relationship between cottage program goals and the size of the inmate population. Large inmate populations may generate more intense custodial practices by increasing pressures toward regimentation and mass processing, thereby limiting opportunities for effective interaction between staff and inmates. Our data lend some support to the hypotheses relating increased size to increased custodialism. Table 1–8 presents the number of inmates, the number of staff members, and staff-inmate ratio in the various cottages. The custody cottages had considerably larger inmate populations than did the treatment-oriented cottages. With only slightly fewer staff, the treatment cottages enjoyed a substantially better staff-inmate ratio. Actually these staff-inmate ratios are somewhat deceptive, since the staff coverage was divided into two 8-hour shifts, seven days per week. In terms of effective contact, the staff-to-inmate ratio in Cottage 9 was more like 1:10, contrasted with "I Belong" which was closer to 1:3.

Although there appears to be some relationship between the number of inmates, the staff-inmate ratio, and the cottage goals, a low population and favorable staff-inmate ratio are probably necessary conditions—but insufficient by themselves—for the development of a therapeutic program. Population size and staff-inmate ratios place constraints on the types of treatment programs that can be used. The treatment cottage staff people were aware of the deleterious impact of large populations on programs, and they tried to limit the number of inmates. Since treatment staff were better able to control the cottage population inputs than were the staff of the custody cottages, this suggests that staff action and program orientation determine cottage population size, rather than the size of the population determining the program.

Table 1-8. Cottage Population and Staff-Inmate Ratio

	Custody-Oriented Cottages						Treatment-Oriented Cottages			
	Group	Individual					Individual	Group		
	Cottage 9	Cottage 8[a]	Elms	Westview	Lancaster		Topsfield (co-ed)	Sunset	Shirley	"I Belong"
					Putnam	Clara Barton				
					(female)[b]					
Number of inmates	27	15	40	29	28	22	15	15	16	8
Number of staff	9	16	15	10	5	6	9	5	16	8
Staff-inmate ratio	1:3	1:1.1	1:2.7	1:2.9	1:5.6	1:3.7	1:1.7	1:3	1:1	1:1

[a] Cottage 8 was in the process of being closed at the time of our study. During the year prior to the closing of Shirley, the population of the open-school cottages was likely to be about twenty-five, and thus much more typical of custody-oriented cottages.
[b] Lancaster was not decentralized to nearly the same degree as were the Shirley and Lyman cottages. In addition to the staff members assigned to these individual cottages, several other teachers and supervisors serviced these cottages and others as well. Since we aggregate our Lancaster data for most purposes, our staff $N = 14$, unless the analysis is restricted to each individual cottage.

SUMMARY

In this initial chapter we have defined our basic research objectives and described the institutions in which this study was conducted. The principal focus of this study is subcultural violence—the physical, psychological, and verbal aggression that inmates inflict upon one another—and the organizational structural features that increase or decrease it. We have described briefly the research settings in which the opportunity to explore these problems arose, focusing on the institutional changes introduced by Commissioner Miller.

It is important to appreciate the extent to which institutional decentralization produced a number of autonomous cottages within the former training schools—veritable "mini-institutions" within the larger settings. The comparative research design enabled us to analyze systematically the organizational factors associated with the various treatment programs that staff implemented within these mini-institutions.

Finally, we introduced the subjects—the cottage residents and staff—whose adaptations and interactions provide the basis for this study. This initial introduction was static: a description of their background characteristics.

In the ensuing chapters we will examine the sources of treatment variation, the organizational structural implications of alternative intervention strategies, and the ultimate impact that cottage treatment programs have on their residents.

Chapter 2

Organizational Structure and Program Characteristics of the Cottages

The organizational structure and program characteristics of the ten cottages in our sample will be examined here. The cottage sample is presented by means of an organizational typology that classifies correctional facilities on the basis of both their custody or treatment goals and their group-oriented or individual-oriented intervention strategies and social-control techniques.

There have been several attempts to classify the variations found in correctional organizations—both juvenile and adult. One common classification scheme groups organizations on the basis of their goals, distinguishing, for example, between custody and treatment [1]. Studt suggested four different organization models for treating offenders—custodial, educational, psychotherapeutic, or group treatment—describing for each the corresponding staff ideologies and intervention strategies [2]. Street, Vinter, and Perrow classified juvenile correctional organizations according to their goals—obedience and conformity, reeducation and development, or treatment—arrayed on a continuum from custody to treatment [3]. Ohlin suggested an alternative typology for youth correctional institutions, distinguishing between protective custody, treatment, and therapeutic community models [4]. Ohlin's models resemble those of Street et al., although Ohlin distinguished between individual treatment and group or therapeutic community treatment models to highlight the significant differences between these two types of correctional organizations. Ohlin's protective custody model merged Street's organizational distinctions between obedience/conformity and reeducation/development to emphasize the authoritarian and paternalistic style of both kinds of institutions. The typology proposed here incorporates Ohlin's treatment-organization distinctions and Street's custody-institution distinctions, resulting in the four types of organizations described by Studt.

Juvenile correctional organizations are typically located on this custody/treatment continuum according to the organizational emphasis they place on control and containment, and education, vocational training, and work experience, as opposed to clinical or group treatment. The intervention strategies used to accomplish these custodial or therapeutic goals may be located on a continuum ranging from those that are group- or group-process-oriented, to those that are oriented toward individual characteristics. Group-oriented strategies reflect efforts to change or control an inmate based on the group of which he or she is a member, while individual strategies focus more directly on the individual apart from the larger grouping.

The typology used here identifies four different types of organizations, reflecting the various combinations of means and ends. Both axes of organizational variation—custody/treatment goals and group/individual means—reflect a continuum, and these may vary independently. These four different organizations constitute markedly different correctional strategies that in turn reflect variations in staff assumptions about the causes and cures of delinquency. These variations are reflected in many aspects of the formal organizational structure, the treatment programs used, the social control practices, the nature of staff-inmate relationships, and the like. Ultimately, these structural differences are reflected in the articulation of the inmate subculture as well.

The combinations of goals and means yield the typology shown in Figure 2-1, with the four cells reflecting the combinations of goals and means. These four types of organizations correspond to the treatment models Studt described, while making clearer the relationship between organizational goals and intervention strategies. Although this typology was developed to analyze systematic variation in juvenile correctional settings, the goals/means framework should also aid in understanding other types of total institutions, such as adult correctional and mental health settings.

The alternative treatment strategies indicated in the typology parallel the historic development of juvenile correctional institutions. The group-custody or maximum-security model is based on assumptions of inmate free-will and deterrence, with historical analogues to the earliest institutional response to juvenile deviance in the nineteenth century. The individual-custody organization or industrial training school model, based on assumptions of inadequate socializa-

Figure 2-1. Correctional Typology

Organizational Means	Organizational Goals	
	Custody	Treatment
Group-Oriented Intervention Strategy	**Group Custody** Custodial[a] Obedience/conformity[b] Protective custody[c]	**Group Treatment** Group treatment[a] Treatment[b] Therapeutic community[c]
Individual-Oriented Intervention Strategy	**Individual Custody** Educational[a] Reeducation/development[b] Protective custody[c]	**Individual Treatment** Psychotherapeutic[a] Treatment[b,c]

[a]Organization corresponding to typology in Elliot Study, Sheldon L. Messinger, and Thomas P. Wilson, C-Unit: *Search for Community in Prison* (New York: Russell Sage Foundation, 1968), p. 12.
[b]Organization corresponding to typology in David Street, Robert Vinter, and Charles Perrow, *Organization for Treatment* (New York: Free Press, 1966), p. 12.
[c]Organization corresponding to typology in Lloyd Ohlin, "Organizational Reform in Correctional Agencies," in Daniel Glaser, ed., *Handbook of Criminology* (Chicago: Rand McNally, 1974), p. 1000.

tion, can be traced to the juvenile reformatories of the last third of the nineteenth century, which were organized around the cottage plan and emphasized moral development and vocational education. The individual treatment institutions, based on assumptions of individual pathology and a medical model, can be traced to the influence of Freudian psychology and the emergence of professional social work at the beginning of the twentieth century. The group-treatment model, based on assumptions of peer group dynamics, has only gained prominence within the past half-century [5].

The typology identifies four types of organizational alternatives for "rehabilitating" juvenile offenders. Every correctional organization confronts essentially similar problems of defining who its clients are, what "caused" them to be adjudicated delinquent and institutionalized, what they should be like when they are "rehabilitated," what the goals of the organization are, and what types of intervention strategies and social-control practices are required to achieve these goals. Analytically, these questions identify a number of basic and interrelated variables that, taken together, constitute the organizational structure. These variables include a staff ideology as it defines the inmates and their needs; organizational goals as a directive to meet these needs; staff intervention strategies implemented through institutional programs and social control practices; and staff relationships with inmates as the ultimate source of client change.

The organizational and intervention alternatives identified in the typology represent different answers to the same questions. Staff members who have varying assumptions about the causes of delinquency and the end product of rehabilitation will pursue dissimilar correctional goals using the intervention strategies, programs, and social-control techniques that are consistent with their particular assumptions. Because of the relationship between ideology and behavior, staff assumptions and practices will tend to be internally consistent and will produce distinctive organizations with significantly different structures and programs. To the extent that the inmate subculture is responsive to organizational variability, these organizational differences will be reflected in the characteristics of the respective inmate social systems.

STAFF IDEOLOGY AND GOALS

In the course of institutional decentralization Commissioner Miller had provided some general outlines of a therapeutic community program and had constantly emphasized that the goal of the Department of Youth Services was to do "good things for kids." The various autonomous cottages and their staff within the DYS facilities used a wide range of disparate and almost contradictory intervention strategies and techniques of social control in pursuit of this goal.

In this section we will identify some of the ideological sources of program variation and indicate how they relate to the substantial differences in strategies of change. Our discussion of staff ideology and goals is keyed to Table 2-1, which provides twelve selected indicators for measuring the custody/treatment attitudes of cottage staff. The table represents a condensation of an extensive analysis employing multiple indicators and scales based on both survey results and coded interviews. The condensation is possible with relatively little loss of information because of the great degree of internal consistency in the larger analysis. The additional items and scales reiterate the patterns shown in this table [6].

A correctional ideology explains what an inmate is like, how he or she became that way, what the appropriate correctional strategies for resolving these difficulties are, the likelihood of intervention success, and what the inmate will be like when the necessary changes have occurred [7]. It includes staff assumptions about the nature and causes of criminal behavior as well as prescriptions and proscriptions for how inmates should be treated. Correctional ideologies are important because staff people who believe otherwise and act on those alternative beliefs will pursue alternative change goals and use different types of intervention strategies.

In the field of corrections there are several ideological explanations of who the clients are and how they are to be handled and changed. In a very important respect the process of institutional decentralization initiated by Miller provided a setting in which diverse ideologies could flourish and the programmatic implications of these differences emerge. While there was some ideological diversity among cottage staff, the processes of recruitment, cottage assignments, and self-selection, coupled with socialization into the work role and selective turnover, produced relatively homogeneous beliefs among cottage personnel about what they were trying to accomplish in their respective programs [8]. Staff team meetings in the various cottages further helped to forge a consensus among personnel.

We traced the variations in the decentralized cottage programs to differences in the underlying assumptions staff held about delinquency and change. A variety of questions were designed to measure ideological perspectives among cottage staff. Not surprisingly, we found fundamental differences between cottage personnel on a number of ideological dimensions. We examined some elements of authoritarianism, as reflected in an emphasis on obedience, respect for authority, reliance on external controls, and a preference for the status quo; psychological or nonpsychological views of deviance and treatment; views on the relation of free will to deviance; views of inmates as dangerous and untrustworthy; and optimism about the likelihood of positive inmate change. Interview materials also elaborated staff perceptions of the "kinds of kids" they were treating, and the type of inmate change sought. These attitudinal variations help to explain the differences in staff choice of cottage programs.

One component of a correctional ideology may include elements of an authoritarian perspective—with emphasis on domination and obedience, submission to external authority, and a preference for the status quo. Custody staff appeared to be much more concerned with obedience and respect and to place a greater emphasis on external controls to achieve conformity than did treatment staff (see Table 2–1, scale 1). Among the custodial cottage personnel, authoritarian views tended to predominate, while among the treatment cottage staff, such views were subordinate or absent. Substantially more of the custody-oriented staff people were concerned with respect for authority than the staff in the treatment settings, and they were more likely to endorse external controls to curb delinquency.

Custody personnel were also much more likely to be resistant to

Table 2-1. Selected Indicators of Staff Ideology and Goals *(percentages)*

	Custody-Oriented Cottages					Treatment-Oriented Cottages			
	Group	*Individual*				*Individual*		*Group*	
Scale	Cottage 9	Cottage 8	Elms	Westview	Lancaster (female)	Topsfield (co-ed)	Sunset	Shirley	"I Belong"
1. Respect for authority	89%	88%	73%	67%	54%	11%	0%	25%	25%
2. Authority vs. psychology	78	75	73	50	36	0	0	13	13
3. Free will and deterrence	79	81	60	78	50	0	40	38	13
4. Delinquents cannot be understood	67	75	67	67	43	0	0	19	13
5. Inmates are dangerous	67	63	47	56	43	0	20	38	13
6. Optimism that positive change will occur	22	31	36	25	69	78	80	94	88
7. Conformity to staff orders	56	69	71	63	50	0	20	6	13

8. Negative staff perceptions of informal inmate groups	75	75	43	29	30	0	0	11	13
9. Custody-oriented goals	37	34	32	37	38	15	13	21	10
10. Personnel acting in clinical capacity	0	18	7	10	21	56	20	44	50
11. Group orientation	56	31	50	14	50	38	50	56	67
12. Entire staff has authority	0	0	0	38	5	50	75	89	88

innovation. Personnel at Lancaster—the female setting—tended to be more like the custody-oriented staff than the treatment-oriented staff on these dimensions, although their views were more moderate. Cottage staff also differed in their reliance on psychological or nonpsychological explanations of delinquency causation (see Table 2-1, scale 2). Staff members in the treatment-oriented cottages were more than twice as likely as the custody-oriented staff to perceive their charges as "rejected children who need help" and as suffering from emotional or psychological problems. Individual treatment staff were more likely to perceive inmates as "sick" than their group-oriented counterparts, since individual treatment relied more closely on a medical model of delinquency. With the exception of the Lancaster staff, custody cottage personnel did not regard the bulk of their inmates as suffering from emotional or psychological problems. When staff people were forced to choose between an authoritarian response and a more clinical response, the differences between custody-oriented personnel and treatment-oriented personnel emerged in stark relief, with the custody-oriented staff about six times as likely as treatment staff to prefer "stricter laws and more law enforcement" over "understanding problems."

Custody staff were more inclined to identify the individual's exercise of free will as the source of deviance, while the treatment staff pointed to psychological conflict or environmental factors (see Table 2-1, scale 3). The propensity of custody staff to attribute deviance to individual free choice derives from their nonpsychological orientation and their reliance on external controls to enforce conformity, while treatment staffs' attribution of inmate deviance to emotional or psychological conflict follows from their more psychological and deterministic orientation. The custody staff people were more than twice as likely as treatment staff to see delinquency as a product of free will that can be deterred by a relatively simple pleasure-pain mechanism.

Custody staff, rejecting assumptions of psychopathology, which might make delinquent or bizarre behavior more explicable than assumptions of rationality, found delinquents considerably more difficult to understand than did treatment staff (see Table 2-1, scale 4). Similarly, custody and treatment staff differed over the extent to which delinquents were "incapable" of normal relationships. Custody staff were substantially more likely than treatment staff to believe that delinquents "cannot be friends among themselves" or form normal relationships with young people or adults. The custody-treatment staff differences also prevailed with respect to their belief that "delinquents are incompetent," with a majority of the custody staff seeing inmates as incompetent to "make decisions even about everyday living problems." Staff were also asked whether they regarded the inmates in their cottages as "hard-core delinquents" who posed "serious control and management problems," and custody-oriented personnel were about four times as likely as treatment staff to accept this characterization. On most dimensions Lancaster staff views were very similar to those of staff members in the individual male custody cottages. Custody staff people were more than two and a half times as likely as the treatment staff to see their charges as dangerous and untrustworthy, although individualized program strategies tempered this view (see Table 2—1, scale 5).

The Lancaster staff regarded their female inmates as almost as dangerous as male delinquents. To some extent the custody staff perceptions of inmate dangerousness may reflect something of a self-fulfilling prophecy. Inmates in the custody settings may have been less cooperative or reliable and more prone to violent outbursts than those in treatment settings, and the staff perceptions of these qualities may well have been accurate. But these differences fail to take into account the extent to which the expectations and treatment strategies in the custody programs may actually create or exacerbate these tendencies. Since the inmate populations were matched to minimize client differences, to the extent that there is a relationship between program structure and inmate responses, the differences reported by custody staff may be a product of inmate reactions to staff behavior rather than an independent characteristic of the inmates. Treatment staff were from two to three times more optimistic than custody staff that their efforts would result in positive changes among inmates (see Table 2—1, scale 6).

Staff attitudes were probed by means of interviews as well as questionnaires. Staff in custody cottages tended to describe their charges as repeated criminals, unpredictable, or dangerous, while staff in the treatment cottages tended to describe them as suffering from family, personal, or psychological problems. Although there was some overlap in their coded responses, the results were consistent with the previously noted attitudinal differences.

The group custody staff shared an almost undifferentiated perception of the boys in Cottage 9 as bad, unstable, and untrustworthy. A preoccupation with unpredictability and unreliability characterized most of their responses. "They're alright until they don't get their way, then they get a little disturbed and do something wrong. . . . Most of the kids here are no good. . . . When they get excited, they are extremely unreliable and untrustworthy, and most of the kids sent here are capable of flying off the handle. . . . We used to be able to categorize them as mean or vicious or sick, but now, with the drug problem, they can be charming and disarming one minute and vicious the next...."

There was somewhat greater diversity among the individual custody staff perceptions, with some recognition of the relationship of home and family problems to the inmates' current difficulties. These staff described the inmates as "a little bit of everything.... The boys' records speak for themselves.... Several types: homeless types, they've been here for years, like vegetables; then there is the element that no one can straighten out; and the element that no one but age can straighten out.... Some are just full of the devil. Some will lose it as they grow, some won't." A mood of passivity and pessimism characterized these responses. Staff described children "who've gone astray," "who are full of devilment," "who may or may not straighten out as they mature." There was an air of fatalism; whether or not the child could be rehabilitated was determined by factors beyond the control of the staff.

The staff at Lancaster shared many of the same custodial views, although they also attributed many of their inmates' difficulties to home and family problems, or psychological or emotional disturbances. These inmates were perceived as somewhat less "bad" or "dangerous" than their male counterparts, but somewhat more disturbed or problematical.

Consistent with the questionnaire data, treatment staff regarded the youths as suffering from personal problems or as similar to other adolescents. They also showed a greater sensitivity to the labeling process in the juvenile justice system. On the whole, treatment staff evinced a much greater awareness of family and psychological problems. "We have kids with problems.... I'd say these kids' internal coping ability does not match the stress of their environment.... We see these breakdowns of coping abilities in terms of drugs or transgressions with the law." They were much more likely to offer clinical descriptions of their charges. In addition, they were more positive in their assessments of the boys' reliability and trustworthiness.

We also asked the cottage staff, "What do you think causes kids to get in trouble and end up in a place like this?" to identify where they located the causes of delinquency and the complexity of the causation model they used. While there was fairly widespread consensus among all staff members that the primary causes of delinquency were family-related—broken families; inadequate parenting; working mothers who provided little supervision—custody-oriented and treatment-oriented staff viewed the consequences of family inadequacies differently. Personnel in the custody-oriented cottages emphasized the children's failure to learn discipline and respect for authority as a consequence of this family breakdown, while the treatment-oriented staff saw family breakdown as compounding other influences by not providing a backdrop or insulation against other delinquency-causing factors. Custody and treatment personnel also differed in the complexity of their delinquency causation model, with most of the custody-oriented staff relying on a single factor to explain delinquency, almost invariably the family. The treatment-oriented staff saw delinquency causation as a much more complex process.

Not only does a staff correctional ideology explain deviance and its correction, it also includes a picture of the end result. Staff people have an image of the product they seek and the behavioral responses an inmate must show to indicate his or her "rehabilitation." They employ various criteria to evaluate an inmate's institutional behavior as an indicator of readiness to return to the community. The custody staff were about six times more likely than treatment staff to favor inmates who followed orders and kept out of trouble, reflecting the relative emphasis that staff members placed on external controls versus internal controls (see Table 2–1, scale 7). In one of the staff questionnaire items, they were asked to choose between an inmate who was obedient and conforming and an inmate who was an active problem-solver. While more than a third of the custody-oriented staff preferred inmates who did not break rules and kept out of trouble, all of the treatment-oriented staff wanted inmates to gain understanding.

We also asked the staff, "What makes a good kid?" and "What makes a bad kid?" to further identify institutional criteria that staff people use for evaluating inmate behavior. Staff in the custody cottages were more concerned with obedience, conformity, and deference, while staff in the treatment cottages were more concerned with their inmates gaining insight and self-awareness and acting responsibly toward others. Custody cottage staff placed much greater emphasis on an inmate's demeanor, politeness, manners, and ability to follow orders, on the theory that conformity in the institution will lead to submissive law-abiding behavior after release. Treatment staff emphasized inmate participation and involvement in the change process, on the theory that resolution of their internal conflicts will reduce the prospects of subsequent deviance.

Staff perceptions of inmates were also reflected in the types of relationships they encouraged between inmates (see Table 2–1, scale 8). Custody-oriented staff frowned on informal inmate associations, preferring inmate self-isolation, while treatment staff encouraged inmate involvement with other inmates. We asked the staff people if "the boy who gets the most out of his stay here keeps to himself and doesn't get too close to the other boys." A third of the Cottage 9 staff and nearly a quarter of the individual custody staff endorsed inmate self-isolation, while none of the treatment-oriented staff approved of it. That custody staff encouraged this adaptation probably reflects their general perception of inmates and their apprehensions about inmate collusion against staff people.

Personnel in individual custody settings were not as likely as Cottage 9 staff to perceive informal inmate groups negatively or to expend as much effort separating them. For most of the individual custody staff, however, informal inmate groups were problematical. "In some cases groups will hurt. Bad kids can influence good kids, and that's bad." Their primary concern was that unsupervised associations would reinforce negative behavior, such as running away from school, creating disturbances, or the like. When staff observed clusters of boys "conspiring" together in small, furtive circles, their response was similar to that of Cottage 9 staff: separate the members of the group, supervise them more closely, and deny them opportunities to connive.

Lancaster staff followed a similar pattern. When a negative group emerged, they attempted to separate the trouble-makers and instigators to minimize their influence on other inmates. This tendency to disrupt groups was also reinforced by their concerns about the emergence of homosexual relationships among the girls. Their sensitivity to this caused them to be vigilant in watching girls who consistently clustered together.

While a substantial proportion of custody-oriented staff regarded inmate groups as undesirable, less than 10 percent of the group treatment staff shared this view, in part because their principal intervention strategy required the mobilization of the inmate group. Despite their general preference for inmate involvement, when groups began showing a negative influence the staff responded similarly to their custody counterparts—disrupt the group. So even the group treatment staff, whose efforts to mobilize the inmate group was a basic part of their treatment strategy, stood ready to neutralize the less helpful aspects of inmate associations. However, staff concern with the undesirable character of groups did not center around the dangers of "cooking something up" against staff, or planning runaways, but rather on the adverse influence the group might have on a susceptible inmate. They separated inmates to counter this deleterious impact.

Informal inmate groups were less problematical for individual treatment staff. Since they were not as sensitive to group processes, they paid less attention to groups and most found it difficult to generalize about groups. The primary danger they perceived was the tendency of groups to insulate individuals and prevent the staff from reaching them and developing therapeutic relationships. Despite these potential dangers, however, individual treatment staff did not actively disrupt inmate groups.

To the extent that staff ideologies influence organizational behavior, we would expect these competing explanations of delinquency to guide staff in pursuing different goals. The multiplicity of correctional purposes and justifications—retribution, incapacitation, special and general deterrence, reformation, resocialization, psychological treatment, protection, and so on—are all broadly subsumed under the rubrics of "custody" or "treatment" (see Table 2–1, scale 9). The cottages selected for this study were chosen because the combinations of custody and treatment goals pursued by their staff provided a continuum that corresponded to our theoretical model. Our initial selections were based on observation, but in addition we used several other indicators to refine the cottages' relative positions. Staff people were asked to choose and rank a variety of goals commonly associated with institutions for delinquents. The alternatives ranged over a wide area of correctional goals, and they were asked to weight their choices. Of eleven alternatives, six items—three clearly treatment-oriented and three clearly custody-oriented—were chosen by about 90 percent of the staff.

Treatment staff tried to facilitate community adjustment by helping delinquents "gain an understanding of the kind of things that got them into trouble," and by helping them "learn how to get along better with other people" to a much greater extent than custody-oriented personnel. These clinical goals were supported by cottage programs of community meetings, daily small-group therapy sessions, and, in one cottage, additional individual counseling. Custody-oriented personnel did not emphasize these goals, either theoretically or in daily practice. Taken together, these results strongly corroborate the cottage-goal placements that we made on the basis of observations.

The bulk of the custody-oriented staff attributed custodial purposes to their cottages: isolation, respect and discipline, and training and educating. According to Cottage 9 staff members, their purpose was "to try to prepare a kid to accept the responsibility of what he has done, and to prepare him with an education or a trade to go back and face the world."

It depends a lot on the kid himself. Some kids don't accept responsibility on their own part, and don't change. They've got to have a place to put these kids that break the law. Second, try to rehabilitate them. But nobody knows how to do that. These kids are so irrational from one day to the next, it's puzzling what to do.

In addition to describing relatively limited custodial or educational goals, these comments also underline the relationships between ideology and goals. They convey the sense of irrationality and unpredictability that made it difficult for staff personnel to engage in any real rehabilitative endeavors. There is the sense of willfulness, in which change is ultimately dependent on the inmate, and staff efforts become almost secondary.

Individual custody staff described their cottages' purposes in much the same way. They saw themselves as serving a dual function. On the one hand, their purpose was to provide "a place to detain them, to get them off the streets. You can't let them run in society...." At the same time, they also saw their goals as "to help kids. If you had them any length of time, it would be to give them some training, to teach them morals, manners, and good upbringing, although that's different from what they're used to." Again, the relationships between staff ideology and cottage goals emerges: the belief that the inmates are dangerous and should not be allowed to "run free in society"; the idea that they are different from other people, particularly because they have not learned discipline and respect for authority; and the conclusion that providing them with the personal discipline and skills demanded by the dominant culture will resolve their problems.

The Lancaster staff resembled the male individual-custody staff in their emphasis on the school's custody-oriented purposes. They also endorsed the isolation of the school as a kind of protective paternalism. "They have to have a little corner to hide people, and put them out of anyone's view." Several also suggested the school's purpose was to "protect the community against the kids." They also indicated the importance of education and training.

In addition, however, several Lancaster staff suggested more therapeutic and clinical purposes than did male custody personnel. Some indicated that the purpose was to "try to give a girl a chance to deal with herself and gain some insight, so she can deal with the community and make an adjustment when she goes back." Others said they tried to help their residents "learn to understand themselves and their family a little better." Despite the somewhat greater emphasis on treatment-type purposes, however, several staff members noted that the custodial goals predominated. "This place serves as a holding place for kids, and therapy is kind of secondary." To a greater extent than the male staff, the Lancaster personnel also emphasized the protective functions of the institution. They described their girls as the products of chaotic living experiences and subject to abuse, and they hoped the school could mitigate the deleterious impact of the community. For them the school's purpose was "to protect them. Gives the kids a chance to get away from their environment and the family, and gives them time to get settled and get organized."

By contrast, the treatment-oriented cottage staff members were much more concerned with treatment goals: helping inmates learn how to relate to other people; preparing them to readjust to society; and helping them develop insight and self-awareness. As one treatment staff member said, "We're trying to get the kids to face their problems. Maybe not solve them, but at least face them. Teach the kid to handle his community." In keeping with their treatment ideology, which recognized the complexity of delinquency causation, these staff members posited a number of interrelated goals for their cottages: "To have them try to understand their environment and their family problems, as well as their socioeconomic problems, and at the same time to be gaining insight into themselves and building up their own self-esteem in the structure as well." The group-process orientation of these staff appeared in their concern with the ways in which an individual related to the group, and the manner in which he interacted with others. Many treatment staff members indicated their cottage purpose was "to get the guys to think about how they relate to other kids, other people.... It's to learn something about themselves, how they come across, in what situations they blow up, what situations will get them in trouble, and how to avoid those."

We further identified organizational goals by examining the manner in which resources were allocated to achieve institutional purposes. In people-changing organizations, staff is the primary resource that can be allocated to treatment tasks. An organization pursuing custodial goals will allocate this major resource to control and containment personnel, or to educational or vocational staff (see Table 2—1, scale 10). Thus an organization pursuing treatment goals will devote a larger proportion of its resources to clinical and treatment personnel. The custody-oriented cottages had their personnel concentrated in the categories of line staff and education, while the treatment-oriented cottages had a much greater proportion of treatment staff, with a commensurate reduction in purely supervisory staff.

Cottage 9, the group custody setting, was comprised exclusively of custodial staff, with no clinical or educational personnel. Their daily program consisted exclusively of custody and supervision. The individual custody cottages were dominated by line staff, primarily cottage masters and matrons, and vocational instructors. Elms, Westview, Sunset, and Shirley cottages all had approximately the same number of cottage masters, assisted by their wives or other female line supervisors. Elms and Westview, the Lyman "trade cottages," also had the largest proportions of personnel in vocational instruction and inmate work supervision.

The major personnel difference, however, is reflected in the much larger proportion of clinical personnel associated with the treatment-oriented cottages. Shirley, Topsfield, and "I Belong" used the bulk of their staff in a clinical capacity, as compared with about 10 percent in the custody cottages. Lancaster was similar to the other individual custody cottages in staff role allocation, although they also used more clinicians to provide individual counseling to the girls.

Corresponding to custody-treatment distinctions, an organizational tension also exists between tendencies toward bureaucratization and those toward individualization. The pressures of bureaucratization lead personnel to deal with inmates according to gross characteristics. The pull toward individualization, on the other hand, leads to nonroutinized treatment, with potentially disruptive organizational consequences. The nonuniform nature of individual behavior results either in individualized, nonroutinized staff responses *or* in an effort to increase predictability through regimentation. While bureaucratization increases regimentation and clearly defined expectations of inmate behavior, individualization requires either specifying norms for every eventuality or delegating discretion and authority to low-level staff to enable them to deal with unpredictable situations and individual variation. The resolution of these countervailing pressures constitutes a primary source of organizational variation. Staff orientation toward groups or individuals presents a critical variable in explaining organizational behavior.

Organizational intervention strategies were refined by probing the extent to which staff dealt with inmates individually or as part of a group (see Table 2-1, scale 11). "I Belong," Shirley, and Cottage 9 yielded clear majorities favoring group-oriented strategies to change or control inmates. Elms, Sunset, and Lancaster occupied an intermediate position with respect to individualized or group-oriented change strategies. The response of the staff in Topsfield, Cottage 8, and Westview became progressively more oriented toward the individual. The relative cottage positions based on these responses reinforced our earlier location of the cottages through observation. "I Belong" and Shirley were consistently group-process/treatment-oriented cottages. Cottage 9 staff used group-oriented management strategies almost exclusively, because they provided an effective way of maintaining a high level of mass supervision and control. We classified these three cottages as using group-oriented change strategies.

Sunset and Elms cottages and Lancaster occupied intermediate positions on the group/individual continuum. Although programmatically Elms cottage emphasized vocational education and work experiences on an individual basis, it also had the largest cottage inmate population. Group management and mass processing techniques appeared to be an unavoidable by-product of a large population. Sunset, on the other hand, had previously relied heavily on group therapy treatment strategies, but because of staff shortages and a decline in the program, the consistent group-process approach was diminishing. The situation at Lancaster was similar. Although the cottage was heavily programmed, and inmates received a number of individualized educational, vocational, and clinical assignments, the staff also used group-oriented management and control strategies as well, such as group lock-ups and marching as a unit.

Topsfield, Cottage 8, and Westview were located toward the individualization end of the spectrum. Although treatment-oriented, Topsfield was not as group-process oriented as either Shirley cottage or "I Belong." The cottage directors and certain key staff members relied upon more individualized treatment—individual counseling and psychotherapy—to supplement the standard group-oriented programs. The location of Cottage 8 and Westview at the individual end of the intervention continuum was entirely consistent with our observations.

Based upon these various measures we are able to place the cottages in the study in relation to each other, in terms of their goals—custody or treatment—and in terms of the intervention strategies—individual or group—that staff used to achieve these goals. This placement is shown in Figure 2-2.

Although the presence of competing demands, extensive organizational co-mingling, the imposition of one treatment model upon another, and the prevalence of "rehabilitative rhetoric" in even the most custodial settings made identifying the goals of an organization and placing its location on the custody-treatment continuum extremely difficult, the emphasis staff placed on control and containment, education and vocational training, or clinical and group treatment offers a starting point. The initial placement of our sample

Figure 2–2. Cottage Position within the Organizational Typology

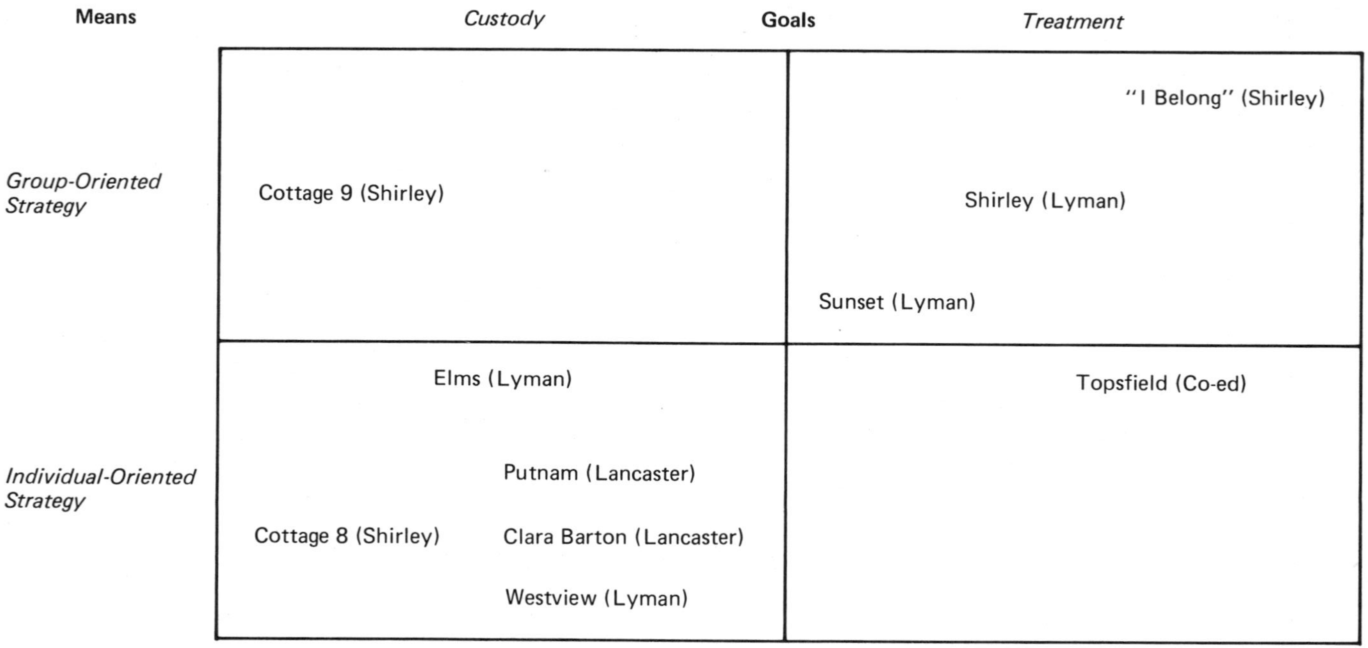
Means
Custody
Goals
Treatment
Group-Oriented Strategy
Individual-Oriented Strategy
Cottage 9 (Shirley)
"I Belong" (Shirley)
Shirley (Lyman)
Sunset (Lyman)
Elms (Lyman)
Putnam (Lancaster)
Cottage 8 (Shirley)
Clara Barton (Lancaster)
Westview (Lyman)
Topsfield (Co-ed)

cottages was guided by observation and interviews, and further discrimination followed the range of indicators of staff ideology and goals.

Figure 2-2 indicates the location of the cottages in our sample within the organizational typology. While the cottage positions are necessarily approximate, there are striking internal consistencies which corroborate these placements on the basis of organizational characteristics. Reading across the figure, the cottages are arrayed on a continuum from custody-oriented goals to treatment-oriented goals. Reading down the figure, one moves across a continuum from group-oriented strategies to individual-oriented strategies. A cottage's placement reflects its relative position on both these axes simultaneously.

In Figure 2-2, Cottage 9 most clearly marks the custodial pole on the custody-treatment continuum, while "I Belong" most clearly reflects the treatment end. Using the continuum of group- or individual-oriented intervention strategies, Cottage 9 and "I Belong" reflect the group-oriented pole, while Westview occupies the most individual-oriented position. Most of the cottages are located in either the individual custody or group treatment quadrants of Figure 2-2. The cottages in the individual custody quadrant reflect the institutional treatment most delinquent youths received in Massachusetts prior to Miller's arrival. The cottages in the group treatment quadrant reflect Miller's primary emphasis on the development of therapeutic communities as part of the process of institutional decentralization.

Thus far we have established that the staff in the respective cottages shared relatively homogenous, internally consistent beliefs about the types of inmates in their charge and the types of change they wanted to induce. This is also reflected in the types of goals they specified for their organization. These findings indicate that the cottage staff had sufficient institutional flexibility under Miller's policy of decentralization to pursue radically different correctional objectives. The result was the clearly graduated transition of cottage strategies from the purely custodial to the strongly therapeutic.

The differences in staff ideology, goals, and cottage programs were also reflected in corresponding variations in the cottages' decision-making processes and staff interdependence. In theory, all of the cottages were decentralized under the administration of a cottage director, and staff people were supposed to participate collectively in the development of the cottage program and the evaluation of inmate progress. In fact, attributions of influence by staff reflected the extent to which the previous hierarchical institutional structure had been transformed into a participative and egalitarian one (see

Table 2-1, scale 12). Even after decentralization, in the custody-oriented cottages control over cottage policy and the disposition of inmates was lodged either in the institutional bureaucracy or the cottage director rather than in the entire staff. While nominally decentralized, these cottages still operated as they had in the earlier period as one part of the larger industrial training school, and influence was still hierarchical. By contrast, decentralization was virtually complete in the treatment-oriented cottages, and the cottage staff team was the principal decision-making unit. It was only in the group-treatment cottages, organized on a collective problem-solving model, that true staff teams emerged to any appreciable degree.

This organization/program shift was also reflected in differences in staff interdependence. As organizational goals become more complex, the amount of information about inmates that staff must share increases accordingly. We asked staff members how much contact they had with personnel occupying other roles. In the custody-oriented settings, staff with different responsibilities were effectively isolated from each other and contact was limited to supervisory and line staff. In the treatment-oriented settings, on the other hand, the use of a staff team greatly increased the amount of contact that staff with different formal roles had with each other.

The programmatic changes introduced by Miller had far-reaching organizational consequences. Although it appeared initially that he was only deemphasizing vocational programs and emphasizing more clinical or group-treatment programs, the shift in program focus brought major changes in organizational structure, staff role definitions, and allocations of decision-making influence.

While it was possible to conduct vocational training and education within traditionally structured departmentalized institutions, group treatment implemented by a staff team could not take place in a segmented structure. The need to coordinate all staff members having contact with inmates to assure consistency in staff response generated increased interdependence and cooperation. One consequence of increased contact was role diffusion, in which traditional institutional definitions of staff roles and responsibilities had less salience and every member of the treatment team was involved in the collective enterprise. Decentralization facilitated the emergence of integrated staff teams in which all members participated regardless of formal role definitions. Those cottages where the reduction of institutional control was most successful—Shirley, "I Belong," and Topsfield—were also the ones that were newly formed or transferred from other settings, thereby breaking links with prior programming and departmental constraints.

COTTAGE PROGRAMS AND SOCIAL CONTROL STRATEGIES

There is necessary complementarity between cottage program strategies and staff social-control practices since alienating compliance practices are incompatible with intervention strategies requiring inmate commitment. Staff control strategies influence the types of relationships they can develop with inmates and consequently the subculture which emerges. We rely on Etzioni's compliance framework as a basis for analyzing the differing social-control techniques in the cottage groupings [9].

The principal control strategies available to staff included: (1) the threat or use of physical coercion; (2) the threat or use of transfers to less desirable units, such as isolation settings or discipline cottages; (3) the use of a "privilege" system; and (4) informal or formal collaboration between staff and inmates to maintain order. Physical coercion and transfer or isolation are self-explanatory control techniques. A privilege system consists of a set of rules and regulations, conformity to which earns rewards or privileges, and disobedience of which results in the loss of privileges or the imposition of penalties [10].

Informal collaboration between staff and inmates to maintain order is a well-documented correctional control technique. Lacking complete and total physical domination of inmates, staff rely on the inmate elite to maintain social order, in return for which the staff allows the elite certain privileges and immunities [11]. Formal collaboration between staff and inmates as a means of social control occurs when a facilitating social structure allows both to participate, at least to some degree, as members of a common group in either defining deviance, determining the appropriate sanctions, or both. Formal collaboration differs from informal collaboration in a number of critical respects. It is explicit and overt, with parties visibly engaged in the process. Since the process is formalized and given organizational sanction, it is legitimate and consistent with the declared principles of the organizations, rather than covert, *sub rosa*, and in a sense subversive of the formal organization. Perhaps most importantly, it is universalistic and democratic with all members of both groups involved, rather than elitist and particularistic, confined only to the inmate leadership.

Group Custody: Cottage 9

Cottage 9 was the discipline cottage at the Industrial School for Boys. Despite Miller's constant attention, its primary function—discipline and punishment—and the techniques to achieve these goals resisted his reform efforts. Until it was finally closed, Cottage 9 operated as a maximum-security, exclusively custodial juvenile setting.

The disciplinary unit was similar to the other residential cottages, although it was somewhat smaller and contained a number of additional security features. The building contained a basement-level locker-room much like that of a gymnasium, where each boy was assigned a locker to keep his towel, toothbrush, and the few other personal possessions he was permitted. An adjoining area contained communal sinks and urinals, unenclosed toilets, and an open area of showers. The shower area was enclosed on three sides by the walls of the building; on the fourth side stood a three-foot high wall that allowed staff to supervise the boys during their showers. The mirrors on the wall in the bathroom were made of metal rather than glass and hardly cast a reflection. This type of communal toilet facility was typical of all the boys' units. There was also a storage area for dirty towels, linen, and blankets, which in other cottages contained a ping-pong table or provided some other recreational opportunities.

The first floor contained a kitchen, dining room, staff area, and a reading room. In Cottage 9, unlike the open-school cottages, the boys ate their meals in the cottage and food was sent from the cafeteria to the kitchen for preparation and serving. The dining room had four tables each seating six boys arranged in a horse-shoe shape with a separate staff table at the open-end of the horse-shoe. Staff always ate facing the boys. The reading room in other cottages also housed the television set, which provided one of the central focuses of cottage life. In Cottage 9, however, the television was removed as punishment and the reading room was simply used to contain all the boys in one place. The staff quarters in other cottages consisted of a small living room–den and an adjoining bedroom, which was a vestige of earlier days when the cottage masters slept in. In Cottage 9 this was an office area with a desk, telephone, and chairs.

The second floor of the typical cottage held two large dormitories, each capable of accommodating twenty-five or more beds. In an attic-like alcove overlooking the dormitory was a room for the guard–night watchman. This room had windows which allowed the guard to look into the dormitories to see anything taking place. There was an open bathroom in the dormitory, since the boys were locked in for the night. In Cottage 9, however, what would have been the second dormitory was occupied by the "Tombs," which consisted of small rooms, each perhaps five by seven feet. Used for the isolation and solitary confinement of "troublemakers," they were literally rooms-within-rooms—four walls, perhaps seven feet high, built in the middle of the floor with a ceiling covered by a very heavy mesh wire. This allowed the night watchman to look down into the room from his guard tower.

Cottage 9 had other distinctive security features as well. Unlike the other cottages, which generally allowed free physical mobility within the unit, every room in Cottage 9 had a locked door with a heavy metal frame covered by screen-mesh security wiring. This security mesh covered every window in the building as well as the doors. Every room was locked with a separate door and access between rooms was extremely restricted. An accompanying guard had to open the door to each room.

The staff itself was a security feature of Cottage 9. In the open-school cottages older married couples served as the primary supervisory cottage staff. Only men worked in Cottage 9. Most of them had been in the Marine Corps; several were former football players or professional boxers. They were physically much larger than staff in the other cottages, and looked as though they could handle any difficulties the boys might present.

Boys were sent to Cottage 9 from the open-school cottages at Shirley for disciplinary infractions. The most frequent and typical violations were running away from the institution or fighting. Running away, or attempting to run away, resulted in mandatory confinement for at least three weeks before a boy was returned to his open cottage. Since many boys ran away from the school, and there were no discernible differences between those who did and those who did not, the Cottage 9 population characteristics were similar to those of other cottages.

A boy was placed in Cottage 9 for close supervision and, accordingly, activities were much more static and limited than in the open-school cottages. When a boy arrived in the cottage his clothes were taken, tagged, and stored, and he received a blue work shirt, chino pants, sneakers, and institutional underwear. Wearing uniforms rather than their own clothing was only the beginning of the differences between inmates of Cottage 9 and those in other settings. Smoking cigarettes was prohibited—a severe deprivation. Matches and virtually all personal property were contraband. Cottage 9 was a punitively spartan setting with no amenities to offset the institutional deprivation.

There was no program. The boys received no vocational training or academic education and only infrequent counseling. There was no recreation. Despite a back yard with a volleyball court, and some horseshoe pits completely enclosed by a high fence topped with barbed wire, during our seven weeks of observation at the cottage, neither facility was ever used. The absence of programming made the day extremely boring. The boys passed their time in the reading room, seated on hard wooden chairs around large tables playing cards, shredding two-year old *Reader's Digests* that somebody had contributed, "ranking"—verbally denigrating—the staff and each other, and beating-up the low-status "punks"—all under the watchful eye of the cottage staff. Meals presented the only break in the daily routine of enforced idleness.

The Cottage 9 intervention strategy was punishment and deprivation. The enforced boredom was interrupted only for meals, routine clean-up, and cottage maintenance. Cottage chores were performed by the boys as a group. No counselors were assigned to Cottage 9, although the boys received some minimal counseling if the counselor assigned to their open-school cottage visited them. Contact with any outside community was limited to those few boys who received visitors on visiting day—Sunday between 1:00 and 4:30 P.M. Visits were closely supervised by the guards to assure that no contraband was smuggled into the building. Only about one boy in five received visitors on any given Sunday, and a relatively small number of boys received a disproportionately large number of visitors.

All the cottage activities took place in a highly controlled, structured environment, and virtually all activities took place in a group setting. Every boy's actions were subject to close scrutiny by the staff. This resulted in an extremely unpleasant, oppressive situation which the boys had no choice but to endure. The cottage program consisted of negative experiences to condition the boys to conformity and obedience, implemented almost exclusively within a group context.

Staff relied primarily on physical coercion and transfer to isolation units to achieve obedience, conformity, and respect. These techniques of social control were feasible since inmate program involvement was irrelevant and staff domination made it practicable. Other control techniques were virtually absent: there were no privileges to be lost; mass handling prevented the individualized relationships necessary for informal collaboration from emerging, and the extreme separation, mistrust, and alienation between the staff and inmates precluded formal collaboration.

Early in his administration, Miller had categorically denied to staff the use of physical coercion as a means of control. This prohibition was a constant source of complaint for the Cottage 9 staff who felt that they were expected to control inmates without the necessary authority. "Even if a kid's hostile and violent, they tell you, you can't touch them. 'Oh, don't touch him or you're fired.' And so you can't deal with the problems they create for you. And nine times out of ten, they'll take the words of the kids before they'll believe us. You wonder who's in jail, us or the kids." Miller also drastically restricted the use of isolation rooms or solitary confinement as a means of securing order. Despite these prohibitions, the Cottage 9 staff often beat inmates or locked them in the Tombs to maintain order.

Physical coercion or isolation normally followed a major rule violation: fighting, provoking fights, or participating in the frequent disturbances that occurred in the dormitory at night. These riots were the most blatant challenge to staff control, occurred with some regularity, and incurred the heaviest sanctions. Shortly before this study, the entire inmate population had escaped from Cottage 9 when they overcame the guards and stole the keys during the course of such a disturbance. The Cottage 9 staff response to these challenges were twofold: isolation or transfer, and physical beatings. Boys participating in riots were often locked in the isolation rooms for several days at a time. Troublesome inmates were occasionally transferred to a detention center that provided security features, or removed to the school hospital and handcuffed to a bed. When staff responded to these disturbances, they physically "handled" the boys as well, since they had to secure control. While the force used was usually not unreasonable or excessive, staff members sometimes used these opportunities to punish particularly trying inmates.

Inmate aggression against other inmates—fighting or provoking fights—was a common social-control problem, which staff also dealt with by threats, physical coercion, or isolation. These heavy sanctions were also used by Cottage 9 staff to secure inmate conformity to rules, and to maintain inmate respect, deference, and obedience. A "bad attitude," inmate recalcitrance, questioning staff authority, failing to obey orders promptly, or responding disrespectfully often elicited a physical response from staff. One inmate's disrespect prompted a staff member to grab the boy around the neck and drag him down a flight of stairs, saying, "I don't like you and the next time you act up and step out of line, I'm going to lock you up for a long time." Choking was sometimes used by staff because it was effective and also did not leave tell-tale marks.

Possession of contraband could also result in physical beatings or isolation. Almost everything was contraband—cigarettes, matches, personal possessions, any potential weapon or means of escape, as well as the ordinary institutional contraband such as drugs and alcohol. When a boy was found with contraband, the staff member who found it decided what punishment to impose. Most staff members considered it reasonable for a boy to spend a day in the Tombs for possession of contraband. Physical force was typically used if the boy did not divest himself of contraband voluntarily.

One situation that provoked physical punishment in several custody-oriented settings including Cottage 9 involved inmates circumventing the normal lines of authority, by taking intracottage problems to the institutional administration. A boy's complaint to the institutional administration about his treatment by cottage personnel was likely to be punished. After several boys had complained to a school administrator that the staff was not giving them enough to eat, a staff member grabbed the complaining boys by their hair and banged their heads together threatening to "crack them like walnuts next time you complain. One more time out of you, and I'll take you up in the Tombs and bounce you off the walls." When a weaker boy complained to the administration that the staff did nothing to prevent his being beaten by other boys, the cottage master threatened that "no matter what they [the other boys] do to you, you complain again, and we'll do worse."

Social control in Cottage 9 was a brutalizing experience for inmates and for staff. The staff had an extremely limited repertoire of control mechanisms—physical coercion and isolation—as their response to major types of deviance, such as riots and fights, inmate provocations, disrespect, recalcitrance, or failure to obey promptly. These tactics alienated the inmates, who attempted to minimize their contacts with staff. Because these control techniques were grossly disproportional to less serious kinds of deviance, the staff ignored a considerable range of inmate misbehavior. If major deviance occurred in their presence, they were forced to respond. But they neither sought out nor encouraged inmates to report deviance occurring outside of their presence. As we shall see in the discussion of the cottage subcultures, this tendency to avoid confronting inmate deviance contributed to the violent and aggressive inmate culture by leaving the inmates at the mercy of other inmates with minimal protection by staff.

Individual Custody: Cottage 8, Elms and Westview Cottages, and the Lancaster Cottages

The programs, structures, and operations of the individual-custody cottages were essentially similar to each other, with some minor variations. The individual custody cottages included Cottage 8 at Shirley; Elms and Westview cottages at Lyman; and Clara Barton and Putnam Cottages at Lancaster.

The physical facilities in the individual custody cottages for boys were alike, and similar to those of Cottage 9 except for the security features. The girls' cottages at Lancaster had their toilet facilities and individual bedrooms on the same floor. There were no dormitories in the girls' cottages. At night each girl was locked in her own room, and a pail was provided to make it unnecessary for the matron to unlock doors until morning. The toilet facilities in Lancaster were enclosed and private; the showers had curtains across the front, and the toilets were enclosed in stalls, unlike the facilities in the boys' cottages, which were communal and completely exposed.

In general the individual custody cottages allowed considerably greater personal freedom and physical mobility than Cottage 9. Although the girls were allowed to retain some personal clothing, for the most part they were institutional uniforms. The boys, however, retained many more personal possessions. They wore their own clothing and, in Cottage 8 and Elms, they carried their own cigarettes. In Westview and Lancaster, inmates were not allowed to possess cigarettes and the staff doled them out at periodic breaks and as rewards. Because the boys retained many more personal items and clothing, there were locks on the lockers to prevent thefts, and most boys wore their keys on a string around their neck.

The physical settings were not nearly as oppressive as those in Cottage 9. More furniture was available, and the matrons put curtains on the windows and pictures on the walls in an effort to lighten the institutional environment. The cottage parents furnished the staff rooms with sofas, chairs, and rugs, and created a more homelike environment than was found in Cottage 9.

There were physical differences in the staff as well. The individual custody cottages for boys were staffed primarily by cottage parents, husbands and wives working together as supervisors. Normally, several couples were assigned to each cottage, supplemented by some additional cottage masters, matrons, and a counselor. Typically, one cottage couple was on duty in the cottage, aided by an additional supervisor or two. In all the settings, about half of these cottage couples were fifty years of age or older, and the vast majority of staff were white. Effective supervision was limited by the practice of cottage matrons having to remain exclusively on the first floor of the cottage because of the communal toilet facilities. They spent most of their time with other matrons or staff in the staff quarters or in the kitchen. Male staff members divided their time between the staff quarters and periodic inspection tours around the cottage to investigate what the boys were doing. Although the cottage staff was supplemented by vocational and academic instructors who were assigned to the particular cottage as part of institutional decentralization, these personnel conducted their activities in separate school buildings and shops and were not integrated into daily cottage life.

The cottage staff at Lancaster was exclusively female, mostly middle-aged or older, and white. Two matrons were on duty for each shift. Since the girls at Lancaster ate in the cottage, one of the two took charge of the kitchen and had four to six girls preparing meals under her supervision for the rest. The kitchen work was a full-time activity, and the kitchen matron had relatively little contact with the other cottage residents. As a result the cottage matron was the dominant staff person. She was in charge of all matters involving the girls outside of the kitchen, and spent most of her time supervising the girls within the cottage, making certain that they went to their assignments promptly and returned to the cottage at their conclusion. In addition to the matrons, one counselor was assigned to each cottage. Although physically present in the cottage, their heavy individual counseling caseloads and the inevitable administrative paperwork reduced their impact. The academic and vocational instructors were nominally assigned to the various cottages, but they spent the bulk of their time in the separate school building. There were also several men on the institution staff who were general handymen, responsible for institutional maintenance, and not assigned to individual cottages. In addition, two were specifically designated as security, and remained in the administration building in case of a call for assistance in handling an unruly girl. They also served as chauffeurs, driving the girls between the cottages and other buildings on the grounds, since normally the girls were not allowed to walk about unescorted.

The process by which a newly arrived inmate was inducted into a cottage was also similar in these settings. At Shirley and Lancaster, assignment to the open-school cottages was based primarily on which cottage had less current residents at that time. The process was almost as simple at the Lyman school, where the older boys were assigned to Elms, Westview, or Sunset, the three cottages we studied. Boys who volunteered to work in the cafeteria program were sent to Westview. Boys who chose to work on the other institutional maintenance and life-support services were sent to Elms. The remaining boys were sent to Sunset. When particular trades or programs were short-handed, boys were strongly encouraged to volunteer. For research purposes, the unsystematic process of cottage assignments—on the basis of available space or the personnel needs of various trades—produced reasonably comparable cottage populations. Although assignments were not random, there were no apparent systematic biases.

After a resident received his cottage assignment he was taken to the cottage master. There was no formal process for acquainting a resident with the cottage or the school programs, although Lancaster girls informed us that they received an orientation lecture from the school supervisor, the essence of which was that the best way to get along at Lancaster was "to obey the matrons and behave, regardless of what the other girls may say." The orientation process for new boys and girls was similar; new arrivals were ignored by staff and other residents until they eventually learned their way around. It was assumed that they would learn the institutional rules from other residents on an informal basis.

Although the cottages varied considerably in the range, quality, and demands of their programs, the individual custody settings we studied all used vocational training as their primary intervention strategy. When we first began studying the Industrial School in June 1970, the institution had seventeen trade programs, virtually all of them connected to the school's maintenance: a laundry, a cafeteria, custodial and maintenance work, and landscaping. Typically, vocational training staff supervised boys who performed routine chores. Vocational education was deemphasized by Miller, and by the following year the vocational training program was minimal. Of necessity, the laundry was washed, the food prepared, the buildings swept, and the grass cut, and some boys assisted in this as an alternative to boredom. The vocational instructors became much more involved in institutional maintenance and services than before. Several staff members suggested that one reason the vocational instructors opposed Miller so vociferously was because they realized that they would have to do the work previously performed by the boys themselves.

While there were more activities and clearly more freedom available to boys in Cottage 8 than to those in Cottage 9, there were no consistent, ongoing vocational educational programs that could be regarded as a strategy to change delinquent offenders. Miller's deemphasis of vocational education and his efforts to close the facility disrupted many of the vocational instruction programs. Even after the prematurely announced closing was rescinded, the vocational instructional staff regarded the boys as simply waiting for reassignment to other treatment programs. Accordingly, they made little effort to revive their own programs. By the time of our study in June 1971, only seven of the original seventeen trade programs remained, and only four—auto-shop, cafeteria, laundry, and janitorial staff—had three or more boys assigned to them. These were also the services most essential to ongoing institutional functioning. No formal instructional component existed for boys who did work in these programs, and staff supervision of the work was desultory at best.

Elms cottage ran a trade program, but after Miller's orders against coerced or compulsory work, boys were not required to participate. Most of them participated, however, since the alternative was lounging around the cottage the whole day. Boys who were discharged from their trade because of misbehavior soon tired of their enforced leisure and sought reinstatement to combat boredom. Older boys were assigned to Elms on the theory that by participation in a trade they would acquire some discipline and skills of practical value to them after release. The major trades or work experiences in which the Elms boys were involved included the laundry, the storeroom, the printshop, the delivery truck, and custodial services. There were two or three other trade programs, created as institutional demands required trades. With the exception of the printshop, none of these chores involved any formal instruction. As at Shirley, the trades taught served institutional life-support rather than providing skill training for jobs. Most of the boys worked in a trade program simply to help their time pass more quickly.

The other trade cottage at Lyman was Westview. The boys in this cottage were assigned to the cafeteria program, which was by far the most articulated and rigorous training program available. The director of the cafeteria tried to make the program as rewarding as possible, enrolling boys in correspondence courses on food and nutrition, providing them with instruction and work experiences as fry cooks, salad chefs, short-order cooks, bakers, and the like. The Westview cottage population was divided into morning and afternoon shifts with similar duties: cleaning the cafeteria, washing the dishes, preparing the kitchen for the next meal, and cooking the meals. Unfortunately, the volume of meals served and the large number of boys in the program reduced the level of instruction and the amount of responsibility that each boy could assume, and militated toward a routinization of tasks.

Lancaster also relied heavily on vocational training programs as a major intervention strategy. Girls received instruction in sewing, grooming and beauty care, baking, laundry, and child care. Like the boys' schools, the labor of the girls was used to make the institution self-sufficient. The institutional bakery made the bread for the cottages; the uniforms made in the sewing shop provided the staple garments of the institution. During the summer there was an extensive farm program for these primarily urban youngsters. The girls planted a large variety of fruits and vegetables, and they spent a great deal of time cultivating, harvesting, and canning produce. Assignments to a particular job or program were based on requests submitted to the program director of the institution, who filled requests as space permitted, rotating assignments monthly. About six girls normally worked in the kitchen or the laundry of each cottage, where they could earn credit for a one-year home economics class in the event that they returned to school (and the school was willing to grant credit).

Minimal academic and clinical programs were available in some of these individual custody settings to supplement the vocational educational programs. In Cottage 8 the academic and clinical programs were as moribund as the vocational programming. Most of the academic instructors had either transferred to the treatment-oriented cottages, or resigned, and the academic program was effectively discontinued. The clinical program was correspondingly weak. Although several counselors on the institutional staff were assigned to Cottage 8, the bulk of their time was spent handling administrative paperwork, and they had minimal contact with the boys.

There were no regularly scheduled individual counseling sessions, and boys initiated contact with the clinical staff only when it served their own interests; for example, when they wanted to expedite a weekend pass or to try to obtain an early parole. Although Miller's goal in decentralizing the institutions had been the creation of therapeutic communities, the counselors responsible for conducting community meetings held them only sporadically. The counselor was the only staff member who even attended the community meetings, while the other staff members visited together in the staff quarters or on the porch. The meetings only lasted long enough for the counselor to call the roll and ask if anybody wanted to discuss any problems. After one ten-minute meeting, several of the boys complained about the "marathon" session.

During the regular academic year, a few Elms and Westview boys participated in a program of formal academic instruction in a classroom setting. This was discontinued for the summer, and there was no academic instruction. Although a counselor was assigned to each cottage, the clinical programs in Elms and Westview were decidedly subordinated to the trade program and general cottage life. One counselor in Elms was supposed to provide individual counseling for the thirty or more boys in residence, while simultaneously preparing parole reports, weekend passes, and other administrative paperwork. The counselor in Westview operated under similar organizational constraints, with the priority of the cafeteria program determining all other cottage activities. In Elms, the demands of the job, the number of inmates involved, and the ideology of the cottage director rendered the counselor ineffective. He had almost no impact on the cottage or on policy formulation, and provided little more than adjustment counseling for an occasional inmate.

The counselor in Westview was only slightly more effective. Apart from weekly meetings to discuss progress in the cafeteria and in the cottage, no group treatment meetings were conducted and very few individual counseling sessions were scheduled. The relative absence of academic or clinical programs is consistent with custodial organizations utilizing vocational instruction as the primary intervention strategy.

Lancaster was much more heavily programmed than the boys' schools. In addition to the more extensive vocational programs, there was also a summer academic program emphasizing remedial reading and mathematics to supplement the regular junior high school academic program. Girls under fourteen were enrolled the whole day in school; fifteen-year-olds spent a half day; and girls sixteen and over worked, unless they were going to return to school upon their release. The clinical program at Lancaster received greater emphasis, although ultimately it suffered from the same shortcomings as those in Elms and Westview. The majority of the counselors' individual caseload consisted of girls in the cottage to which the counselor was assigned. However, the counselors' efforts to deal with a girl's problems on an individual counseling basis was hampered by the pressures of routine paperwork and record-keeping. Despite this workload, counselors met with about twenty girls a week for counseling on an individual basis. By the summer of our study, the counselors also had begun to run weekly cottage community meetings but, because they lacked experience, the counselors sometimes lost control of these meetings to the more vocal, oppositional girls.

As a result of the comparatively greater freedom and the need to secure some degree of inmate cooperation, staff in individual custody settings relied primarily on a privilege system, enforced by threats of transfer to less desirable settings such as Cottage 9. The staff also relied on inmate leaders to maintain order, and manipulated the privilege system to confer additional status and rewards on the inmate. The privilege system used in the individual-custody cottages was called "steps" or "levels of freedom," a security-graded system in which boys at different levels were afforded different degrees of freedom and privileges, with accompanying restrictions and responsibilities associated with each level. Passage from one level to the next was strongly related to the amount of time served and general behavior and conformity. Misbehavior could result in being dropped to a lower level with a concomitant reduction in privileges. The ease or difficulty with which boys changed levels varied from cottage to cottage, as did the process by which they were raised or lowered. The underlying rationale was that a combination of time served and proper behavior was rewarded by certain freedoms and privileges within the cottage.

Staff initially assigned a boy to a low level of freedom with periodic reevaluations of his behavior and progress. As long as a boy conformed and avoided "messing up," he advanced up the ladder. A step system contained four or five levels, with the highest level indicating readiness for parole and all corresponding institutional privileges, and the lowest level corresponding to a loss of almost all privileges, or even disciplinary confinement. The steps in between provided gradations of freedom and privileges. The ultimate privilege—parole—was tied into this system. Conversely, the time a boy spent in the disciplinary cottage—the lowest—was "dead time," which was not applied when computing the three months required as a minimum institutional stay. By virtue of their influence over the levels of freedom a boy reached, the staff appeared to have considerable leverage over parole eligibility. Their influence was more apparent than real, however, since time served was the principal determinant of parole eligibility.

Short of parole decisions, staff influence over a boy's level held greater significance. Privileges and freedoms within the cottage and the school depended on a boy's step assignments. Visiting privileges, both weekend furloughs and off-ground trips with parents, were contingent on reaching a certain level. Eligibility for certain activities, freedom of movement around the school, and the like, were tied to the levels of freedom.

The process of raising or lowering a boy's level varied somewhat among these three boys' cottages, and differed significantly from the process used in the treatment-oriented cottages, which also used a step privilege system. In Cottage 8, staff had little influence over a boy's level. In the absence of egregious misconduct, the passage of time moved a boy through the system. In Elms a boy's level was set by the cottage director, occasionally after consultation with the other cottage masters or the counselor, but essentially unilaterally. The primary criterion was obedience and conformity around the cottage and at work. In Westview the decision was made by the cottage director in consultation with the counselor, although the latter's contributions were not clinical but behavioral. A boy's behavior in the cafeteria program also affected his level.

Granting or withholding privileges was used to control a variety of rule-breaking situations. If boys ran away from the cottage, the remaining boys lost certain privileges, such as visiting off-grounds or evening activities with the girls' cottage, on the theory that other inmates who were aware of the planned run should have prevented it. In some individual custody cottages, rules prohibited inmate possession of cigarettes or money, and staff conducted periodic shakedown searches to discover contraband. Money or cigarettes were confiscated and used to provide cigarettes for boys who could not afford their own. Possession of contraband also resulted in step reductions, with corresponding losses of privileges.

Transfer to the discipline cottages was a logical extension of a privilege system, and a common sanction for the most serious forms of rule-breaking. Running away from the school invariably resulted in confinement in a setting like Cottage 9 for several weeks or more. A boy could be transferred to a discipline unit for serious or persistent fighting. As assault on a staff member invariably resulted in extended disciplinary confinement. Major insubordination such as refusal to obey a number of repeated orders by a staff member or creating a disturbance in the dormitory could also result in disciplinary transfers.

Disciplinary transfer was reserved for more serious violations, because of both space limitations and a reluctance by staff to admit their inability to maintain control. Almost every use of disciplinary transfers—runs, fights in the cafeteria, riots in the dormitory, assaults on staff members—involved highly visible misconduct. The staff tried to keep instances of misconduct from the institutional administration and to maintain discipline within the cottage. Only when this was unsuccessful would more visible sanctions like transfers be employed.

The individual custody staff members also used some physical sanctions to punish misconduct, although not as frequently or as severely as those used by Cottage 9 staff. The director of one cottage used a plastic baseball bat called the "Teacher" to administer "whacks" for minor types of misbehavior such as cursing, lying, and the like. Whacks were accumulated and administered in the evening in the locker room to all boys who had earned them during the day.

While such formalized physical sanctions were not used in all the individual custody settings, lying, swearing, and disrespect often resulted in a slap, a choking, or some other minor physical punishment. However, the amounts of staff violence directed towards inmates was both quantitatively and qualitatively less than that employed by Cottage 9 staff.

As was also the case in Cottage 9, the individual-custody staff frequently dealt with situations by ignoring them. Because of the multitude of incidents and the limited number and effectiveness of available sanctions, staff members exercised considerable discretion in the rules they enforced, against whom, and under what circumstances. Less serious forms of inmate misconduct which did not challenge staff authority were routinely ignored, although this varied with the staff member on duty and the social position of the offending boy in the inmate hierarchy.

The combination of a privilege system and selective enforcement reached its ultimate refinement as informal collaboration between staff and inmate leaders to maintain social control. Such informal relations between staff and the inmate elite are common in individual custody settings because of the greater availability of privileges, the increased discretion vested in staff to grant or deny such rewards, and the greater difficulties for staff in maintaining order because of program individualization and increased inmate freedom.

The prevalence of informal collaboration between staff and inmate leaders was probably the most significant difference in control strategies between group-custody and individual-custody staff. Older line staff reported that for many years prior to Miller's administration this relationship was quasi-formalized in a "duke" system or "king of the cottage," whereby an inmate-leader assumed many control and supervisory functions in return for a privileged position. In return for a variety of privileges and immunities, inmate leaders performed diverse order services for staff: keeping other boys in line; supervising the work and chores of other boys; preventing runaways; keeping the level of violence and deviance down; and the like. Westview had the most elaborate system of informal collaboration, followed by Elms. Cottage 8, with its program void and limited staff-inmate relations, also had the least refined collaborative system. This partially explains why Cottage 8 also had the most negative, violent subculture of the three individual-custody cottages for boys, with the most serious disturbances and the least staff control.

The Lancaster staff used many of the same social-control techniques employed by their male individual custody counterparts. Their primary control mechanism was a privilege system, although it was not as elaborate as the steps or levels of freedom used for boys, and Lancaster staff had fewer privileges to offer girls. Decentralization at Lancaster had not proceeded to the point where institutional practices had been significantly changed. Many of Miller's policies regarding inmate grooming, personal clothing, coerced work, and the like were not yet in effect. The girls wore institutional uniforms and the staff controlled cigarettes, so these were not viable privileges. The girls were subjected to tighter security and had less mobility around the school grounds, so privileges related to freedom of movement were precluded. Paroles were determined by the institutional administration and the DYS so staff could not appear to manipulate departure.

The staff did, however, try to offer some positive incentives to induce inmate conformity. Matrons wrote up daily reports on each girl in which her conduct, deportment, and work were evaluated and given either an "A" or a "D." Daily reports were cumulated on a weekly basis. If a girl received all "A"s, then she was eligible for the "A party" at the end of the week, a Sunday evening social event where the girls played records, ate special snacks, and received additional cigarettes. If a girl received one "D" in a week, she missed the "A party." Girls receiving several "D"s also lost the option of going to the school movies in the evening and were bolted in their room instead. A girl who received six "D"s lost all evening activities and was locked and bolted into her room every night after dinner. Staff conceded that there were some weaknesses in their privilege system; once a girl received her first "D" of the week, she had little incentive to conform thereafter. Moreover, the privilege earned—the "A party"—was not necessary as attractive as some other incentives might have been.

The Lancaster staff compensated for their lack of more effective privileges with significantly greater reliance on lock-ups and isolation rooms. Each girl had her own room, and each cottage had several security rooms that were similar to the girls' bedrooms, but with only a mat on the floor and heavier security screens. Inmate misconduct was often dealt with by locking the girl in her room. Most of the minor rule-breaking that in male settings would be dealt with by a slap or a loss of privileges were handled by lock-ups. A girl who destroyed property or was disrespectful might spend a day bolted in her room. Girls who ran away were normally locked in their rooms for three days following their return. Most types of inmate recalcitrance and disrespect met with lock-ups. These room lock-ups were in addition to the hours that all girls spent locked in their rooms after meals, waiting to go to assignments, and many evenings.

Physical control was maintained by "security men" called in from outside the cottage. Whenever a girl began acting-out or was recalcitrant or threatening, the matrons could call in these reenforcements. Because of the greater concentration of power in the institutional administration, staff felt less compunction about resorting to administrative assistance for internal order than did the male staff in individual-custody settings.

Even though Lancaster girls had fewer personal possessions or amenities, a limited privilege system maintained a relatively high degree of obedience and conformity. Most of the female residents were status offenders and appeared to be somewhat more docile and acquiescent than their male counterparts. The relatively weak privilege system was reenforced by much greater access to lock-ups and room isolation than was available to male staff to control boys. The girls spent more time alone, locked in their rooms, and the inmate culture in Lancaster was somewhat more atomized than in the comparable male settings.

Social control, however, appeared to be somewhat more problematical at Lancaster. The dearth of privileges and the greater acquiescence of most of the female inmates reduced the staff's need or ability to co-opt the inmate leadership. It was also easier, however, for a recalcitrant girl to resist being involuntarily confined, since cottage staff had to summon outside help if they needed to subdue a girl. Since the female inmate leadership had many of the same aggressive and violent characteristics as did the males, the lack of informal collaboration placed them under somewhat less effective staff control than in comparable male settings.

The result was a less stable inmate culture in which verbal and aggressive girls intimidated other residents. While in most respects Lancaster's cottage social structures were "objectively" similar to Westview's or Elms's in terms of staff attitudes and programs, due to the weakness in their social controls the inmates lived in a somewhat more anomic subculture, comparable to that of Cottage 8.

Individual Treatment: Topsfield

Topsfield was intended to serve as both a treatment center for youth and a training center for staff. The staff training component was intended to teach techniques for developing and working in therapeutic communities. The treatment component involved the development of a model of a therapeutic community treatment setting. We studied only the treatment aspects of the organization, and the staff and children involved with treatment. Because it was part of a new facility, the treatment program was able to develop without any preexisting limitations or institutional constraints. One consequence was that many of the staff roles and programs typically found in more traditional institutions were absent.

After several abortive starts the treatment program began in earnest when two boys and two girls took up residence about three months before our study. The numbers of residents gradually increased, so that when our study began in July 1971, seven boys and nine girls were enrolled in the program.

Compared to Shirley and Lyman, Topsfield was well staffed, with a large cadre of full-time people assisted by a number of part-time and summer employees. More than half the staff members were clinicians or worked in a treatment capacity. They were considerably younger and better educated than those employed in the more custody-oriented cottages. Topsfield had no vocational education program, and thus no vocational instructors. Similarly, apart from a few children who worked in the local community, there was no program of work experience. Institutional life-support and maintenance, the primary source of inmate "work experiences," were performed by displaced staff members from other institutions. There were no cottage parents in the custodial sense of that role. Moreover, there was a great deal of staff role diffusion with personnel performing several tasks and functions.

Many of the residents at Topsfield originally came from other institutions, although some arrived directly from reception centers. Regardless of where they came from, the reception process in the treatment-oriented cottages was similar. A new resident was introduced to the cottage at the first community meeting after arriving. Thereafter they learned the details of cottage life from the other residents in the program.

With treatment the primary focus, other programs, such as academic instruction, had to develop around this core. Topsfield staff used the entire panoply of treatment modalities: community meetings, small-group therapy sessions, and individual counseling. Community meetings were conducted every morning, with additional meetings scheduled as needed. These meetings were generally confined to cottage business—scheduling daily activities, sharing information, and identifying problems. The staff dealt with problems of interpersonal relations to a lesser degree in community meetings than did those in group-treatment settings.

Group psychotherapy sessions were held immediately after the community meetings five days per week. The cottage population was divided into two groups, with boys and girls in each group. The group-treatment process focused on gaining insight into personal problems, using techniques that were essentially "individual therapy in a group setting" [12]. Each inmate was also assigned to a counselor, and they met together for individual counseling sessions several times a week. The staff members who conducted the group therapy and individual counseling sessions were more psychoanalytically oriented, more neutral in their questioning, and more concerned with individuals gaining insight and self-awareness than were the more group-oriented treatment cottages.

A strong academic instruction component reenforced the treatment thrust. Staff members offered instruction in a wide variety of traditional and innovative curricula, ranging from mathematics to psychology to sculpting. Each youth enrolled in two courses and received twelve hours of instruction per week. Instruction took the form of self-directed group discussions and presentations by staff or inmates, or individual tutoring. An active music program provided instruction in musical instruments and appreciation.

In keeping with individual-treatment philosophy, the Topsfield program was very free and open, with relatively few restrictions. The children kept their own clothes, personal possessions, and cigarettes. Staff attempted to minimize deprivations and maximize gratifications to encourage inmate participation. Individualized treatment ideology eschews universal rules, and clinical considerations may dictate different dispositions for like-situated persons. The lack of structure occasioned frequent complaints by staff and inmates about the lack of consistent enforcement of rules and the staff's inability to confront children for misbehavior.

The Topsfield staff relied almost exclusively on a rich privilege system. Although the threat of transfer to a less desirable setting was the ultimate sanction for major inmate deviance, this penalty was never imposed. Formal collaboration between staff and inmates was less extensive than in the group-treatment settings. Additional clinical sessions were prescribed to reinforce the privilege system—not as sanctions but as supports. Physical coercion and collaboration between staff and inmate elite was minimal.

Topsfield used a step system of graded privileges with considerably more rewards and fewer deprivations than in the individual custody cottages. Many of the privileges subject to manipulation in custodial settings—possessing cigarettes, wearing personal clothes, and the like—were rights Topsfield inmates retained. Being dropped a level mainly affected freedom of movement and the degree of supervision, but did not normally entail any loss of amenities of institutional life. Parole was implicated in the privilege system, since a child had to attain the highest step in the order to be eligible, but parole eligibility was not as closely connected to "doing time" as in the custodial settings.

It was clear that the amount and kinds of controls employed at Topsfield were significantly less than in any other setting. The unstructured nature of the program prompted one inmate to comment, "When I first saw this place, it blew my mind. Anywhere else, if a kid told a staff member to fuck off, he'd get his head busted open. This place is like a dream." Unlike custody-oriented settings, numerous instances of inmate recalcitrance and disrespect occurred with no discernible consequences. Treatment staff were not only unconcerned with deference and respect, but actively encouraged expressions of feelings, even hostile feelings, and social control to coerce respect was almost nonexistent.

There was, if anything, a serious problem of laxity and nonenforcement of rules at Topsfield. Residents objected to a rule obliging everyone to write down instances of rule-breaking in the Book, a daily log which provided the basis for group discussions, clinical conferences, and individual evaluations. Individualized treatment rationales also prompted frequent discussions about inconsistency in enforcing the rules and writing up violations. The staffs' clinical orientation made it very difficult for them to put themselves in an authoritarian position vis-à-vis the children. Typical of this ambivalence was the complaint of one staff member who objected to "running around playing the heavy. I'm a clinician, not a cop."

Group Treatment: Sunset Cottage, Shirley Cottage, and "I Belong"

There were three group-treatment cottages in our sample. Their programs were developed during Miller's tenure as a result of institutional decentralization. Although they all shared a group-treatment orientation, Sunset provided primarily "humane care," Shirley cottage supplemented its well-structured group-treatment program with vocational education and work experiences, and "I Belong" reenforced its group-treatment strategies with an academic educational component. These programs, along with the one at Topsfield, distinguished institutional treatment in the Miller regime from that of his predecessors.

Sunset. Sunset cottage was physically similar to Elms and Westview, built at the same time and located immediately adjacent to Westview. The staffing patterns were also similar, consisting primarily of line staff, although the Sunset staff was substantially younger. Three cottage masters, one of whom was the cottage director, provided primary staff coverage. The one cottage master on duty at any given time was assisted by a counselor, a teacher, and occasionally in the evenings by part-time summer personnel. Because of the extremely limited number of staff members available, the counselor and the teacher acted in a supervisory capacity, much like the cottage masters, despite their formal job designations. This skeleton staff was not supplemented by vocational instructors, work supervisors, or cafeteria personnel as were the staff complements associated with Elms or Westview.

New inmate arrivals were assigned to Sunset by a process that was similar to that used for Westview and Elms. Once a boy was assigned to Sunset, he received his locker and state clothes. He wore a state uniform during his first week in the cottage and had to remain in the presence of staff for the first day, to insure that he did not run away. There was no formal orientation process, and a boy learned the cottage routine by asking questions or following the lead of the other boys. Cigarettes were turned in to the cottage masters who doled them out at various times in much the same fashion that Westview staff controlled cigarettes.

There was no regular program in Sunset cottage. The Lyman school vocational programs were filled almost exclusively by the boys from Elms or Westview. Several Sunset boys worked on a ground-clearing project at the Lyman School, while a few others volunteered to work in the school laundry, which had difficulty recruiting enough assistance from Elms during the hot summer months. These activities were voluntarily undertaken to help pass the time, and there was no pretense of instruction. For the majority of boys there was no work other than occasional routine cleaning chores around the cottage. Since the Lyman education program followed an academic school calendar, there was also no academic program in operation from June to September. The academic teacher functioned as a cottage master during the summer.

The primary intervention emphasis of the cottage, then, was the development and maintenance of the "therapeutic community" treatment setting. A consulting psychiatrist who assisted the staff in this venture noted the vocational and academic program deficiencies. In a memorandum to the administration several months before our study, he observed that "the school and activities program at Sunset is not as well organized nor as elaborate" as those in other cottages. But he also reported daily community meetings, small-group therapy sessions, and an effective treatment program: "I believe the rare components of truly therapeutic milieu are present: warmth, caring, humor and liveliness are freely exchanged between boys and staff in an atmosphere of mutual respect." By the summer of our study, however, the clinical program was sharply curtailed by staff limitations. The community meetings, which had been held daily, were now conducted of an irregular basis, primarily in response to a cottage problem. The small-group treatment sessions were also discontinued during the summer. This curtailment resulted from staff shortages, which pressed the teacher and counselor into more traditional supervisory roles.

Almost by default, the boys spent several hours a day in athletic and recreational activities; playing basketball in the gymnasium, swimming in the pool, or playing baseball on the field across from the cottage. The program in Sunset cottage had deteriorated into little more than "humane care," a model in which

> custodial practices have been largely discarded but therapeutic ones barely developed, despite considerable effort. The resulting program emphasizes "humane care.... The humane care model retains the goal of "therapeutic intervention"... but failing to evolve and apply these techniques, they are left with a fairly permissive environment in which sanctions and deprivations are reduced and friendly relations may obtain between personnel and inmates. But the basic task of personnel is to provide care rather than therapy [13].

While Sunset staff did not have a specific program or intervention strategy, their previous experiments with a therapeutic community prepared them to relate to inmates in a less authoritarian fashion than previously. Despite the program deficiencies, other aspects of the cottage structure encouraged a relatively benign subculture.

Shirley. The Shirley cottage had been transferred from the Industrial School to Lyman in March 1971, in anticipation of Shirley's closing. The cottage staff had been organized as a staff-team since institutional decentralization had begun at Shirley. The cottage director had been the chief psychologist at Shirley and the other staff were Industrial School personnel who were assigned to the cottage when decentralization occurred. Under his guidance and supervision they developed a stronger cottage team identity, as well as a more systematic treatment program, than did any of the other cottages at Shirley. They received additional training as a problem-solving team from a clinical consultant hired by the Department of Youth Services. Because they were committed to the treatment model, when Shirley's closing was announced they requested a cottage unit at Lyman to allow them to continue their program before moving to a community-based setting. Fifteen staff members and thirteen boys transferred to the Lyman School.

The Shirley cottage was administratively autonomous from the other cottages at Lyman. All of its programs were cottage-based and cottage-administered, obviating any formal participation in activities by the boys from Shirley with boys from Lyman. Even informally they did not engage in joint athletic activities or other recreational programs. The concomitant institutional decentralization at Lyman also contributed to the insulation of Shirley cottage. Perhaps symbolically, there was a self-imposed boundary around the cottage to further minimize contacts between Shirley boys and those in other cottages. The boundary was partly administrative and party ideological. Shirley boys enjoyed greater freedoms, and one condition set by the Lyman administration on Shirley cottage was that its residents minimize their contacts with the Lyman youths. The Shirley staff agreed because they believed they would be insulating their boys from the more custodial influences of the Lyman school.

The staff of Shirley cottage was the most diverse of all the staffs we observed. There were three young academic teachers, as well as three older cottage couples recruited from the Shirley line staff. Six people functioned as counselors, or group therapy leaders, regardless of their formal job designations. Although the cottage masters and matrons functioned in a relatively traditional supervisory manner, there was considerable role diffusion among the other staff members, who performed two or even three different functions within the cottage—clinical, academic, vocational, and recreational. An active summer program provided several additional people and programs during the evenings and on weekends.

The boys originally in Shirley cottage transferred with it. Boys entering Shirley cottage later came directly from the reception centers, rather than through the normal Lyman intake process. A counselor, accompanied by several boys, visited the reception centers whenever the cottage population declined, or when impending paroles would soon reduce the population. Since the DYS administration believed the Shirley cottage staff had a relatively successful treatment program, there was some pressure for them to accept more difficult boys. At the reception centers they interviewed older, repeated offenders or boys known to boys already in the cottage program.

Once a boy was interviewed, had the program explained, and agreed to enter it, he was taken directly to the cottage. There, he received his state uniform, which he wore until the cottage community raised his level of freedom and voted him additional privileges. During this initial period he was restricted to the cottage unless accompanied by a staff member. He kept his cigarettes and other personal possessions, and there were no special restrictions or deprivations imposed.

A new boy was introduced to the cottage at the first community meeting after his arrival. Shortly thereafter, he was assigned to one of three smaller groups to begin group therapy. He was under immediate pressure by the other boys to talk about himself, to tell his "life-story." The treatment rationale was that by "forcing" a boy to reveal himself and to trust his peers, he would make a personal commitment to the program. It was intended to establish an initial precedent of honesty. The boys in his small group were expected to explain the cottage routines and rules since, in a number of respects, boys were responsible for each other.

During the school year an academic educational program used individual tutoring, programmed instruction (Job Corps materials), and group discussions to provide a range of instruction from remedial assistance to high school equivalency degree preparation. Several other staff members supplemented the academic regime with vocational education and work experiences in carpentry and in auto mechanics. Indicative of the primary therapeutic thrust of Shirley and the staff role diffusion, two of the three academic teachers and the automotive instructor also functioned as counselors and group leaders.

During the summer the academic and vocational educational programs were discontinued and replaced by half-day work experiences in the institution or in local communities, for which the boys were paid. Funds from the Neighborhood Youth Corps program enabled them to work for the state in nearby Westboro on a ground-clearing project. More responsible boys worked on a construction project in Worcester. Boys who were not ready to work in the community were compensated for clearing underbrush for the state's Department of Fish and Game.

Group treatment was the primary cottage program. Cottage community meetings were held five days a week (with additional shorter meetings on weekends to resolve any troublesome incidents), followed by small-group therapy sessions. The community meetings generally lasted between one and two hours. A daily log provided the agenda for the community discussions. Staff and boys were encouraged to write any notations, observations, complaints, or recommendations about incidents that required community attention.

As part of the strategy of structuring the organization so that all interactions were part of the therapeutic regime, staff tried to integrate the boys' work activities and cottage living experiences into the meetings. If an employer had difficulties with a boy, he could attend the community meetings and present his position. Boys' parents occasionally attended cottage community meetings, as did other outsiders such as parole officers or people trying to arrange job placements for boys. Shirley staff members also provided some family counseling, with the parents of several boys participating in group therapy meetings and individual counseling sessions.

The cottage masters also participated by actively bringing difficulties in cottage living to the attention of the cottage community. One of the most significant organizational changes was the extent to which these traditionally custodial personnel were integrated into the treatment regime. The original staff-team training, reinforced by weekly staff-team meetings, continually reaffirmed the importance of full participation by all of the staff team members. Community meetings were of such importance that they would be postponed to await the arrival of boys returning late from work. The morning and afternoon staff shifts changed during the meeting. Many staff members coming on duty arrived early to participate in the community discussions.

The cottage population was divided into three smaller treatment groups, with two counselors assigned to each. These groups met daily, immediately after the community meeting, to work on problems of interpersonal relations and to discuss any problems raised in the community meetings that required additional attention. During these one-and-a-half-hour treatment sessions staff used a variety of group treatment strategies, especially Guided Group Interaction, a treatment process utilizing peer influences.

The small groups were the basic treatment unit of the cottage. Boys worked with other members of their group, lived with them, and were responsible for each others' behavior. Accountability was often structured on a group basis, with collective liability. The initial determination that a boy was eligible for a weekend furlough or parole was made by his group, which then recommended action to the full community.

In addition to the work and clinical programs, summer activities were an integral part of the cottage program. Extra staff members were present to supervise the boys on swimming trips or at athletic events, and there was an arts and crafts program as well. Furthermore, of all the cottages studied the Shirley program contained the most community contact. In addition to the weekend furloughs, which were the primary source of community contacts in all cottages, the summer enrichment program at Shirley afforded additional opportunities to leave the school. About half the boys left the school every morning for their jobs, greatly increasing their community contacts and reducing the levels of deprivation normally associated with incarceration. And whenever staff members left the school grounds on errands, boys accompanied them for the ride.

"I Belong." The third group treatment cottage we studied was known by its inhabitants as "I Belong." Although located on the

Shirley Industrial School grounds, the program was autonomous and independent of the rest of the school. It was geographically isolated from the other open-school cottages, although, ironically, it was situated closest to Cottage 9, its polar opposite. Its physical plant was roughly similar to other cottages. In "I Belong" what served as staff quarters in other cottages had been converted into two rooms for holding small-group therapy meetings or staff meetings. Although the boys slept in a dormitory setting like the other cottages, as at Topsfield, the regular cottage staff took overnight duty on a rotating schedule rather than using a nightwatchman. There was a staff bedroom located adjacent to the dormitory. The nightwatchman's tower was converted into an arts and crafts room. A small pond was situated behind the cottage, and boys and staff used it for recreational and educational purposes.

The "I Belong" eight-member staff was the product of a two-week intenseive training session conducted at Shirley in February 1971. Several academic teachers and some other newer and younger staff were trained in group processes and program development by a clinical consultant hired by DYS. Their training was similar to that provided to the Shirley cottage staff members, but this team was less representative of institutional personnel since only two were drawn from the prior regime.

After training ended, Commissioner Miller provided the staff with a vacant Shirley cottage and the institutional support to begin operation. Staff-team, institutional administrator, and Miller agreed that the program would be autonomous from the rest of the school. The program was completely cottage-based. Meals were eaten in the cottage, with the food delivered from the cafeteria by the same truck that serviced Cottage 9. When "I Belong" used institutional facilities, they were scheduled so as to minimize contact with the other boys in the school. Their geographic isolation also allowed the cottage program to develop in an independent fashion.

The atmosphere in "I Belong" was very different from that of the other Industrial School cottages. The boys had complete freedom of movement inside and outside the cottage. They wore their own clothes, carried their own cigarettes, and had much greater contact with the surrounding communities. They were freer and less regimented than the open-school boys. The staff were much more involved with the boys; one was as likely to find a boy with a staff member as with another boy. Interaction among the boys and between the boys and staff was much more open and there was a sense of friendliness and liveliness that did not exist in other Industrial School cottages. At the time of our study, eight boys made up the

"I Belong" population, out of an original group of eleven that the staff had selected when they began operations in March 1971. During the six weeks we studied this cottage, no new boys entered the program, and none of those present left it. None of them had yet been in residence long enough to be eligible for parole.

The basic treatment model envisioned by the staff was a problem-solving group working together in a stable family environment. The cottage name was selected to reflect the concept of community and interdependence among staff and boys. The program strategies of "I Belong" were similar to those of Topsfield, with primary emphasis placed on academic education and clinical treatment. There was no vocational training or work experience other than routine cottage maintenance and chores. Unlike Topsfield, where even maintenance was performed by staff, the boys of "I Belong" were involved in the care of their home, painting and repairing it.

The academic education program included programmed instruction and individual tutoring in remedial subjects. The boys spent several hours each day working at their own speed on reading or math instructional programs. A second component of the educational program was group learning. The staff-inmate problem-solving group was utilized in the academic program, and the boys read stories about adolescent conflict situations—hypothetical or real problems involving dating, peer loyalty, delinquent activities, or the like—and then discussed the moral-ethical questions the stories raised, with staff and boys examining their thoughts and attitudes about these subjects. Group field trips provided another option.

The primary cottage program was treatment: community meetings, small-group therapy sessions, and individual counseling. Every afternoon inmates and staff participated in a one- or two-hour community meeting. As in Shirley cottage, the agenda of the meetings was determined by the entries recorded in the cottage log-book. The agenda included any complaints, proposals, or problems raised by boys or staff, covering any area of life. The cottage's program philosophy stated: "In our therapeutic setting, all house programs and activities are geared toward one specific goal. That is, developing the habit of using the process of problem solving whenever difficulties arise."

On particularly troublesome days when the agenda might contain a dozen or more items, the community meeting might last for several hours, or it could be continued after the evening meal. Although community meetings were not intended to be group therapy sessions, the inmate and staff group was sufficiently small that when the occasion warranted, the meeting could quickly assume all the features of the small-group therapy sessions. Particularly when a number of incidents recorded in the log involved the same individual, the group might conclude that the infractions were symptomatic of a deeper problem. Small encounter groups were conducted by the staff following the community meetings. The group treatment techniques were similar to those used in Shirley cottage, although the sessions were not held on as regular a basis. Individual counseling provided an adjunct to the group treatment process, with a consulting psychologist providing clinical services for a few boys in the cottage.

Social Control in the Group Treatment Setting

The primary means of control in the group treatment setting was formal collaboration between staff and inmates in the community meetings and in the therapy groups. Formal collaboration uses the group problem-solving process to define and enforce collective norms and to mobilize group pressures to deal with specific instances of deviance. Staff and inmates collaborated to create the rules governing cottage life and participated in their enforcement via an elaborate privilege system. Formal collaboration reduced the need for, and efficacy of, informal collaboration or physical coercion to maintain order. Temporary transfers to a discipline cottage was another control available through formal collaboration.

The amount of inmate participation in formal collaboration varied among the treatment cottages: The inmates of Sunset cottage participated in the formulation and enforcement of cottage norms far less than did those in either Shirley or "I Belong." They all used a privilege system in which inmates participated in assigning fellow inmates to particular levels of freedom. Unlike the custody settings, a boy's movement from one level to another was much more dependent on his performance and participation and much less determined by the amount of time served. The gradations of privilege and freedom were much more explicit and applied to virtually every aspect of institutional life as well as to parole eligibility. The privileges and responsibilities associated with each level were consistently and energetically enforced.

Social-control practices differed somewhat among the three group treatment cottages owing to differences in programs and the degree of formal collaboration. Sunset staff granted or withdrew privileges more unilaterally than did the staff of Shirley or "I Belong."

Boys could lose a level of freedom and the corresponding privileges for fighting, threatening other boys, sniffing lighter fluid, destroying state property, not doing their jobs properly, arguing with staff members, stealing from other inmates, or failing to report other boys who engaged in any of the above activities. While custody-oriented staff used a variety of control strategies to deal with different kinds of behavior, formal collaboration to restrict freedoms and privileges was the group treatment response to almost every form of deviance. Temporary transfer to a discipline cottage was reserved only for runaway boys and aggressive, acting-out boys who posed a serious threat to the other boys and the staff.

Despite the emphasis on formal collaboration, the boys were sometimes reluctant to punish their fellow inmates. The strength of formal collaboration was the staff pressure on boys to put pressure on other boys. The concept of responsibility was central to this process. A boy was responsible both for his own progress and for that of other boys. The higher his level of freedom, the greater his responsibilities for himself and others. This is a crucial distinction from social control in individual treatment settings, where inmates were primarily concerned only with their own progress. For group treatment boys, "being responsible means working with other people and helping yourself as well. Like if you think someone is going to run, you try to talk them out of it, and if you can't, you tell a staff member so they can talk to him." The principle of third-party responsibility effected a major transformation in the subculture norms governing informing, with much greater inmate acceptance of "dime-dropping" than in other types of settings.

In order for formal collaboration to succeed, the staff had to maintain consistent pressure on the boys and support them in their efforts to change others. The inmates could not maintain the pressure on other boys alone. A lack of staff support could lead to a breakdown of control while the reintroduction of staff support could reinforce the inmates' ability to maintain control through formal collaboration. When the staff was able to reinforce the group, the boys were able to confront and control each other, enforcing the levels of freedom and the corresponding privileges.

Consistent with the group treatment orientation, many of the control pressures were directed toward either the small treatment groups, the basic unit of boys in the cottage, or the total inmate population, rather than individual boys. The Shirley cottage population was divided into three smaller treatment groups, with group members responsible for their members' completion of cottage chores and the like. If the group failed to pressure a boy to do his work, the whole group could be dropped a level. There was also third-person responsibility. If boys were aware of deviance, even if they were not participants, their failure to take action or report it to staff could result in being dropped a level. Collective responsibility was basic to the operation of the cottage. When several boys questioned sanctions for the group on account of one individual's deviance, the cottage director reiterated the philosophy of the cottage, that one boy's irresponsibility was the whole group's problem. "The philosophy of the cottage is that kids should get it as a group. There are group consequences, and there should be. Do we want to put the pressure on a guy individually, or do we want to put pressure on the group as a whole to be responsible for him? We all have to be responsible for each other."

In the group treatment settings, an egalitarian participative community of staff and inmates collaborated together to maintain discipline and control within the cottage. Virtually all issues were resolved collectively with staff and inmates defining the rules and imposing the sanctions. This marks a major transition from the more authoritarian, hierarchical controls used in the custody-oriented settings. In the treatment cottages, the role of staff was to encourage and reinforce boys' efforts to assume responsibility for and help change other boys. The cottage social structure and programs were designed to facilitate and support this type of inmate responsibility for the actions of others.

SUMMARY

We began this chapter with an analysis of the ways in which staff used the opportunities afforded by institutional decentralization to define their own cottage treatment programs. In the absence of explicit guidance, staff assumptions about the causes and cures of delinquency inform their behavior. Our analysis of correctional ideologies suggests the ways in which their beliefs led staff to pursue markedly different goals for the rehabilitation of delinquent youths. They selected program and social control strategies that were consistent with their goals.

Ultimately, people-changing organizations bring about client change by structuring relations between staff and inmates. The nature and quality of staff-inmate relations depends upon the intervention strategies used, since program and social control techniques influence the types of social relations and interactions that can occur. Personnel in the various cottages sought different types of inmate change and structured their relationships accordingly.

Staff-inmate relations in Cottage 9 were highly problematical. There were very few opportunities for positive interaction between staff and inmates in this punitive setting. The program, or more properly the absence of one, did not require inmate commitment nor did it provide opportunities for interaction with staff on any basis other than domination and submission. The staffs' heavy reliance on physical coercion alienated inmates who avoided staff if they were able. Moreover, the staffs' mass-handling strategies precluded the emergence of informal interactions between staff and inmates. Finally, staffs' concern about the possibility of inmate collusion to "overthrow" the guards led them to discourage informal inmate associations and encourage self-isolation and splintering within the subculture. As a result of these programs and control strategies, there was an enormous gulf and cleavage between the staff and inmate social systems.

The strategy of encouraging residents to form positive associations with adults through individualized programs of training and education fostered more personal contacts between staff and inmates in the individual custody settings. Although these relationships were defined narrowly, they tended to reduce the enormous staff-inmate schism observed in Cottage 9. Occasionally, staff members developed close relationships with a particular boy or girl, although the majority of vocational training and work relationships were perfunctory, indifferent, and domineering. The typical pattern of staff-inmate relations was one in which authoritative, paternalistic adults exercised considerable control over inmates. Inmates were expected to do their work, obey orders promptly, demonstrate their reliability and dependability in shop, school, and cottage assignments, and respond to adults with respect and deference. Staff sought inmate conformity but lacked the physical resources to achieve direct domination as in Cottage 9. The uneasy accommodation of custody and co-optation resulted in a staff-inmate social system that remained essentially bifurcated with occasional bridges across the gulf. Lancaster staff relations with inmates were similar to those in the male settings in most respects, with staff relating to inmates almost exclusively on an authoritative, formal basis.

There was a marked reduction in the separation between staff and inmates in the individual treatment setting. Staff domination was minimal and the permissive, relaxed, and open setting facilitated the development of warm relationships between inmates and staff in both clinical and other contexts. While the lack of emphasis on formal collaboration retarded the integration of the inmate and staff social worlds, relations were still considerably more extensive and rewarding than in the custody settings.

It was in the group treatment settings that staff and inmates most closely achieved an integrated social system in which both were members of the same group. While there were differences between cottages, formal collaboration between staff and inmates in the treatment program and as a process of social control greatly increased the quality and quantity of staff interactions with inmates. It increased the openness, visibility, and consistency of staff encounters with inmates. The community meeting provided a forum in which all members of the cottage community were encouraged to participate on an open, democratic, and egalitarian basis. Staff related to inmates primarily as older, more responsible people whose greater experiences enabled them to help the residents.

In this chapter, we have described the organizational consequences that followed institutional decentralization. The various cottage staff groups used a variety of change strategies which structured their relationships with inmates in different ways. In the following chapters, we will explore the implications of these different intervention strategies for subculture dynamics as these define the organizational context to which the inmates must adapt.

Chapter 3

The Inmate Subcultures

Inmate subcultures develop within the confines of correctional or other total institutions and exhibit all the characteristics of a subsociety. Its norms and values reflect the focal concerns of institutional life. Inmate roles and subculture stratification reflect conformity to or deviation from these norms. Newly entering inmates are socialized into this system and adapt to the expectations of their fellow inmates. Of necessity, their peers are their primary reference group. This informal social system often mediates the effectiveness of the formal organization, aiding or thwarting staff in the pursuit of their goals [1].

THEORIES OF SUBCULTURE FORMATION

Most early studies of adult maximum-security prisons were in agreement about the predominant characteristics of this prison culture: a two-caste system separating inmates and staff, with inmates united in opposition to staff values. Researchers described a variety of illicit activities that took place as inmates tried to lessen the deprivation of their imprisonment and to secure the materials, status, and power denied by the staff. A variety of argot roles evolved, organized around the core values of the inmate code. The feature that most pervades these early studies describing "oppositional" quality of the inmate culture is the hostility and antagonism between the inmates and the staff [2].

Two alternative models were offered in these early studies to explain the source and content of the inmate code and social system.

Commonly referred to as the indigenous-origins model and the direct-importation model, they attributed the organization and content of the inmate culture to different sources and social processes. The indigenous-origins model provided a functionalist explanation that related the values and roles of the subculture to inmates' responses to the problems of adjustment posed by their deprivations and pains of imprisonment. The formal organization of the prison was seen as the shaping force [3].

According to the indigenous-origins model the inmate social system is a creative adaptation to a variety of institutionally posed problems of adjustment, among them lack of freedom, constant surveillance, the deprivation of material goods and services, the lack of heterosexual relations, the psychological problems stemming from societal rejection, and threats to self-esteem [4]. The inmate system, responding to these problems, provides a collective mechanism for reducing or alleviating their impact. Since the problems are inherent in the prison regime itself, the solutions almost necessarily circumvent the goals of the formal organization and the activities of the staff.

Early studies characterized the inmate subculture as one of "solidary opposition," in which the inmates joined together in unified resistance to the institution's staff and goals. Not only was the subculture itself portrayed as negative and hostile to staff values, but new inmates quickly adopted these perspectives. This process reinforced the very value system and deviant interaction processes that prison was intended to modify [5].

Several recent functionalist studies have qualified the solidary opposition model. One group has reported that the oppositional inmate culture is not monolithic. Rather, an inmate's role in the subculture, his institutional socialization, or his integration into a primary group affects the extent to which he adopts oppositional values [6]. A second group of studies found that variations in organizational structure or treatment goals resulted in significantly different informal inmate social systems [7]. These studies suggest that variations in the organizational goals are related to variations in the inmates' social organization. The study by Street et al. of six institutions for delinquents represents one of the more systematic attempts to link differences in organizational goals and structure to variations in subcultural orientations and individual adaptations.

Comparing institutions arrayed along a custody-treatment continuum, Street et al. found systematic subcultural variations that corresponded to the goals and programs of the institution. The differences in subculture structure were related to the types of control systems used and the ensuing levels of deprivation and gratification that resulted. Variations in the severity of sanctions and the levels of deprivation were reflected in the inmates' attitudes toward the staff and institution and the types of change they attempted.

Unfortunately, this study is subject to several methodological criticisms arising from the noncomparability of the institutions in the sample [8]. Although several other studies have corroborated the relationship between treatment goals and subcultural variation, others have failed to find a relationship between an organization's custody or treatment goals and variation in the inmate subculture, reporting results more consistent with a solidary-opposition model [9].

The discrepancy between the earlier studies, which consistently found solidary-opposition subcultures, and the more recent ones, which suggest a relationship between the organizational goals and the informal inmate organization, is not as great as might first appear. Most of the earlier institutional studies examined heavily custodial institutions such as adult maximum-security facilities. The more recent studies have included treatment institutions as well as custodial settings. Since these studies also support a solidary-opposition model in custodial institutions, it has only been with the advent of treatment institutions that the variability of the relationship between organizational goals and subcultures has emerged. While the more recent studies have suggested the existence of a structure-subculture relationship, generally they have not explored the features or processes that produce this result.

A second model, the direct-importation theory, viewed the normative order of the prison as reflecting the values held by inmates prior to their incarceration. According to this theory the characteristics of the inmate population determine the nature of the subculture. The mechanism by which the roles and values of the external culture are imported into the inmate social system is that of "latent culture," the shared membership in a group other than the group in which the member is now participating and which influences his conduct in the present system [10]. For many prison inmates the latent culture is that shared with other members of the criminal subculture in the larger society [11].

Irwin and Cressey have offered a major statement about the importation thesis. They suggest that the adult prison inmate culture is actually an amalgam of a thief subculture, a convict subculture, and a conventional subculture [12]. They argue that inmates who are professional criminals (the thief subculture) bring with them an identification with and commitment to the larger society's criminal subculture which is not erased when they enter the prison, and that the values of the criminal subculture provide a source of identity and orientation while they are in prison. In the convict culture, one shared by reform school graduates and persons with extensive adult prison experience, the institutional subculture is the primary source of orientation and identification, and "the most manipulative and most utilitarian individuals win the available wealth and such positions of influence as might exist." Persons with neither a professional criminal background nor extensive institutional experience make up the conventional subculture.

Other researchers have questioned the existence of three distinct subcultures, noting that the basis for inclusion or exclusion from the hypothesized subcultures are unclear, that there is significant similarity in the three subcultures, that the indicators used to establish membership in the thief subculture are invalid, and that ultimately, regardless of their prior experience, inmates must still come to terms with the manifest pains of imprisonment [13]. Despite the apparent shortcomings of this first formulation, it is clear that the inmate does not enter the institution as a *tabula rasa*, and that his or her prior experiences will influence present perspectives and the alternatives seen as solutions to the circumstances of imprisonment.

Since subcultures arise when people in effective interaction with one another face similar problems of adjustment, then organizational difference would be expected to generate different problems of adjustment and provide various motives and opportunities for interaction. The inmate social systems should vary accordingly. One of the critical aspects of organizational variation that conditions the character of the inmate social systems is the extent to which the staff and the organization they structure succeed in neutralizing inmate violence and exploitation, thereby freeing inmates to endorse staff social values. Organizational variables influence the prevalence and intensity of inmate violence and exploitation in several ways. Institutional deprivations may provide some inmates with an incentive for exploitative and predatory behavior directed at their fellows. The organizational structure may also provide the circumstances and opportunities under which such exploitation may be carried out more or less successfully.

Violence among inmates, unfortunately prevalent, is an efficient and economical way for some inmates to alleviate the conditions of their own incarceration at the expense of other inmates. Moreover, many of the inmates in correctional institutions come from violent backgrounds where toughness and protection of physical integrity is at a premium. One aspect of our analysis of the cultural importation thesis will be a consideration of the extent to which differences in the presenting culture prepare some inmates better than others for adaptation within violence-based subcultures. In view of the potential for violence within the subculture, organizational structure becomes paramount as it increases or decreases the incentives and the circumstances under which violence can be fruitfully employed.

A clear relationship was found between the formal organizational structure and the type of subcultures that emerged in the cottages studied here. In the punitive group-custody setting, inmates suffered the greatest deprivations and tended to be the most alienated from other inmates and staff. Residents of this setting were also most likely to resort to predatory violence and exploitation of their fellows. Inmate alienation precluded the development of common defenses to exploitation. The prevalence of violent exploitation fixed an extremely rigid, hierarchically stratified inmate subculture in which aggressive inmates dominated their subordinates. To a considerable degree the authoritarian basis of the subculture paralleled the structure of the formal organization.

In the individual custody settings, the staff's use of a privilege system, coupled with informal co-optation of the inmate elite, brought potentially aggressive inmates under some degree of staff control. This provided some limits on the effectiveness of inmate violence and exploitation, although aggression remained the dominant mode of interaction within the subculture. The available roles and the stratification of the subculture remained essentially authoritarian and hierarchical, although inmates were not as brutally suppressed or alienated as in the group custody setting.

In the treatment-oriented cottages, especially in the group treatment programs, formal collaboration between inmates and staff considerably reduced the overall level of inmate violence. The therapeutic rationale for informing made the workings of the subculture much more visible to staff. This, combined with the lesser deprivations inmates experienced in these settings, reduced the necessity for and effectiveness of inmate aggression and exploitation. The reduction of violence in turn permitted the emergence of a more egalitarian subculture in which inmates were able to enter into relationships voluntarily rather than coercively and support more pro-social norms.

INMATE PERCEPTIONS OF COTTAGE PURPOSE

In the following analysis, we will attempt to clarify the linkages between the organizational characteristics and the features of the inmate subcultures in the respective cottages. Inmate perceptions of the purposes and goals of the cottage constitute a primary factor in defining the organizational context to which they must adapt. Their perceptions are important as well in assessing the degree of organizational alienation they experience, and helps to lay the groundwork for an assessment of the relative degree of deprivation they suffer.

Through questionnaire and interview items we examined the inmates' views of organizational purposes and staff expectations. Table 3-1 contains several indicators of inmates' perceptions of cottage goals. Table 3-2 presents their coded responses to the interview question, "What do you think this place is supposed to do for you?" The responses to these two independent measures of organizational purpose indicate clearly that the inmates in the custody-oriented cottages regarded those cottages as places for punishment, while the residents of the treatment-oriented cottages regarded their setting as places for treatment and gaining understanding and insight into the causes of their incarceration.

The questionnaires asked the inmates what they thought the *staff believed* the purpose of the organization to be, and then what they themselves thought were the purposes of the institution. As the first item in Table 3-1 indicates, the residents of the treatment-oriented cottages were more than twice as likely as the inmates in the custody-oriented cottages to describe the staff goals as treatment. Conversely, the inmates in the custody-oriented settings were more than five times as likely as those in treatment-oriented settings to describe the staff purpose as punitive. The Lancaster residents' intermediate position on these dimensions may reflect the ameliorating effect of organizational paternalism, which made the female settings somewhat less punitive.

For the second item the inmates were asked to define the purpose of the cottage. An even larger proportion of the inmates in the custody-oriented cottages thought the cottage purpose was punishment. From the perspective of the inmates in the custody-oriented cottages, regardless of what the staff thought they were doing, their purposes were experienced by the inmates as punishment. The highest level of punishment was reported by the residents of Cottage 9, the disciplinary cottage. The Lancaster girls were identical with males in the custody-oriented cottages in believing that the institutional purpose was punishment. A clear majority of inmates in the treatment-oriented cottages, on the other hand, thought that the purpose of their cottage was to aid them in gaining insight. The differences clearly indicate that these staff members communicated their treatment purposes to their inmates and, more significantly, created a situation that the inmates themselves experienced as creating treatment expectations rather than punishment expectations.

To further assess the differences in organizational purpose and staff expectations, we asked the inmates whether the staff sought conformity or insight, since these staff expectations would color the adaptive strategies pursued by the inmates. Earlier, we had asked the staff the same questions, and found clear-cut differences between custody and treatment cottage staff. The inmates in the custody-oriented settings, responding to staff expectations, were more than twice as likely to view the staff as expecting conformity, while the inmates in the treatment-oriented settings were almost three times as likely to view the staff as expecting them to gain insight and understanding. The girls at Lancaster, like the inmates in the male individual custody settings, overwhelmingly agreed that the staff expected conformity. Initially, then, we find that the differences in cottage purposes were experienced by the inmates and reflected in their perceptions of the organizational demands.

We also asked the inmates "What do you think this place is supposed to do for you?" The coded responses to this open-ended probe, shown in Table 3-2, correspond closely to the questionnaire results, which showed major differences in inmate perceptions. The responses were coded into four primary categories: (1) punishment; (2) isolation; (3) rehabilitation; and 4) problem-solving. Since inmates sometimes indicated multiple purposes, the cottage totals may exceed 100 percent. As coding categories, punishment and isolation are self-explanatory. Sometimes an inmate said the cottage was supposed "to help me." For coding purposes we distinguished between help in "going straight," "keeping out of trouble," or "stopping crime," and help in "solving problems," "dealing with feelings," "relating to other people," coding the first set as rehabilitation and the latter as problem-solving.

As expected, a substantially greater proportion of the inmates in the custody-oriented cottages than in the treatment-oriented cottages saw the purposes of those settings as punishment and isolation. They said that the purpose of the school was to:

> punish you to teach you a lesson not to do crime no more. Makes you think about how it is in here, and how nice it can be outside. Keep you off the streets so you won't get in trouble. Put you out of commission for awhile. Supposed to teach you a lesson for what you did. You did something so you got to pay, so they just send you to stay here. It's not supposed to do anything, just stay out of trouble and stay away from home.

Table 3–1. Inmate Perceptions of Cottage Goals *(percentages)*

	Custody-Oriented Cottages					Treatment-Oriented Cottages			
	Group		Individual			Individual	Group		
	Cottage 9	Cottage 8	Elms	Westview	Lancaster (female)	Topsfield (co-ed)	Sunset	Shirley	"I Belong"
1. What would you guess the staff thinks this place is for? Do they think it is:									

a) A place that helps kids understand the things that got them into trouble;	15%	14%	33% ⎫
			   [26]
				21% ⎭	43%	67%	60% ⎫
							   [61]
								50% ⎭	86%

b) A place to train and educate them;	4	14	10	7	13	13	7	25	0
c) A place to teach them respect for authority;	22	29	28	41	19	13	27	13	14
d) A place to punish kids for the things they did wrong.	59	43	28	31	26	7	7	13	0
2. What is this place trying to do for you, what do you think it is for? Is it:									

a) A place that helps kids understand the things that got them into trouble;	11%	20% ⎫
		   [23]
			23% ⎭	24%	28%	73%	53% ⎫
							   [63]
								63% ⎭	86%

b) A place to train and educate them;	11	7				13	7	13	

c) A place to teach them respect for authority;	0	13		21	13	13		14	
d) A place to punish kids for the things they did wrong.	78	60	64 [60]	55	60	0	27	13 [16]	0
3. What do you guess the staff thinks is more important for you while you are here?									
a) To obey the rules and not get into any trouble;	63%	86%	74% [78%]	79%	73%	7%	46%	43% [37%]	0%
b) To understand your personal problems.	37	14	26 [22]	21	27	93	54	57 [63]	100

Table 3-2. Coded Interview Response: "What do you think this place is supposed to do for you?" (percentages)

	Custody-Oriented Cottages					Treatment-Oriented Cottages			
	Group	Individual				Individual	Group		
	Cottage 9	Cottage 8	Elms	Westview	Lancaster (female)	Topsfield (co-ed)	Sunset	Shirley	"I Belong"
Punish: punish; teach a lesson; discipline	40%	57%	15% [21]	25%	23%	0%	7% [3]	0%	0%
Isolate: remove from community; keep off streets	24	29	21 [17]	10	12	0	0	0	0
Rehabilitate and reform: stop doing time; help you keep out of trouble; straighten out; go straight	52	57	77 [71]	80	60	18	71	38 [53]	50
Solve Problems: solve problems; deal with feelings; get head together	0	0	8 [6]	5	5	82	36	88 [68]	75

The Lancaster inmates were similar to their male individual-custody counterparts in the proportions describing punishment or isolation as the purpose of the institutions. By way of contrast, scarcely any of the inmates in the treatment-oriented settings ascribed these purposes to the institution.

A majority of inmates in almost every setting reported that the purpose of the cottage was to rehabilitate them so that they could return to the community without engaging again in further delinquent conduct. For the inmates in the custody-oriented settings, rehabilitation was the primary purpose of their incarceration. "Supposed to straighten me out. Stop stealing. Supposed to change me. Try to break you away from things you do on the outs, things that get you in trouble. Supposed to make you change your mind about getting in trouble." Even as they described the rehabilitative rationale, however, many of them observed that the school was failing to accomplish this mission. "It's supposed to help you go straight. Supposed to rehabilitate, but it doesn't rehabilitate anyone. It's not set up for rehabilitation. Most kids go back to doing things they were doing before."

Many of the inmates in the treatment-oriented cottages also described the purposes of the institutions as "rehabilitation" and "stopping crime." "They're trying to help us. Trying to get us to stop stealing cars and stuff, stop going to jail, cut down on our swearing. Not run away from home. To rehabilitate you so you can stop stealing and doing B&Es." They were much less likely, however, than were the inmates in custody-oriented settings, to add critical comments about the ineffectiveness of the programs.

By far the greatest contrast was in the proportion of inmates in the treatment-oriented cottages who described the purpose of the cottage as helping them solve their personal problems, relate better with other people, gain insight, and the like. For them the cottage was designed to:

> Help me solve my problems. In the small groups, they say "let's talk about your problems," "why are you here," "how do you get along with other people?" They see if you're telling the truth. If you ain't, they'll come back to you the next day and the next. They'll stick with you until you are telling the truth. When I first came here, I didn't get along with the kids here, didn't get along with the staff either. Now I'm better. I get along better with the staff and the kids, and I'll be better with people on the outs.

> Help you on your problems with others. To find out why you did the things you did. Help us solve our problems. Find out the root of it, question the kid about it, and then get into it. It's supposed to solve my problems, tell me what my problems are and how to solve them.

Only a small proportion of the male or female inmates in the custody-oriented programs thought the purpose of their cottage was to aid them in dealing with personal problems or difficulties in interpersonal relations.

PROBLEMS OF ADJUSTMENT AND MOTIVES FOR EXPLOITATION

Differences in organizational structure and staff behavior influence the types of deprivations and problems confronting inmates and the circumstances under which they can resolve these problems. It is our hypothesis that the organizational differences will determine both the degree of the "pain of imprisonment" that inmates experience, and the conditions under which the inmate group can ameliorate them. These two factors are related to the levels of inmate exploitation. In this section we consider the problems that confront the inmates in the various settings.

Many of the problems confronting these inmates are shared by all residents of total institutions and result from the inherent nature of incarceration. These include deprivations of liberty by confinement, the accompanying involuntary isolation and separation from family and friends, the implicit community rejection involved in institutional confinement, sexual segregation, the loss of autonomy and freedom with a corresponding increase in dependency and submission to authority, reductions in the material goods and services available, boredom, confinement with other inmates, and the like. These problems are not present uniformly, and organizational variation determines the degree to which they are salient.

To identify what the cottage inmates regarded as problems associated with their incarceration, we asked them, "What's the toughest part of being here? What kinds of stuff do you miss having the most?" Table 3-3 contains their coded responses. We distinguished between the external problems, such as separation from family and friends, that were inextricably associated with being incarcerated, and the internal problems, such as material deprivation, that were more situationally determined by the characteristics of a particular setting.

By virtually every measure, the inmates in the custody-oriented cottages reported far more extensive and more severe problems and deprivations than did the inmates in the treatment-oriented cottages. Those differences were expected, since treatment staff were more concerned with minimizing the unpleasant, alienating aspects of institutionalization and their programs than were custody-oriented staff.

Table 3-3. Coded Interview Response: "What's the toughest part of being here?" (percentages)

	Custody-Oriented Cottages					Treatment-Oriented Cottages			
	Group	Individual				Individual	Group		
	Cottage 9	Cottage 8	Elms	Westview	Lancaster (female)	Topsfield (co-ed)	Sunset	Shirley	"I Belong"
External Factors									
Incarceration per se; lack of freedom to leave	48%	43%	48% [42]	32%	49%	18%	21%	44% [34]	38%
Absence from home and family	28	29	59 [53]	53	56	0	71	25 [47]	50
Absence from friends, boy/girl friends	12	29	62 [58]	63	58	27	50	13 [32]	38
Internal Factors									
Living with other inmates	4	14	10 [7]	0	9	0	0	0	0
Material deprivations; lack of things used to having	40	43	24 [25]	21	19	0	14	0 [5]	0
Boredom	16	43	14 [22]	26	2	9	7	4 [5]	0
Staff, rules, and regulations	8	0	31 [22]	16	14	27	7	19 [11]	0
Therapy and treatment	0	0	0	0	0	64	0	25 [11]	0

For all the inmates the loss of freedom and the isolation from family and friends were the most troublesome problems. The relative discomfort caused by these external deprivations differed by cottage type: in the group custody setting, incarceration and the accompanying loss of freedom were seen as the most severe. The boys missed "not being able to be free and not going out and playing when you want, coming in when you want. You got to sit down in the room, and you can't move around too much, or even go to the bathroom." The absence of family and friends, while painful, paled by comparison with their extensive loss of freedom.

The loss of freedom was painful for the inmates in the individual custody cottages as well, especially for the girls at Lancaster. Many complained that "you can't go out or walk around whenever you want. You can't go wherever you want to." For them, separation from friends and family was even more difficult. Many of the inmates in these settings found that the toughest part of being in the institution was "Being away from society, from friends, getting adjusted to being away from my family, and missing my friends and family." Although the differences were slight, the girls at Lancaster were somewhat more likely than their male counterparts to find their loss of contacts with family and friends painful. This is consistent with the suggestions that cultural differences in female socialization increase their needs for affectional relationships.

Inmates in the treatment-oriented cottages found incarceration and the absence of friends and family considerably less painful than did their peers in custody-oriented settings. The treatment programs were freer, and more open and permissive than the custody-oriented programs; inmates probably suffered less real loss of freedom than did the custody-oriented cottage residents. Moreover, the treatment-oriented inmates had substantially greater contacts with the community, families, and friends because of the more frequent weekend furloughs, home visits, off-ground trips, and work opportunities, which helped to reduce their isolation.

All the youths shared the problem of removal from their homes to varying degrees, but institutional living posed additional problems. Among the more common problems of imprisonment described in the literature of adult prison subcultures is the deprivation of material goods and services and the loss of the amenities of life. Institutional living also poses problems of coping with boredom, living with other inmates, and following the rules and regulations imposed by staff. We found major differences in the situationally determined internal features confronting the inmates.

Those in the custody-oriented cottages reported more severe deprivations and problems than did those in the treatment-oriented cottages. For the boys in Cottage 9, material deprivation ranked just behind incarceration itself as the major problem confronting them. In this setting the boys were denied virtually all personal possessions: they wore only state-issued uniforms, were prohibited from smoking, and were allowed to eat only at regularly scheduled meal times. They were denied television or recreational opportunities. Many boys complained bitterly about these deprivations. The extensive material deprivations also provided some inmates with a motive to exploit other inmates for the few amenities that the system permitted as well as for any contraband.

In the individual custody cottages, about a quarter of all of the inmates complained of material deprivations. The complaints were similar to those made by the boys in Cottage 9—lack of cigarettes, snacks, and similar amenities. Their deprivations were somewhat less severe than those in Cottage 9, because the staffs' privilege system allowed the residents to retain some of their personal possessions in their lockers. As one boy said, "I get the smokes, that's all I care about. I don't miss candy or tonic." The deprivations experienced by the girls at Lancaster were similar to those of their individual-custody male counterparts.

Among the inmates in the treatment-oriented cottages, only those in Sunset cottage complained at all about material deprivations. Because of its moribund program, it was more like Elms and Westview, the other Lyman School cottages. The general absence of complaints reflects the greater availability of resources and amenities as part of the treatment program privileges, as well as their increased contacts with the community which enabled them to buy additional goods.

Institutional living posed other problems in addition to material deprivations. A small but significant proportion of the inmates in the custody-oriented cottages complained about difficulties in living with other inmates and problems of "getting along with the other kids." One boy saw the problem as "being locked up with a bunch of maniacs. Sometimes I feel more mature than the others here." Another complained of "having to live with all of these creeps" and "avoiding fights." This aspect of institutional adjustment appeared to be as problematic for the girls at Lancaster as for the boys. Several girls expressed difficulties in "getting along with the other kids" or getting along with "the ones that boss everybody around."

None of the inmates in the treatment-oriented cottages expressed this complaint. These complaints by residents in custody-oriented cottages reflect the greater degree of physical violence in these settings. The prevalence of violence in the subculture and its control by staff again and again arises as a key factor in distinguishing among the inmate cultures. The concentration of complaints about living with other inmates in the custody-oriented cottages is one indicator of such differences.

About a fifth of the inmates in the custody-oriented cottages had to face the problem of boredom. For these inmates, waiting, sitting, and just "doing time" were major difficulties of institutional life. They complained of "waiting until your time is up, just doing your time. . . . It gets boring just sitting around doing the same stuff every day." Boredom and the absence of engaging activities provided the residents of the custody-oriented cottages with more opportunities to "get into trouble," since fighting at least helped to pass the time. The girls at Lancaster did not suffer from boredom because the school was so heavily structured and programmed. Similarly, a much smaller proportion of the inmates in the treatment-oriented cottages suffered from a lack of regular activity.

Complaints about rules and regulations reflect another problem of institutional adjustment. Although inmates in both treatment- and custody-oriented cottages voiced complaints about rules and regulations, the substance of the problems differed. In the custody-oriented cottages the inmates objected to regimentation and being ordered around. These inmates objected to the staffs' emphasis on obedience and conformity. "Following the rules is the toughest part; I'm not used to following rules." In the treatment-oriented cottages the complaints pertained to the treatment process itself. A large majority of the inmates in the individual treatment program and a quarter of the inmates in the most consistent and structured group-treatment setting, Shirley cottage, had complaints that fell into this category. These inmates found it difficult to relate openly with each other. Several observed that the "toughest part about being here is trying to be honest." Others found group meetings a threatening experience, and they complained about the constant exposure of their behavior to public scrutiny and criticism. The rules on honesty and confronting inmate deviance compounded these difficulties.

In summary, the inmates in the treatment-oriented settings confronted somewhat different and considerably less severe problems of adjustment than did the inmates in the custody-oriented settings. While these settings were similar in their external features, there were major internal differences. These were clearly related to the programmatic differences in the various organizations. As part of the basic program, the treatment cottage staff attempted to reduce many of the deprivations of institutionalization and to make the experience more gratifying. Custody cottage staff, because of their program orientation, had less of a commitment to ameliorating the impact of institutionalization. As a consequence of these program differences the residents of the custody-oriented programs were provided with an incentive to alleviate their conditions by means of violent and aggressive behavior.

INMATE COOPERATION WITH INMATES OR STAFF: OPPORTUNITIES TO RESOLVE PROBLEMS OF ADJUSTMENT

The problems of adjusting to institutional life influence inmates' motives for interaction, but the means available to them to resolve their problems are of equal significance in determining the form and character of the inmate subculture. Correctional programs and change strategies require staff to structure their relationships with inmates. Similarly, to resolve the problems of the informal organization, residents attempt to control and structure their relationships with staff and other inmates. The relationships inmates enter create a variety of opportunities to alleviate the problems they confront.

The collective solutions available will obviously depend upon inmate perceptions of staff and other inmates. Depending upon the circumstances, cooperative relationships can occur between inmates and staff, inmates and inmates, or both. We assume that negative perceptions will detract from cooperative relationships, while positive perceptions will enhance them. The patterns of relationships that arise are one of the prime determinants of subculture organization. Inmate cooperation with staff augers for a more open, visible, and manageable social system. If staff cannot obtain inmate cooperation, either formally or informally, a more closed, subterranean, and violent social system may emerge.

INMATE PERCEPTIONS OF STAFF

We found a very strong correlation between the staffs' perceptions of inmates and the inmates' views of staff. In those settings where the staff held negative views of inmates, describing them as dangerous, unreliable, abnormal, or incorrigible, the inmates held correspondingly negative views of staff, regarding them as untrustworthy, unhelpful, and indifferent. Conversely, in those settings where the staff expressed more favorable views of the inmates, regarding them as essentially like other adolescents and capable of normal relationships, the inmates shared more positive perspectives of the staff.

The degree to which inmates hold strong positive or negative views of staff is a measure of their alienation from staff. It is also related to the probability that they will cooperate with staff members either in the attainment of the staff's goals, or in the solution of their own institutional problems. Thus, inmate perceptions of staff are both an indicator and determinant of the emergence of an oppositional or cooperative inmate social system.

We measured inmates' perceptions of staff reliability, trustworthiness, and concern for inmates through questionnaire items and interviews. These results are summarized in Table 3—4. Several items reflecting staff concern for inmates and commitment to helping them were merged into the scale "Staff do not help or care about inmates." The differences in inmate assessments of staff concern and commitment emerged with startling clarity. Virtually every inmate in the group custody setting, and well over half the inmates in the individual custody setting, felt that staff were neither concerned nor helpful, as contrasted with fewer than a fifth of the inmates in the group treatment settings and an even lower proportion in the individual treatment setting. The Lancaster girls' perceptions of staff were nearly identical with their individual custody male counterparts.

These differences clearly follow from the previously reported variations in inmate perceptions of cottage goals, since it is easy to equate punitive programs with unconcerned staff and therapeutic programs with committed staff. These perceptions of staff commitment and concern should affect the extent to which inmates will cooperate with or rely upon staff to help them in their institutional adjustment.

Another measure of the nature and quality of inmate-staff relations was the degree to which the inmates regarded the staff members as trustworthy and reliable. The scales "positive perspectives of staff" and "negative perspectives of staff" contained several items that measured inmate perceptions of staff helpfulness and trustworthiness. None of the inmates in the group custody setting and less than a third of the inmates in the individual custody settings had positive views of staff, as contrasted with about three-quarters of the inmates in the treatment setting who shared positive views. At the other end of the continuum, 85 percent of the inmates in Cottage 9 and about half of the inmates in the individual custody cottages had negative perspectives. Among the individual custody group, the inmates in Elms and Westview cottages had somewhat more positive and correspondingly fewer negative views of the staff than did those in Cottage 8. This suggests that the vocational training programs in these cottages fostered greater inmate contact and interaction with staff, which helped to reduce the negative stereotypes each held of

The Inmate Subcultures 109

Table 3–4. Inmate Perceptions of Staff (percentages)

	Custody-Oriented Cottages					Treatment-Oriented Cottages			
	Group	Individual				Individual	Group		
Scale	Cottage 9	Cottage 8	Elms	Westview	Lancaster (female)	Topsfield (co-ed)	Sunset	Shirley	"I Belong"
1. Staff do not help or care about inmates	96%	87%	46% [58]	59%	51%	13%	20% [18]	25%	0%
2. Staff treat inmates unfairly	78	67	44 [54]	62	68	40	21 [32]	56	0
3. Positive perspective of staff	0	0	39 [30]	35	40	80	73 [74]	63	100
4. Negative perspective of staff	85	80	44 [49]	41	49	13	13 [13]	19	0
Coded Interview Responses									
Positive Response: Fair, concerned, committed to helping	8	0	21 [22]	32	14	45	21 [19]	6	38
Neutral Response: all right, OK	69	57	54 [54]	53	67	45	64 [68]	75	62
Negative Response: unconcerned, indifferent, self-centered	23	43	25 [24]	15	19	10	14 [13]	19	0

the other. As will soon be seen, the staff people in these two cottages were also able to reach a more effective informal accommodation with the inmate leadership and thereby exercise greater control over the levels of violence in their subcultures. The female inmates at Lancaster were similar to the individual custody males in their positive and negative perspectives on staff. Again, by contrast, less than one inmate in seven in the treatment-oriented cottages had a negative view of staff.

These attitudinal differences were corroborated by the inmate responses to the interview question, "What do you think of the staff here?" The coded responses appear in Table 3-4. The inmates in the custody-oriented cottages gave the largest portion of negative responses. Their complaints centered on staff indifference, lack of concern, and cultural separation, since the custody-oriented staff were considerably older and more conventional than treatment-oriented staff. Again, the inmates in Elms and Westview had a somewhat less negative view than those in Cottage 8. The inmates in the treatment-oriented settings were much less likely to make negative, disparaging comments about staff. Thus, the interview responses support the inference from the questionnaire measures that the inmates in the treatment-oriented settings were less alienated from staff than those in the custody-oriented settings.

Their responses provide a view of the inmates' perceptions of staff in the various settings. Several of the boys in Cottage 9 complained, "They never really do anything for you. They say all this stuff, but then they just come in, sit down, and don't do anything." Another said, "Some just work for the money and they don't care about the kids." Although complaints of lack of concern and indifference were heard in varying degrees in all of the cottages, they were more frequent in the custody-oriented settings. The boys in the individual custody cottages complained that "some of them just come in and work. What the hell, they don't give a shit. A good staff member would help you. He wouldn't say 'line up, shut up, do this, do that.' They're too bossy. Kind of bullshit like that gets you pissed off." The female inmates at Lancaster complained that the cottages were not fairly run because of staff favoritism. "I like most of the matrons, but they have favorites. There's usually one girl they're interested in, but not the rest. They pick on kids more than they would pick on their favorites." Very few of the inmates in the male cottages complained about staff favoritism.

In addition to complaints about unfairness, indifference, and lack of commitment, another common complaint in the more custodial cottages was that the staff members were too old to understand or relate effectively with their young charges. Since more than half the staff members in the individual custody cottages were over fifty years of age, this criticism was especially pronounced in these settings. As one boy complained, "They don't know what they're doing. They don't care about you. They're too old and grouchy. You need younger people around here. These ones are too old for the job. All they like to do is sit around and enjoy the last years of their life while we suffer." Another boy added, "They're so old, they don't understand the kids. They're not the right people for this place. They're old fashioned. If you make noise, he can't stand it. They like everything to be quiet. You need young dudes who know how a kid feels."

Although age and cultural differences between staff and inmates were present in all of the cottages, they were much less pronounced in the treatment settings. The inmates at Topsfield, which had one of the youngest staffs, regarded their staff's youthfulness as a virtue. "A lot of the staff is really cool. Some of them are too much into psychology—as soon as something happens, they look for the reason —but a lot of the staff are really good. A lot of the younger staff are really into a lot of the stuff the kids are."

In sum, there were real, clear-cut differences between the cottages in the inmates' perceptions of staff. The inmates in the treatment-oriented cottages were substantially more likely to credit staff members with good intentions and making a sincere effort to help inmates, and they were more inclined to regard them as trustworthy and reliable. These positive perceptions were much less prevalent in the custody-oriented settings; especially in cottages 9 and 8, where the inmates were extremely alienated from staff. Moreover, age and cultural differences posed an additional barrier to inmate relations with staff in these settings.

Inmate differences in perceptions of staff commitment and reliability should also be reflected in differences in cooperative relationships between residents and staff. To assess whether perceptual differences were also reflected in actual differences in interactions with staff, we included several questionnaire items measuring the quantity and quality of inmate contacts with staff members. The results are contained in Table 3-5. We asked the inmates whether they "talk with staff members more than most kids or less." Very few inmates in Cottage 9 indicated they talked to staff members more than other inmates, and almost three-quarters indicated that they avoided staff. In view of their negative perceptions of and alienation from the cottage staff, this reaction is not surprising. Most of their contacts with these staff people were unpleasant and punishing.

Table 3-5. Inmate Contacts with Staff (percentages)

	Custody-Oriented Cottages					Treatment-Oriented Cottages			
	Group	Individual				Individual	Group		
	Cottage 9	Cottage 8	Elms	Westview	Lancaster (female)	Topsfield (co-ed)	Sunset	Shirley	"I Belong"
Do you think you talk with staff members more than most kids or less? More than most	8%	27%	21% [20]	17%	21%	27%	27%	38% [28]	13%
Less than most	73	20	44 [36]	35	38	20	27	50 [30]	0
Do you ever talk serious with your counselor about things that get you into trouble, personal problems, that sort of thing?	27	20	14 [19]	24	48	91	27	62 [45]	43
How well do you think your counselor understands you? Very well or fairly well	36	47	69 [61]	60	59	82	77	81 [83]	100
When you really need something can you count on him to help you out? Most of the time	5	20 [30]	27 [30]	42	30	46	36	38 [43]	71

Comparing the remaining cottages, a larger proportion of the inmates in the treatment-oriented cottages than in the custody-oriented cottages indicated greater contact with staff. Conversely, a larger proportion of the inmates in the custody-oriented cottages than in the treatment-oriented cottages indicated that they had less contact with staff. The girls at Lancaster had about the same level of staff contact as did their male counterparts. Thus, we find that the inmates' perceptions of staff were closely related to the quantity of staff contact.

We also attempted to measure the quality of contacts and the degree of trust and confidence that inmates placed in staff by asking them how often they talked with their counselors about personal problems or serious issues, as distinguished from procedural matters such as preparing papers for weekend furloughs, home visits, and the like. The inmates in the treatment-oriented cottages were more than twice as likely as their custody-oriented counterparts to talk with their counselors about important personal matters. In part this difference reflected basic programmatic emphases, since the treatment-oriented staff placed a greater premium on clinical relationships. On the other hand, the fact that twice as many treatment cottage residents as custody cottage inmates were in a position to enter into a trusting relationship with a staff member made inmate identification and cooperation with staff that much more likely. To explore these differences, we asked the inmates whether they thought their counselor understood them and could be relied on if they needed help. A substantially larger proportion of the inmates in the treatment settings than in the custody settings believed that their counselors understood them and could be relied upon. Thus, the differences in inmate perceptions of staff were also discernible in the quantity and quality of contacts they had with staff members.

Another indicator of subcultural differences regarding staff contacts was reflected in the normative injunction, "Don't be a suck-ass," which was prevalent in the custody-oriented cottages. The inmate alienation and negative perceptions of staff in the custody cottages led residents to minimize their contacts with staff. This norm against playing up to staff was much more pronounced and prevalent in the custody cottages than in the treatment cottages, where the pejorative "suck-ass" was employed to denounce inmates attempting to curry favor with staff. It was permissible for a boy to protect his own interests by "getting in good with the [cottage] master, but don't go sucking their asses." This meant that "you have to get along with them, but that doesn't mean you have to agree with them." Thus, the differences in inmate perceptions of staff were reflected in the nature of contacts with staff and, in the custody cottages, an injunction against unnecessary communication or ingratiation with staff.

INMATE PERCEPTIONS OF OTHER INMATES

The character of the subculture also depends upon whether inmates can enter into cooperative relationships with other inmates to facilitate institutional adjustment. As a result of philosophical differences in techniques of implementing change, the staff in different cottages pursued several alternative strategies in response to informal inmate associations: encouraging them, discouraging them, or perhaps ignoring them. Staff efforts to atomize and isolate inmates or to integrate them with each other should be reflected in inmate perceptions of fellow inmates. In this section, we consider whether the inmates perceived their fellows as trustworthy and reliable, since this should influence the types of social relationships they have with each other.

We asked inmates whether they thought other inmates could be trusted and would help fellow inmates. These results are summarized in the scales presented in Table 3—6. Their views of other inmates closely parallel their perception of staff. The inmates in the custody-oriented cottages reported substantially lower levels of trust and concern on the part of other inmates than did the residents in the treatment-oriented settings. Only 7 percent of the inmates in the group custody setting had a positive view of their fellow inmates, as did only about one-third of the inmates in the individual custody setting. These were also the settings in which staff discouraged informal inmate associations. The female inmates were similar to their male counterparts on this dimension. By contrast, over half the inmates in the group treatment settings indicated a positive assessment of their fellows, as did nearly all the inmates in the individual treatment setting.

Positive views of fellow inmates should encourage them to enter informal associations voluntarily, on the basis of friendship. Of equal relevance for analyzing subculture character is the strength of negative perceptions, since these could deter inmates from entering into cooperative relationships. On this dimension, even stronger differences emerge between the cottages. The inmates in the custody-oriented settings were almost twice as likely as those in treatment settings to have negative views of their fellow inmates. Stated another way, the inmates in treatment cottages were more than twice as likely to view fellow residents positively as negatively, while the inmates in the custody-oriented settings were more likely to hold negative views

Table 3-6. Inmate Perceptions of Other Inmates (percentages)

	Custody-Oriented Cottages					Treatment-Oriented Cottages			
	Group	Individual				Individual	Group		
Scale	Cottage 9	Cottage 8	Elms	Westview	Lancaster (female)	Topsfield (co-ed)	Sunset	Shirley	"I Belong"
Positive perception of other inmates	7%	33%	26% [35]	48%	32%	93%	53%	38% [54]	88%
Negative perception of other inmates	70	47 [41]	41	38	51	7	27 [21]	25	0

than positive ones. In Cottage 9 the inmates were ten times more likely to hold negative views than positive ones.

Thus we find that organizational differences are also related to differences in the views that inmates have of one another. These differences in perceptions probably reflect differences in the degree to which inmates were exploited and victimized by other residents, since predatory behavior was much more common in the custody-oriented settings than in the treatment programs. Once this pattern is established, however, modification requires outside intervention, since inmates who have negative views of their fellows are less likely or able to enter into cooperative relationships to curb exploitation than those who hold more positive views.

We predicted that residents of treatment cottages would be more likely to engage in collective solutions with other inmates to resolve a variety of institutional problems than the residents of custody-oriented settings. To test this hypothesis, we analyzed the types of institutional adaptations that inmates made in the various settings.

INMATE ADAPTATIONS

As the previous discussions suggest, cottage staff people shared organizationally distinct expectations of "appropriate" inmate behavior, and these were communicated to inmates. Apart from the formal organizational demands, inmate perceptions of staff members and other inmates also conditioned the types of adaptations that inmates could make. Staff in the custody-oriented settings tended to emphasize overt conformity and obedience, while staff in the treatment-oriented settings tended to emphasize the gaining of insight and the solving of personal problems. These staff expectations mark one set of parameters that inmates must consider in planning their own adaptive strategy.

The possibility of cooperative relationships with other inmates or staff marks an additional set of variables limiting the adaptive alternatives available to inmates. In view of the differences in their perceptions of staff and other inmates, we expected inmates in the treatment-oriented settings to cooperate more extensively with inmates and staff in their institutional adjustment than would the inmates in the custody-oriented settings. Several different indicators of inmate adaptations are contained in Table 3—7. Some of these items indicate whether inmates used adaptive strategies that emphasized obedience and conformity or gaining insight and understanding in response to the demands of the formal organization. Others measured the degree to which inmates isolate themselves, cooperate with other inmates, or with staff. Taken in combination, they begin to show the effects that differences in cottage structure have on the organization of the inmate social system.

We asked the inmates to choose "the best way to get along here" and provided four adaptive alternatives: deviance, conformity, repentence, and insight. In view of the staff expectations communicated to inmates, we expected the inmates in the custody-oriented settings to respond disproportionately in the first two categories and the inmates in the treatment-oriented settings to choose the latter two adaptations. More than a third of the inmates in Cottage 9 chose overt conformity and covert deviance—"get away with what you can —as their optimal adaptation. About a fifth of the male and female inmates in the individual custody settings also chose the "deviant" adaptation, compared with fewer than one in ten in the treatment-oriented cottages. The marked reduction in deviance in the treatment settings is probably attributable to the more benign character of these settings, which reduced the necessity of deviance. The greater legitimacy of staff also probably reduced the impetus to "stay out of the way of the adults."

A majority of the inmates in the individual custody settings chose conformity as the best adaptations, while the largest proportion of inmates in the treatment-oriented settings chose gaining insight. These adaptations were consistent with the inmate responses sought by staff in those respective settings.

To further assess the conformity and obedience adaptation of inmates, several items were summated in a scale measuring a "prisonized adaptation." Well over half the inmates in the custody-oriented cottages agreed that these prisonized adaptations—prompt obedience and self-isolation—were the most appropriate responses to their settings, as contrasted with about a fifth of the inmates in treatment settings. These inmate responses closely parallel the staff responses to these same items, again suggesting the impact of organizational goals and staff expectations on the inmate social system.

Another variation of the prisonized adaptation is the adaptive strategy of "doing your own time," which entails noninvolvement with inmates or staff, avoiding trouble, and having an easy and uncomplicated incarceration experience. To the extent that staff emphasize conformity and self-isolation, as opposed to personal change and involvement, inmates respond by "doing time." As the scale on "just doing time" in Table 3—7 indicates, inmates in the custody-oriented settings were more inclined to do time than their treatment-oriented counterparts. In Cottage 9, where the staff emphasized conformity and self-isolation and the inmates were alienated from

118 Neutralizing Inmate Violence

Table 3–7. Inmate Adaptations (percentages)

	Custody-Oriented Cottages				Treatment-Oriented Cottages			
	Group	Individual			Individual	Group		
Scale	Cottage 9	Cottage 8	Elms	Westview	Lancaster (female)	Topsfield (co-ed)	Sunset	Shirley	"I Belong"
1. Regardless of what the adults say, the best way to get along here is to:									
(a) stay out of the way of the adults, but get away with what you can	37%	7%	23% [18]	17%	20%	0%	13%	6% [8]	0%
(b) don't break any rules and keep out of trouble	26	53	54 [54]	55	33	33	27	44 [38]	50
(c) show that you are really sorry for what you did	0	7	7	10	11	13	13	6	13
(d) try to get an understanding of yourself	37	33	13 [22]	28	37	53	47	44 [44]	37
2. Prisonized adaptation	59	60	56 [51]	38	53	7	40	13 [21]	0
3. Just do time	70	67	40 [51]	59	43	7	60	44 [41]	0
4. The best way to get along here is to:									
(a) keep to yourself	41	27	36 [30]	24	52	7	13	7 [8]	0

(b) get involved with the other kids	37	40 ⌐	26 [33]	¬ 38	11	73	47 ⌐	50 [51]	¬ 63
(c) cooperate with the staff	22	33 ⌐	38 [37]	¬ 38	37	20	40 ⌐	43 [41]	¬ 37

5. Primary Group Integration. Have you developed any close friendships in the cottage since you have been here?

(a) Three or more	37	53 ⌐	58 [58]	¬ 62	39	73	60 ⌐	57 [59]	¬ 63
(b) One or two	37	40 ⌐	22 [29]	¬ 31	54	27	27 ⌐	25 [28]	¬ 37
(c) None	26	7	20	7	7		13	18	

each other, 70 percent endorsed "just doing time." An inmate in a custody cottage told us that the best adaptation is, "Don't start trouble for anyone else. I stay by myself. Keep by yourself and worry only about yourself. Don't try to get involved because it might screw you up." In settings where staff expect personal change and cooperative relationships among inmates, self-isolation, prisonized adaptations like obedience and conformity, and "doing your time" decrease accordingly.

Another method of discerning inmate adaptive strategies was to ask them, "What do you have to do to get a parole or a weekend?" Their responses were expected to indicate the kinds of behavior that were institutionally expected and which therefore shaped their own adaptations. Their coded responses are contained in Table 3–8. The two principal alternatives the inmates articulated were conformity—obeying rules, doing time, and keeping out of trouble—and solving problems—gaining insight, and helping others with their problems.

The inmates in Cottage 9 gave the most prison-hardened responses. In order to secure parole, they said, they had to do time. "Just wait until your time is up. Sit on your ass and wait." Others said they had to obey the staff and stay out of trouble, as well. In short, the staffs' emphasis on conformity and obedience, coupled with the inmates' extremely negative views both of staff and other inmates, led them to isolate themselves and avoid involvement with anyone while they awaited their release.

The overwhelming majority of inmates in the individual custody cottages also agreed that obedience and conformity was the best way to secure release. The formula was a simple one: "Do what you're told to do. Don't give masters any hassle. Don't mess up." According to them, a person would be paroled "if you mind your business and do what you're told to do." Many inmates suggested that it was simply a matter of behaving and doing time, and that parole would follow automatically unless the inmate actively did something to prevent it.

A number of inmates in Elms, Westview, and Lancaster also indicated that they sometimes had to remind the staff of their presence and eligibility for parole. These cottages had the larger populations, averaging twenty-five residents or more, and apparently obedient and conforming inmates could be forgotten or overlooked unless they reminded the staff that they were there. Thus, "time," obedience, conformity, and good conduct were the preconditions for release, although the conforming inmate might also have to remind the staff that he or she was still there. Interestingly, despite the fact that the individual custody cottages used vocational training programs as their

Table 3-8. Coded Inmate Response: "What do you have to do to get a parole or a weekend?" (percentages)

	Custody-Oriented Cottages				Treatment-Oriented Cottages			
	Group	Individual			Individual	Group		
	Cottage 9	Cottage 8	Elms	Westview	Lancaster (female)	Topsfield (co-ed)	Sunset	Shirley	"I Belong"
Do Time: Wait until your time is up; wait three months; do time	56%	71%	26% [25]	5%	28%		21%	6% [11]	
Obey Rules: Conform; follow orders; keep your nose clean; do what you're told	52	43	55 [63]	84	72	45%	57	38 [45]	38%
Learn Trade: Get a trade; learn skill		14	11 [13]	16					
Talk to Staff: Talk to staff; beg; remind them that you're here; plead			34 [23]	11	19				
Help Others with Problems: Work with other kids; help them solve problems						45	36	13 [16]	
Solve Problems: Understand why you got in trouble; solve problems						45	29	81 [58]	63

primary intervention strategies, only a small proportion of the inmates believed that their performance in the trade affected their eligibility for release.

A substantial proportion of the inmates in the treatment-oriented cottages also indicated that obeying rules and behaving was important in securing release, suggesting that conformity was of considerable utility even in the treatment settings. Inmates placed considerably less emphasis on this adaptation, however, than did those in custody-oriented settings, and they assigned much greater importance to gaining insight, solving problems, and helping other residents. These dual demands were described by one inmate who said, "You've got to keep your nose clean. But you've got to talk up too. You can't just keep quiet and shut-up. You got to talk up around the place and become part of it."

The contrast with the custodial settings was marked. Several residents complained about not being allowed simply to do time. Overt conformity is typically an easier adaptation than responding to the demands for change in the more systematic treatment settings, and inmates with previous experience in more custodial settings objected to the additional responsibilities placed upon them:

> I liked it alot better at Shirley [custody], just put your time in and you get out. I mean what the hell, you come up here to do time, none of this fucking groups and level drops. Community meetings, god-damned meetings will drive you up a wall. Anything you do, you've got a problem. Place gets worse and worse everyday. The longer I stay here, the worse I hate it. When I came up here, I didn't mind, I was just going to do my time and get out. But instead of helping me, it made me worse. They come up with that bullshit you're copping out, everything you're doing is copping out, you can't handle responsibility. I know how to handle myself. I don't need none of their fucking help. When I came up here, I had in my mind to do my time and get out and go straight, but now I got other things in my mind.

The staff in the treatment-oriented settings encouraged their inmates to discuss their problems and to help other inmates in solving theirs, and a number of the inmates felt that this was the principal criterion in securing release:

> Show them you can accept your responsibilities. Be responsible when you handle your own problems. Back away from arguments, talk it over when you're arguing. Talk about your problems and answer them. Show you're capable of handling the outside world, by talking in your group meetings, your community meetings, letting them know where you're at. You have

to show you can get along with the kids and participate in community meetings. Try to solve your problems and if you think you got your head straight, you go home.

The treatment ideology's emphasis on participation was clearly communicated to these inmates, who saw involvement and participation as necessary preconditions for release. Even the more cynical inmates who objected to the staff treatment objectives conceded that at least a pretense of "solving problems" was necessary to persuade the staff that one was ready for release. "Play the game, go along with them. Just play the role while you're in here, that's all." Regardless of one's commitment to therapeutic change, going through the motions was still perceived as a necessity.

SOLIDARITY

Inmate perceptions of staff and other inmates, coupled with staff expectations and staff responses to informal inmate groups, will influence the patterns of relationships that develop among inmates and between inmates and staff. To further refine our analysis of institutional adjustment we considered the various ways that inmates can adapt to incarceration by: (1) withdrawal and self-isolation; (2) involvement with other inmates; and (3) involvement with staff. We asked the inmates whether the "best way to get along" was to "keep to yourself," "get involved with the other kids," or "cooperate with staff." In the group custody setting, 41 percent of the inmates chose self-isolation, as did nearly a third of the inmates in the individual custody settings. So did more than half the girls at Lancaster.

To emphasize this contrast, inmates in custody-oriented settings chose self-isolation nearly four times as often as did inmates in treatment-oriented settings. Reflecting this striking difference, a larger proportion of the inmates in the treatment-oriented settings than in the custody-oriented cottages chose cooperating with staff or involvement with other inmates as preferable adaptations. While about a third of the inmates in the individual custody cottages chose involvement with other inmates, over half the inmates in the treatment settings did. The girls at Lancaster either isolated themselves or cooperated with staff, but there was comparatively little involvement with other inmates.

These substantial intercottage differences in the proportion of inmates choosing self-isolation rather than involvement with other inmates or staff clearly reflect the effects of staff practices on inmate behavior. Staff in the custody-oriented settings, especially Cottage 9, sought to control the inmate subculture by isolating the inmates within the cottage and discouraging informal inmate associations. On the other hand, staff in the treatment-oriented settings, especially the group-oriented cottages, actively encouraged inmate involvement with each other and with staff. That nearly every inmate in the group treatment settings chose either involvement with inmates or staff reflects the impact that formal collaboration between staff and inmates has on inmate adaptations.

The findings on isolation versus involvement are also borne out by measures of inmate integration into informal groups. Large majorities of inmates in the group treatment and individual custody settings reported several friendships. A quarter of the inmates in Cottage 9, however, reported no friendships at all, further illustrating the extent to which the strategy of Cottage 9 staff for dealing with inmate groups resulted in isolation and atomization within the cottage subculture.

A related adaptive feature was noted among the girls at Lancaster. A majority of the girls reported having as friends only one or two girls rather than the larger groups prevalent in the male settings. This pattern is consistent with the sex-related differences reported in the female inmate subculture literature, which suggests that women tend to form smaller, more stable affectional relationships within the prison than do men. This tendency for female inmates to avoid extensive involvement with other inmates and to confine their contacts to a few inmates or staff is one of the principal differences in adaptive strategies we found between male and female inmates in comparable settings.

We assumed that differences in the levels of trust, involvement, and mutual concern would also be manifest in the degree of collective solidarity within the inmate culture. Contrary to the suggestions in the literature that the negative, oppositional subculture is characterized by high levels of solidarity, the data in Table 3-9 indicate that greater levels of solidarity prevailed in the treatment cottage subcultures, where the inmates displayed greater levels of trust, more positive perceptions, and more extensive contacts. Larger proportions of inmates in the treatment-oriented cottages than in the custody-oriented settings regarded sharing with their friends as an operative norm and agreed that other inmates could trust them to be "honest and loyal" in their relationships. A larger proportion of inmates in the treatment-oriented settings also indicated that the residents stuck together and were loyal to each other. Ironically, the lowest levels of solidarity were reported in Cottage 9, which also housed the most negative and oppositional inmate culture.

Table 3-9. Inmate Solidarity *(percentages)*

Solidarity	Custody-Oriented Cottages					Treatment-Oriented Cottages			
	Group	Individual				Individual	Group		
	Cottage 9	Cottage 8	Elms	Westview	Lancaster (female)	Topsfield (co-ed)	Sunset	Shirley	"I Belong"
In this institution, a good rule to follow is to share any extra goods with your friends. (strongly agree, agree)	67%	53%	60% [63]	72%	81%	87%	73%	69% [77]	100%
The other kids can trust me to be honest and loyal in my dealings with them. (strongly agree, agree)	63	40	55 [61]	79	72	93	87	69 [77]	75
How much of the time do you think most of the boys [or girls] here really stick together and are really loyal to each other? ("all" or "most of the time")	22	53	36 [37]	31	45	67	60	31 [47]	57

SUMMARY OF INMATE PERCEPTIONS AND SUBCULTURAL ADAPTATIONS

Before we explore the operation of the inmate social systems more extensively in the next chapter—the subcultural norms, the inmate roles elaborated around those norms, and the patterns of interaction between various role incumbents—we will summarize the striking subcultural differences reported thus far.

In the group custody setting, the inmates described punishment and isolation as the purposes of their incarceration. They believed that they had been removed from the community and subjected to unpleasant experiences because of their delinquency. The unpleasantness was manifested in a variety of institutionally related problems of adjustment, including severe material deprivations, extremes of boredom, isolation, as well as living with other inmates under such circumstances. The inmates' estrangement from the community and their deprivations within the institution were the most severe of any setting, thereby giving them the greatest incentive to attempt to violently ameliorate their circumstances.

The staff expected inmates to obey, conform, and accept the undesirable consequences of their delinquencies. Inmates recognized conformity as one model for institutional adjustment, but it was a relatively unsatisfying adaptation under the circumstances, and they instead used covert, deviant activities as a potential resolution to their problems of incarceration.

In attempting to solve their problems and relieve their plight, however, these inmates were effectively cut off from developing collective solutions with either staff or other inmates. They had extremely negative perceptions of staff, whom they regarded as unconcerned, unreliable, untrustworthy, and indifferent. These views reflected the alienation engendered by the brutalizing social-control techniques used by staff and the absence of any programming that might have facilitated more favorable contacts. A similarly negative view also pervaded inmates' perceptions of other inmates, who also were regarded as unreliable, untrustworthy, and indifferent to the plight of their fellows. These perceptions accurately reflected the qualitative subcultural characteristics—the predatory exploitation and violence —which reinforced the inmates' negative views. Staff efforts to disrupt informal associations further isolated residents from each other.

As a result the inmate adaptations to Cottage 9 consisted of self-isolation and overt-conformity. These inmates realized that by following orders, appearing to conform, and avoiding involvement with other inmates and direct confrontations with staff, they could do their time and secure release from this unpleasant setting. The consequence of these processes was an anomic subculture in which inmates were unable to cooperate with either staff or other inmates, and withdrew into themselves, isolated from meaningful activities or positive human contacts.

Within this context of being an oppressed isolated substrata, the inmates engaged in deviant, covert activities to relieve the extreme deprivations and boredom they suffered. In the absence of effective legitimate or illegitimate opportunity structures, it should not be surprising that the solutions these inmates developed were the most negative, exploitative, and violent that we observed.

In the individual custody settings, many of the same characteristics and processes were also present. The degrees of alienation and separation were not as extreme, however, because program individualization engendered greater staff-inmate contacts, increased the levels of freedom, elicited less brutalizing control strategies, and reduced some of the deprivations within the institution. These inmates still experienced incarceration as unpleasant and even punishing, but not to nearly the same extent as did those in Cottage 9. They still perceived staff as demanding obedience and conformity, but because of programmatic differences, obedience and conformity required their more active engagement rather than passive acquiescence. Staff also invested greater energy in obtaining voluntary compliance. Active participation in vocational training programs required at least minimal cooperation and involvement by inmates. This could be induced only in part through coercion, and it also resulted in more positive privileges and incentives: cigarettes, snacks, more relaxed living conditions such as wearing one's own clothing, and the like. Accordingly, while they also reported material deprivations, boredom, and difficulties in living with other inmates, these were not nearly as severe as those reported in the group custody setting.

Although residents still held generally negative perceptions of staff, they were not as negative as were those of the Cottage 9 inmates. Part of their alienation reflected the age and cultural differences between inmates and staff. But in general the social-control techniques that staff employed were not as oppressive and brutalizing as those used in Cottage 9, and even unproductive vocational training programs still fostered greater inmate contacts and communications with staff.

In a similar fashion, although the inmates shared negative perceptions of each other, they were not as extreme as those held by the boys in Cottage 9. The cottage programs required more effective cooperation between inmates, thereby engendering greater contacts among inmates and reducing to some degree their negative stereotypes and isolation. The staff's informal collaboration with, and co-optation of, the potentially violent inmate elite also gave them somewhat greater control over the levels of aggression within the subculture. The comparatively greater freedom under less deprived circumstances provided inmates with an opportunity to interact on a basis of friendship rather than necessity or exploitation.

This was also reflected in the types of adaptations they pursued. Although they responded primarily to the staffs' emphasis on obedience and conformity, the reductions in deprivations and alienation made them less likely to isolate themselves from other inmates. Accordingly, there was some possibility for nonexploitative relationships to develop between inmates and—at least in Elms and Westview cottages where the trade programs enhanced relations with staff— occasionally even between inmates and staff. Accordingly, while the subculture developed in forms inconsistent with many staff objectives, there were still some mechanisms for limiting the most negative, oppositional, and violent aspects of the subculture.

Although some significant differences existed between the perceptions and responses of the female inmates at Lancaster, as compared with the males in the individual custody cottages, the degree of similarity is far more striking. The girls, on almost every dimension, shared similar perceptions and reported comparable adaptations and experiences. Although there was some tendency for the girls to involve themselves in smaller groups than the male inmates, with a corresponding reduction in their participation in the subculture, the similarities between the male and female experiences and adaptations are clearly greater than the differences that emerged.

There was a marked transformation in the inmate perceptions of their incarceration experience, staff, other inmates, and appropriate institutional adaptations in the individual and group treatment settings. This was undoubtedly related to the differences in organizational goals and intervention strategies. The staff successfully communicated their treatment ideology to inmates and, to a considerable degree, they succeeded in elevating treatment expectations over custodial expectations. The inmates perceived the organizational purposes as rehabilitative and designed to facilitate their gaining insight and solving personal problems. The adaptive strategies they advocated included the additional responsibility of gaining insight rather than simply conforming. Incarceration in the treatment settings was less depriving or alienating than that experienced by the custody cottage inmates. The staffs' treatment rationale encouraged community contacts, more rewarding experiences, and a reduction in deprivations and punishment. Their intervention strategy significantly reduced the level of institutional deprivation and, as a consequence, also reduced the concomitant motives for deviant interactions among the inmates.

The effective communication of therapeutic purposes, coupled with the reduction in deprivations, the increased contact and communication with staff occasioned by individual treatment and counseling in Topsfield, and the formal collaboration in the group treatment settings, resulted in markedly more positive perceptions of staff by the inmates. The individual treatment settings, with intense individual and group interactions between inmates and staff, encouraged the most positive perceptions of staff. The frequent positive contacts with staff in the group treatment settings also fostered more favorable inmate views.

The inmates in these settings also had far more favorable views of their fellow inmates than did their custody-oriented counterparts. The reductions in deprivations, the increased freedom and permissiveness, and the support provided by staff through formal collaboration to resist inmate violence combined to foster inmate relationships based on friendship. This was reflected in the greater levels of inmate solidarity in these settings. Moreover, the treatment process required inmates to involve themselves in the processes of their own change and that of others and to participate actively in group and community discussions. This was demonstrated by inmate adaptations in these settings. Although they indicated that obedience and conformity were necessary, participation and cooperation with other inmates and staff were also seen as desirable.

Involvement with others in the treatment process led to greater communication, understanding, and appreciation of their fellows, with a corresponding reduction in negative stereotypes. As a consequence the inmates in the individual and group treatment settings supported more positive adaptations within the institution, and developed subcultures in which the most negative, oppositional, and violent inmates either could be neutralized and controlled, or at least isolated and contained. This, in turn, freed other inmates to participate more positively in cooperative relationships with inmates and with staff.

In the next chapter we discuss the implications of these organizationally related differences for the structure, roles, and processes of interaction within the inmate social system.

Chapter 4

Social Structure of the Inmate Subculture

The social structure of the inmate subculture consists of the interactions among members of the inmate group, the patterned expectations that surround those interactions, the norms that govern behavior, and the corresponding social roles available to individuals within the group. Since inmates within a cottage interact more frequently and intensely with residents of their own cottage than they do with inmates in other settings, the norms, values, roles, and interactions of the cottage assume a critical salience. We have already found that variations in organizational goals and treatment practices are strongly related to differences both in inmate perceptions of other inmates and staff and in the inmate adaptations to the institution. We would expect, then, that correspondingly different norms govern inmate interactions with other inmates and with staff. Inmate roles and the organization of the subculture should reflect these norms.

VIOLENCE AND AGGRESSION

The role of violence and aggression and inmate and staff responses to it is arguably the single most significant variable in determining the character of the inmate subculture. "Ultimate authority in the delinquent world rests upon tough boys dominating inferior boys by physical force" [1]. The prevalence of violence and aggression characterizes most relationships in the inmate culture in the absence of effective intervention. The emphasis on direct action and defense of personal integrity is part of the focal concern of the "culture of violence" from which the bulk of delinquent inmates are drawn [2]. Even a few aggressive inmates immediately make violence an issue of major concern, since "violence, in the cottage picture, is the great *un*equalizer.... Violence is a direct, uncomplicated, pervasive, and economical form of social control" [3]. Violent behavior is also intimately related to other norms within the inmate culture, especially the enforcement of injunctions on informing. Just as organizational differences give rise to normative differences in informing, there is also considerable variation in the prevalence and intensity of violence in various cottage settings.

We relied primarily on participant observation and interviews with inmates to determine the level of violence. We asked about "unwritten rules" among the inmates, as well as about "strong-arming" or "bogarting"—institutional argot for exploitation by force—and fighting. The levels of violence reported and observed were considerably greater in the custody-oriented settings than in the treatment-oriented settings. In the custody-oriented settings, inmates placed an enormous emphasis on toughness, protecting one's individual integrity, fighting back at the slightest provocation, and establishing one's position within the subculture through physical means. For a variety of reasons these emphases were substantially reduced in the treatment-oriented settings.

In the custody-oriented cottages, "you have to fight" was a basic maxim. It was not necessary for an inmate to be a successful fighter, but he had to be willing to fight to protect himself, his position, and his property. The ability to fight was as important for the girls at Lancaster as it was for the boys in the custody-oriented cottages. As one girl told us, "You have to show you can fight not to be strong-armed. It doesn't necessarily have anything to do with size either." Regardless of ability, a resident had to be willing to fight as a response to a challenge; this was the only effective deterrent to exploitation. If one was unable or unwilling to fight, he or she would be victimized by every person who was physically able to do so.

An inmate's willingness and ability to defend personal integrity were tested and established very early during institutional confinement. New residents, apprehensive on entering the cottage, were subtly or overtly challenged for whatever goods they possessed. This immediately determined their exploitability. One boy advised:

> Don't let nobody bully you as soon as you come in. It's too late for kids to start now. You've got to say no. Even if a kid gets beat up, they'll think twice next time, if he fights back. If he doesn't, someone will try to bully him. Weak kids give something to a guy because they think its better than

getting beaten. They're wrong, because kids won't take from kids who are going to fight back.

Boys and girls who responded to potential intimidation by fighting back could establish a reputation that might insulate them from chronic exploitation. Failing to do so would leave them vulnerable.

In part the comparatively greater levels of material deprivation in the custody-oriented settings made the exploitation of others profitable for the more aggressive inmates. Numerous instances of violent exchanges occurred when inmates took the property of another. As part of the norm affirming personal integrity, inmates suggested that one should never relinquish property to another under duress, but only give to friends or those to whom you wanted to give: "If you show that you're afraid, then they'll always be bothering you, trying to take things from you." An inmate who allowed himself to be bullied was marked by the others as a target for further exploitation until such time as he resisted.

Violence in custody-oriented cottages tended to flow in one direction. The inmate social systems in these settings tended to be hierarchical, stratified on the basis of use and response to aggression. Inmate leaders used violence against subordinates, but never the other way around. The lower status inmates had a better perception of the levels of violence in the subculture than did the leaders, undoubtedly because they were the victims of most of it. When we asked against whom the violence was directed, the answer was almost invariably that it was aimed at the lower status inmates.

To some extent those who used exploitative violence also used a technique of neutralization such as "denying the victim" to rationalize their behaviors [4]. Victims were typically described as "those who are lazy, stupid, or let others push them around, suckers, small kids, and new kids." If "suckers" were exploited, it was because "they make themselves this way. All they have to do is fight back, but they give up their stuff instead."

The emphasis on violence and aggression was so extreme in some of the custody-oriented cottages that tough inmates frequently beat up other inmates simply to force them to fight back. This was especially true of Cottage 9 where several low-status boys were virtual punching-bags for the other inmates. As one boy explained, "we beat up on a few kids to try and get them to fight back. [Why?] Because he won't fight back. Punch the shit out of him, and he still won't fight back." Our field notes contain a number of incidents in which tough inmates gratuitously punched lower status residents in an effort to goad them into fighting back or fighting with another boy. In one instance a tough leader tried to precipitate a fight between two boys, threatening to beat them both up if they did not fight each other. When asked why he was so concerned about their fighting, he explained: "It's because they're both punks and one of them has to stand up and fight. I hate to see a bigger kid getting hit on by a little kid and I want to make him fight back." The point was not that either of these boys could fight well, but that they must simply be willing to fight.

While the tough leaders who dispensed violence justified it by claiming that it was for the victim's own good, the frequency and severity of such aggression permits other interpretations as well. They dispensed a considerable amount of gratuitous violence—that is, beatings not for any utilitarian exploitative purpose such as obtaining food or cigarettes, but for more expressive purposes. In the most severe settings like Cottage 9, where all the inmates were victimized by the formal organization and relegated to a disvalued status, some inmates could externalize their own frustration and anger by directing their aggression against those who were incapable of defending themselves. Our later discussion of leader-subordinate role relations will suggest the status-building function of such aggression.

To a surprising degree the normative emphasis on violence in the male custody-oriented cottages was also expressed by the girls at Lancaster. From their responses to the questions about "unwritten rules" and "strong-arming," as well as from our observations, it appeared that the level of violence and their justification for it corresponded to those of the male settings. A girl who capitulated to the force or intimidation of another would suffer the same exploited fate and degraded social position as her male counterpart. As one girl said, "The girls would stop picking on them if they fought back. Fighting depends on if you're scared of them or not. You should still fight with them even if you can't fight."

Perhaps because female socialization in this society does not prepare women as well as males to initiate or resist aggression, it appeared that those girls who could use violence successfully dominated the cottages. The relationship between the norms proscribing informing and prescribing violence also resembled those in male settings. Several girls told us that "the girls will fight with someone they know won't fight back, and then threaten them so they won't say anything. They'll rarely fight with ones that will fight back." We concluded that violence was as prevalent and as great an unequalizer among the girls as among the boys.

In the treatment-oriented cottages, although violence and the emphasis on toughness among inmates had not been eliminated, the two were qualitatively and quantitatively less than in the custody-oriented cottages. Several treatment cottage residents observed: "This is a peaceful place. Most places are a lot more violent than here." Others added: "There was a bit of violence in this program in the beginning, but nothing compared to other places."

There was still something of a physical pecking order in the treatment-oriented cottages, and tougher inmates occasionally beat smaller inmates in the locker room. But aggression took place under much more limited circumstances such as retaliation for informing in group meetings, rather than for material exploitation or status building. Moreover, several residents complained that tougher inmates enjoyed certain prerogatives not generally available to others by virtue of their intimidating presence. Some inmates in the treatment-oriented cottages had aggressive characteristics similar to those in custody settings. But there was a crucial difference: the normative emphasis on fighting was distinctly subordinated in the treatment settings. Virtually none of the inmates in the treatment settings believed that they had to fight, and they condemned it when it occurred.

When asked about "unwritten rules" they were more likely to say, "Don't go pushing everybody around" than they were to endorse fighting, and they were more likely to intervene to prevent exploitation than were inmates in custodial settings: "When I see it, I try to stop it." An incident in which one boy struck another and the boy who was struck walked away from a fight instead of responding illustrates the difference. When we asked others what they thought about the boy walking away, they responded, "We all thought he did the right thing." They contrasted this situation with another incident in which they criticized a boy who fought back. As one boy explained, "Kids know there's not supposed to be any strong-arming. If you walk away, the other guy'll get in trouble, but if you fight, you'll get in trouble too." In the more custodial programs the only "appropriate" response would have been to fight back immediately.

The primary difference in the levels of violence in the cottages and, presumably, the normative support for it resulted from the steps that the staff took to prevent it. The inmate norms on violence were closely related to those on informing, and the staff responses to the two were similar. In the custody cottages, inmates resorted to violence and disapproved of informing. The one was used to control the other. Custody staff did not encourage informing, and in the absence of knowledge about the workings of the subculture they were ineffective in combatting the violence that stifled the flow of information. In the treatment-oriented cottages, inmates approved of informing as part of the therapeutic process, and condemned violence. The availability of channels of communication through formal collaboration provided inmates with a mechanism for controlling the levels of violence.

Staff in the treatment-oriented cottages appreciated the deleterious impact that unrestrained violence could have on their ability to develop cooperative relationships with inmates and, consequently, violence between inmates was severely sanctioned. In Shirley cottage, for example, a number of rules in the cottage log dealt explicitly with the contexts in which violence might arise:

> If there is any violence in the dorm, there will be no off-ground privileges for anyone for a minimum of one month.
>
> If anyone assaults someone as a retaliation for having been honest at an open community meeting, he will be transferred to a reception center or waiting area until there is a vacancy in the cottage again.

Because of the openness that small-group meetings and cottage community meetings fostered between staff and inmates, staff were generally aware of instances in which inmates picked on other inmates, and they were willing to confront these issues directly. Instances in which staff confronted inmates because of aggressive behavior were not uncommon.

But treatment staff could not always respond to violence effectively, and the larger boys still somewhat controlled the smaller ones. The danger always existed of a vicious circle developing in which an inmate who was informed on then beat the inmate who "dime dropped," who then informed on that beating, and so on. Despite the cottage rule that boys should not assault other boys for talking honestly in the community meetings, most of the retaliatory violence that occurred in the treatment-oriented cottages arose from such informing. To a considerable extent, however, the group and community meetings provided an effective mechanism for controlling extra-curricular violence. It was exactly because of the close relationship between informing and retaliatory violence that staff and inmates invested as much energy in its control as they did.

In the custodial settings, however, when staff became aware of inmate violence they often took no steps to prevent its recurrence, or even heightened it by reinforcing the values of the delinquent culture. When one boy had been reduced to tears by a beating he had just suffered, the staff member asked the victim, "Why do you think those kids are picking on you. Because you don't do anything. You're getting hit anyhow, so you better make it cost them." The staff response to inmate victimization was frequently to encourage the resident to fight back and defend himself.

Staff people were unable to deal with most inmate violence because they were unaware of it. The strong inmate norm against informing was enforced by retaliatory violence. In the absence of a sympathetic and supportive staff response to complaints, inmates had no incentive to inform in view of the violent consequences that would follow. As a result, weaker boys in the custody-oriented cottages were left comparatively defenseless to seek whatever accommodations they could with the more violent, unrestrained inmates.

Even when direct physical aggression was absent in the custody-oriented settings, there was a substantial degree of verbal assault—far more than in the treatment-oriented settings. This verbal assault, known as "ranking," provides a mechanism by which relative status is fixed by verbal rather than physical aggression. Polsky describes ranking as "verbal, invidious distinctions based on values important to the group. . . . Ranking fixes antagonistic positions among three or more persons by placing one member in a target position" [5]. The process entails one person making sarcastic, scornful, mocking, or negative statements about another in the presence of a social audience. The subject of the comments can either concur in the negative evaluation or resist the characterization. Concurrence establishes subordination. Resistance, a rejection of the characterization, implies that the person making the statement is either incorrect or lying. The person making the initial negative characterization either reiterates the initial charge or capitulates in the face of resistance. The presence of a social audience is critical, since acquiescence by either party fixes their relative social positions. Accordingly, ranking provides a mechanism short of force by which relative social status may be established. When the verbal resolution is inconclusive, aggression or the threat of aggression may compel one party or the other to accept the characterization in question.

Thus, ranking fixes hierarchical status in the same way that other more direct mechanisms of social control establish social positions. The following exchange is illustrative:

> Several boys were seated around the table, One said to another, "You're a faggot." The second responded, "No, I ain't." The first repeated himself, "You're a faggot." When the second said again, "No, I ain't," the first boy asked him "You want to make something of it?" The second boy then lapsed into silence and looked down at his hands. Another boy at the table then started imitating him with his hands, laughing at him.

As our observers moved from one type of setting to another, either in their field notes or in conversations, several of them noted the significantly greater prevalence of ranking in the custody settings. These differences reflect the underlying bases of subcultural organization. In the custody-oriented settings, boys were critically concerned with their position in the subculture because of its implications for their own potential victimization. Ranking and verbal aggression were means of establishing superiority without recourse to more direct means. In the more treatment-oriented settings ranking was comparatively uncommon and there was a certain self-consciousness and tentativeness when it occurred.

INFORMING

Among the most commonly described norms in the correctional literature are those governing inmate interactions with staff, and especially those pertaining to inmates informing staff of the activities of other inmates [6]. Informing and subcultural violence are closely linked: uncontrolled violence can deter informing and informing can reduce violence if properly encouraged and facilitated. The regulation and flow of information between inmates and staff therefore becomes a critical determinant of inmate roles and subculture structure [7].

We assume that the inmates' views of staff and other inmates and the types of institutional adaptations they make will influence the quantity and quality of information inmates provide to staff. Since inmate views and adaptations are strongly related to organizational differences, we expect that substantially different norms will emerge around the issues of informing, and the inmates' responses to those who inform. The availability of information about inmate activities necessarily conditions the staffs' ability to control the more pernicious aspects of the subculture, and differences in this dimension are of critical importance to many other patterns that develop within the subculture. Accordingly, we gathered data on informing from questionnaires, interviews, and participant observation to identify the extent and nature of cottage variation.

When inmates have negative perceptions of the staff and other inmates, when material deprivations are high, when staff social-control techniques are punitive, and when inmates' adaptations to the institution encompass covert deviance, a norm proscribing informing and nonessential contacts with staff is necessary and desirable as a matter of inmate self-defense. Because of the self-protective function of such a norm, inmates punish violations violently. The instrumental use of violence and aggression, in turn, further retards the flow of information to the staff and increases the prospects of additional covert deviance, which would thereby make the control of information even more important. The result is a cycle of violence that stifles informing, thereby increasing the likelihood of additional violence.

On the other hand, when inmates have more positive perceptions of staff and other inmates, when the consequences for reported inmate deviance are less severe and punitive, when the level of material deprivations reduces the incentives to engage in institutional deviance, when informing is presented in a more positive light because the treatment ideology encourages a full flow of information as an adjunct to treatment, and formal collaboration provides the staff with greater knowledge of and control over inmate violence, then the norms proscribing informing will be weaker and less likely to be punished by inmate violence.

As the scale on "inmate approval of informing" in Table 4-1 indicates, markedly different attitudes toward informing prevailed in the various cottage settings. In the questionnaire we asked the inmates whether "In some situations, it is all right to inform on another kid?" and whether "A kid should not report a rule violation to a staff member if it will get another boy in trouble." When these items were summated, only 7 percent of the inmates in Cottage 9 approved of inmates informing, as did only about one inmate in five in the individual custody settings. A little over a third of the girls at Lancaster approved of informing. By contrast, about half the inmates in the treatment-oriented settings approved. Inmates in the treatment cottages were nearly three times as likely to endorse informing as those in custody cottages.

To further assess normative variation we asked the inmates whether they were "aware of any unwritten rules that boys follow for getting along in the institution?" Although the question was too abstract and a number of inmates simply responded "I don't know," or "I can't think of any off-hand," from the usable responses it was apparent that inmates in the custody-oriented cottages were considerably more likely than inmates in the treatment-oriented cottages to condemn "dime dropping"—the institutional argot for informing. When asked about informal rules, many of the inmates in the custody-oriented cottages responded, "Don't be a dime dropper."

The injunction against informing was expressed in a variety of ways. When inmates were involved in fights, we were told that "the kid should fight back and not have to carry the problem to the staff to settle it." Occasionally "dime dropper" was hurled as an epithet at inmates who engaged in conversations with staff members about even

Table 4-1. Inmate Views on Informing *(percentages)*

Scale	Custody-Oriented Cottages				Treatment-Oriented Cottages			
	Group	Individual			Individual	Group		
	Cottage 9	Cottage 8	Elms	Westview	Lancaster (female)	Topsfield (co-ed)	Sunset	Shirley	"I Belong"
Percent of Inmates Approving of Informing	7%	20%	21% [18]	14%	36%	80%	33%	50% [51]	88%

innocuous subjects. This injunction was also reinforced by the proscription against "sucking ass," which served the same function of limiting contacts between inmates and staff, thereby reducing the flow of information. Many residents of custody-oriented settings condemned unnecessary interaction with staff. In view of the negative perceptions of staff members and the subterranean inmate activities that might unwittingly be revealed, it is easy to understand the salience of these prohibitions. Several inmates suggested the relationship between informing and covering up covert deviance:

> Kids bribe other kids. Like you do this for me, and I'll do this for you, or you do this and I won't say nothing, or you give me a pack of cigarettes, and I won't say nothing.
>
> Like suppose a fork [a potential weapon, or means of escape] is missing and they [staff] come up to you. Just do your time [in isolation] and when you come out, your friend would do that for you.

Thus, our interviews and observations corroborate the questionnaire responses, which show a strong norm against informing in the custody-oriented settings.

By contrast the staff ideology in the treatment cottages provided a rationale that encouraged sharing information to an extent not present in the custody-oriented settings. Informing was therapeutically redefined as "helping" or "being responsible." When we interviewed the inmates on the subject of informing, a number of them objected to our use of the word "dime dropper" or "informer." As they explained, "You're supposed to tell the truth here. It ain't like finking. It's helping the kid out. You find out why he did what he did. We don't call it finking. We're supposed to tell, and sometimes it can help you." Inmates were encouraged to record information in the daily log for consideration at the cottage community meetings or small-group therapy sessions. "You could say everybody finks on everybody else. They put it on the agenda. Everybody tells and they don't think nobody's a fink." They were also encouraged to report potentially troublesome incidents to staff members and they often alerted staff to impending runaways, contraband, or the like. With half or more of the inmates in treatment cottages approving of informing, it was redefined so that what was labeled as informing in other settings was here grist for the therapeutic mill.

Even in the most custodial of the settings, however, a variety of circumstances were recognized by inmates as exceptions to the prohibition against informing. These tended to be situations in which an inmate would suffer personal disadvantage, such as the loss of a parole or furlough, by remaining silent. Several boys said they would inform "if you could get into serious trouble like jamming my parole. Then, no matter how serious the trouble was that the other kid would get into, if it jammed my parole, I would drop a dime."

A great number of inmates in all the settings also approved of informing to protect the entire cottage, and thus indirectly themselves, from a loss of privileges. In the custody-oriented cottages, if inmates ran away the staff would sometimes punish the remaining inmates by denying off-ground visiting privileges or smoking privileges, on the theory that other inmates were aware of the planned run and should have helped the staff to prevent it. Not infrequently inmates would inform to prevent the imposition of such sanctions, and most inmates approved of this. A number of inmates were also willing to inform if the circumstances were sufficiently serious or dangerous. Girls at Lancaster approved of informing "when a girl puts her room on fire. Setting a fire, something that would hurt the other girls." Many inmates also believed it was all right to inform to protect an inmate from self-destructive behavior: "If somebody did something to hurt herself, like jumping out a window. Or if someone does something that hurts another person, or tries to commit suicide, something that's going to badly hurt someone." Thus, despite the general injunction against informing, even those in more custodial settings recognized several exceptions.

Since informing was related to aggression, and since the subcultures—especially those of the custody-oriented cottages—tended to be stratified on the basis of inmate competence in the manipulation of violence, the injunction against informing was differentially enforced depending upon an inmate's social position. Violations of the norm against informing by inmates lower in the subculture power structure were regarded differently than violations by those occupying leadership positions. High-status inmates were "permitted" to inform against lower status inmates in situations where the reverse was not allowed. A number of inmates observed that informing "depends on who the kid is," and several suggested that the norm "only applies with some kids." The girls at Lancaster appeared to be especially sensititve to the relationship between one's position in the subculture hierarchy and one's "freedom" to inform. They placed great emphasis on obeying the inmate pecking order and observing hierarchical prerogatives. Several girls said, "Don't fink on people for smoking or running, unless you want to get into a big hassle. It depends on the person. If [a low-status person] finked on [a high-status person], there would be a hassle, but if it was the other way around, the girls would go along with it." Their comments illustrate the subtle relationship between social position, violence, and informing. A full understanding of the norm against informing requires an appreciation of power relationships and social position within the inmate hierarchy.

In the treatment settings formal collaboration reinforced the therapeutic rationale for informing and gave inmates greater freedom from personal intimidation by decreasing the likelihood of informal pressures from other inmates. Inmates must feel physically safe from retaliation before they will freely provide staff with information. As a result of legitimating and fostering informing in the treatment-oriented settings, an enormous amount of information was made available to staff about the otherwise hidden processes of the subculture. This information, in turn, enabled the staff to control the levels of violence and aggression in the subculture, thereby freeing those inmates who wanted to embrace staff values to do so. If inmate complaints about retaliation fall on deaf ears, of necessity the inmates will move toward the more negative values of the violent inmates within the subculture, rather than toward the values of the staff.

OTHER INDICATORS OF SUBCULTURAL NORMATIVE ORIENTATION

We asked the inmates for their reactions to a series of hypothetical stories concerning common incidents that occur in correctional institutions. The incidents provide further insight into the norms that prevailed in the various cottages. The scaled results are shown in Table 4−2. The items in the scale "negative inmate role behavior" included: (1) an inmate who is cut in a fight and refuses to name his assailant; (2) an inmate who agrees to hide some smuggled drugs for a friend; and (3) an inmate who is caught while helping some friends to escape and takes the entire blame on himself. Cottages displayed substantial differences, with almost seven inmates out of eight in Cottage 9 approving of these oppositional role responses. About half of the inmates in the individual custody cottages approved of this inmate resistance, compared with about a third of the inmates in the treatment-oriented settings.

The items in the scale "positive inmate role behavior" included: (1) an inmate who reports a theft from another inmate's locker to the staff; (2) an inmate who refuses to aid some friends in an escape; and (3) an inmate who defends a cottage master who criticized an-

Table 4-2. Inmate Subculture Orientation (percentages)

	Custody-Oriented Cottages					Treatment-Oriented Cottages			
	Group	Individual				Individual	Group		
Scale	Cottage 9	Cottage 8	Elms	Westview	Lancaster (female)	Topsfield (co-ed)	Sunset	Shirley	"I Belong"
Negative inmate role	85%	67%	48% [48]	38%	36%	14%	47%	25% [33]	25%
Positive inmate role	33	33 [45]	48	48	47	64	60 [66]	56	100
Staff enforcing rules to inmate detriment	11 [23]	27	23	21	36	33	33 [41]	44	50

other inmate. Two-thirds of the inmates in the treatment-oriented settings supported these pro-staff types of behavior, compared with less than half the inmates in the custody-oriented cottages.

The items in the scale "staff enforcing rules to inmates' detriment" included: (1) a counselor who reports a theft that an inmate-client revealed to him; and (2) a cottage master who reports two boys for a fight which may adversely affect their paroles. The inmates in the treatment-oriented cottages were almost twice as likely as their custody-oriented counterparts to approve of the staff actions in these situations.

Taken together these results strongly corroborate the marked differences previously reported in the normative content of the inmate subcultures. A considerably larger proportion of inmates in the custody-oriented settings than in the treatment cottages supported negative, oppositional behavior by inmates, and a substantially smaller proportion supported cooperative, positive inmate behavior. Similarly, a smaller proportion supported legitimate staff activities that adversely affected inmates. These results are also very consistent with those we obtained regarding inmate views of informing, fighting, legitimacy of staff, and the like.

The various measures also indicate the degree of subcultural differentiation. The inmates in the group custody setting were the most alienated from staff and from their fellow inmates. They also expressed the strongest opposition to informing and placed the greatest emphasis on violence. As the scales in Table 4–2 suggest, they were by far the most likely to approve of negative, oppositional inmate behavior, and the least likely to approve of pro-staff inmate behavior. In the individual custody settings the extremes of alienation and negativism found in Cottage 9 were somewhat ameliorated. Programmatic individualization appears to have had some impact on the inmate culture. These inmates were distrustful of staff and their fellow inmates, but not to such a degree that it was impossible for any types of cooperative relationships to develop. Similarly, while they disapproved of informing and supported aggression, it was not to the same degree as did the boys in Cottage 9. Finally, they were not unequivocally committed to negative roles; as the scales in Table 4–2 indicate, they were almost as likely to support positive inmate roles as negative ones. On all of these measures the girls at Lancaster appear to be similar to the males in individual custody settings, albeit somewhat less negative.

As the preceding discussions suggest, major qualitative differences existed between the character of the subcultures that developed in the custody-oriented cottages and those in the treatment-oriented cottages. In view of the consistency across items on various dimensions, the subcultural differences relate strongly to the variations in the organizational structure and staff activities. Staff in the treatment-oriented settings were able to modify the character of the inmate culture by means of their relationships with inmates and by changing the demands they made upon them. On most of these dimensions the inmates in the individual treatment setting tend to be somewhat more favorably disposed to staff than their counterparts in the group treatment settings.

The individual treatment settings used a variety of group treatment strategies that were supplemented by individual treatment methods. The small but consistently more positive results may be related to the additional individualized relationships. The types of adaptations that the inmates made and the orientations they adopted were generally consistent with the staff objectives. Consequently, the inmates in the treatment-oriented cottages were far less alienated from the staff and from their fellow inmates, and were thereby able to enter into more cooperative kinds of relationships. This cooperation was also manifest in a majority of inmates who approved of informing, with a corresponding reduction in the emphasis on violence and aggression. Moreover, as the scales in Table 4−2 suggest, these inmates were twice as likely to subscribe to positive inmate role behavior as to negative inmates roles.

Inmate Roles

The range of roles that an inmate assumes within a subculture reflects the "set of behaviors appropriate to an individual in a given group and expected of him in a given situation" [8]. The appropriate set of behaviors will vary considerably, depending upon the focal concerns of the group and the norms governing conduct. Within any group a stratified social system emerges, with the roles and the prestige accorded to them allocated on the basis of conformity to or deviation from the group norms. Within the inmate group, focal concerns include adjustment to the institution and relations with other inmates and with staff. Norms provide the basis for collective resolutions of these shared problems confronting the group.

Although studies in adult correctional facilities have indicated a number of "argot" roles that center on resolving the pains of imprisonment [9], studies of juvenile correctional institutions have suggested the availability of a much more limited repertory of roles. Polsky identified juvenile inmate roles as "toughs" or "leaders" who use violence to maintain the delinquent values of the inmate culture; "con-artists" who attempt to verbally manipulate and exploit their fellow inmates; "quiet boys" who adjust to the institution while avoiding involvement in the delinquent subculture; "bush boys" who attempt to participate in the delinquent culture but lack the physical or social skills to do so effectively; and "scapegoats" who are chronically victimized [10]. The roles were related to the delinquent values that Polsky found prevalent in the inmate culture, especially the manipulation of violence.

We observed similar inmate roles in the violence-based cottage subcultures. The hierarchy of inmate roles consisted of the leaders at the top, accommodating to, or loosely allied with, other leaders. Somewhat below them were their lieutenants, "con-men," and others who were oriented to and had influence in the inmate power structure. Below them were the low-status "bush boys" who, as a result of interpersonal incompetence, were unable to reach higher positions in the subculture. In a separate low-status group were the "straight" boys who avoided involvement in the delinquent power structure and kept to themselves. At the very bottom were the scapegoats or "punks."

Although the proportion of inmates occupying any given role varied by cottage, the general distribution of roles resembled a diamond-shaped stratification system. Relatively few leaders or punks were at the top and bottom of the social system, perhaps two or three of each in a typical cottage population of twenty. The bulk of inmates occupied a more intermediate status, neither "one-up" nor "one-down." Superior and inferior roles were allocated on the basis of an inmate's ability to "out-fight, out-think, or out-talk" his fellows. Very few inmates were either complete successes or failures. Despite the subtleties of interpersonal status gradations, however, virtually every inmate knew his position in relation to all the other residents in his or her cottage.

Although several aspects of black-white subcultural differences will be described in the next chapter, we should note here that whenever there was a "critical mass" of about three or more black inmates in a cottage, they tended to associate primarily or exclusively with each other, even when their prowess also earned them dominant positions in the overall cottage subculture. In settings where there was a larger number of black inmates, such as Elms or Westview, separate and parallel white and black inmate hierarchies emerged, although an inmate's race influenced the types of roles he was likely to occupy within the overall subculture.

In the following sections we examine the types of inmate roles and the patterns of interaction among role incumbents in the cottages.

Leadership

Inmate relations with other inmates and with staff members were governed by different norms in different cottage settings, and these differences were also reflected in the characteristics of the leadership of the inmate group. To further refine our analysis of the subcultures, we asked residents to identify the cottage leaders and to answer questions about the roles played by those leaders. The scales in Table 4-3 reflect a number of items measuring the qualities of the inmate leadership.

Inmates in the custody-oriented cottages were far more likely than their treatment-oriented counterparts to see their leaders as filling a negative role in cottage life. The individual items in the scale "leaders negative" asked whether inmate leaders were inclined to fight other boys, to minimize their contact with adults, and to look for an easy way to "do time." Toughness and a willingness to fight provide the underlying basis for the authoritarian subcultures in the custody-oriented cottages. On the individual item about fighting, inmates in the custody-oriented cottages were about three times as likely to perceive their leaders as prone to fighting as were those in the treatment-oriented settings. The inmate leaders in the female settings were as disposed to fight as were their male counterparts. Similarly, the custody cottage inmates saw their leaders as somewhat more isolated from the adults in the cottage, and as more inclined to "do time."

In view of the adaptive strategies and norms prevailing in the respective cottages, these differences were not at all surprising. When these items were summated, about half of the custody-oriented inmates attributed negative qualities to their inmate leadership, as compared to only about a quarter of the treatment-oriented inmates. Put somewhat differently, the inmate leaders in the custody-oriented settings, male and female, were almost twice as likely as those in the treatment cottages to be described negatively by other residents.

The items in the scale "leaders positive" reflect more benign qualities of inmate leadership, such as keeping other residents out of trouble and helping them with their problems. About half of the inmates in the treatment-oriented cottages described the leaders in positive terms, contrasted with about a third of the custody-oriented inmates. On both the positive and negative dimensions, the female leaders at Lancaster were similar to the individual custody males. Looking at the two scales together, inmate leaders in treatment-oriented settings were almost twice as likely to be described positively rather than negatively, while in the custody cottages they were more likely to be regarded negatively than positively.

These differences in inmate perceptions of leadership are consis-

Table 4-3. Inmate Leadership Characteristics *(percentages)*

	Custody-Oriented Cottages					Treatment-Oriented Cottages			
	Group	Individual				Individual	Group		
Scale	Cottage 9	Cottage 8	Elms	Westview	Lancaster (female)	Topsfield (co-ed)	Sunset	Shirley	"I Belong"
Leaders Negative	52%	73%	48% ⎤ ——[49]——	38%	48%	13%	33% ⎤ ——[26]——	31%	0%
Leaders Positive	19	7 ⎦ ——[36]——	36	52	22	67	47 ⎦ ——[50]——	44	71

tent with other measures of the character of the cultures. In general the subcultures in the custody-oriented cottages were considerably more oppositional and negative than those in the treatment-oriented settings, as measured both by inmate perceptions of staff and inmates and by inmate adaptations. Since the inmate norms in the custody-oriented cultures were more opposed to the staff values, there was greater inmate support for negative inmate behavior, and it is not surprising that inmate leaders reflected the predominant values of the subcultures [11].

Inmate perceptions of leadership characteristics reflected the substantially different roles the leaders played in the various cottages. In all of the cottages—custody and treatment, male and female—leaders tended to be bigger, tougher, and physically able to impose their will on others. Even in the more treatment-oriented settings where there was less emphasis on direct physical violence, the leaders were still the more physically competent inmates. Black inmates were disproportionately overrepresented as leaders in all the cottages. As the differences in inmate characterization of leaders suggest, however, despite their physical similarities the leaders in the various settings used their power for dissimilar ends.

In the custody-oriented cottages, the leaders physically dominated the other inmates. One of the leaders in Cottage 9 told us that the "bigger kids rule over the little kids." From the viewpoint of one of the smaller boys, this situation translated into the maxim, "Respect power, and do what the bigger kids tell you to do."

The inmate leadership was the most aggressive, violent, and exploitative of other inmates in Cottages 8 and 9. They acted covertly, rather than through informal collaboration with staff. Since there was minimal programming in these cottages, there was also relatively little basis for inmate leadership to cooperate with staff. Moreover, their extremely negative views of staff made it unlikely that they would collaborate to further staff interests. This failure to achieve a stabilizing accommodation between leaders and staff was also reflected in the lack of effective staff social control in these settings, the frequent riots, fires in the dormitories, homosexual assaults, and destruction of facilities and property. The staff people were unable to effectively contain these inmates.

In turn inmate leaders functioned within these subcultures primarily for their own advantage. They terrorized and exploited lower ranking inmates. Boys who received food, clothing, cigarettes, or other presents from home were quickly intimidated into relinquishing them to the leaders. Our field notes contain dozens of instances of leaders in these cottages physically taking things from other inmates. In those relatively few instances where an inmate protested, a threatening glance usually ended the resistance. Some of the most aggressive leaders in these two cottages "shook down" other inmates, extorting protection money from them by collecting debts that they allegedly owed the leaders or other boys. In other instances the leaders ameliorated the most oppressive and deprived circumstances of their own incarceration by forcibly acquiring whatever amenities were available. Inmates, individually or collectively, were unable to combine with each other or with staff to resist these leaders' depredations. Our participant observation data is corroborated by the questionnaire responses in which other inmates describe the inmate leaders in these two cottages as the most negative. The prevalence of predatory exploitation also helps to explain why the inmates in these settings expressed the most negative views of their fellow inmates.

The inmate leaders in Westview and Elms—the Lyman School trade cottages—also physically dominated the other inmates in their cottages, although not to the same degree as did those in Cottages 8 and 9. They were neither as ruthlessly exploitative nor as gratuitously violent. They also performed some positive functions for staff and inmates by maintaining some degree of order and control in those settings, which redounded to the benefit of other residents as well. In these cottages informal collaboration between inmate leaders and staff provided the underlying basis for social organization and social control.

In Westview, the symbiotic relationship between the staff and the inmate leadership was most pronounced. The inmate leaders enjoyed a special status of "house boys," receiving a variety of privileges in return for controlling other inmates and maintaining the smooth functioning of the cottage. The other inmates in Westview clearly recognized the role of the leaders in maintaining order and control and preserving the status quo for staff. As one boy said, "The cottage masters use them as cops. They figure no one is going to screw up trips when they're around. Nobody's going to run." These leaders aided the staff in "taking a count," encouraging inmates to return property missing from the cottage, supervising other inmates if the staff was absent, preventing fights between inmates, and the like. The reciprocity of staff-leadership relationships was apparent to all. "The masters know they can help them straighten out things. They give them fringe benefits because of the services they give. They are allowed to do things."

While the role of the leaders in this setting was beneficial to the staff, it was useful to the inmate group as well. As one boy said, "I'm a little scared of him [the inmate leader] myself. But sometimes he's a good influence on the kids. Sometimes he keeps kids from having things stolen from them, or if a big kid is hitting on a smaller kid." To some degree the leaders reduced disruptions within the inmate group by preventing boys from running away or preventing or controlling fights. In a variety of ways they tried to make it unnecessary for staff to discipline the inmate group. The inmate leaders in Elms cottage occupied a status similar to those in Westview, both within the inmate group and with the staff members. Although their relationship was not formalized with "houseboy" status, they enjoyed privileges from the staff and controlled the operations of the inmate group.

The female leaders at Lancaster resembled their male custody-oriented counterparts in terms of physical aggressiveness and exploitation. The leaders in the Lancaster cottages were often described in our interviews as "strong-arms" who threatened and intimidated other girls for their own advantage. They sometimes beat other inmates for material advantages such as cigarettes or soft drinks, but sometimes just to reinforce their position. On the basis of our interviews and observations, the level of physical intimidation appeared to be somewhat greater than in the comparable boys' settings—Elms and Westview—and the girls appeared to be more sensitive to the nuances of power relationships. The leaders in the female cottages were more like the aggressive, exploitative leadership of Cottages 8 and 9 than the cooperative and informally collaborative leaders of Westview and Elms. Although the leaders occasionally cooperated with staff by answering telephones, conveying messages and orders to other inmates, in general they were not relied upon by staff. One girl told us, "Relations with matrons don't matter for the leaders; they just get along enough to stay out of trouble." In fact they posed a greater threat to the staffs' powers of control than did boy leaders in any settings. They were more prone to challenge staff authority and engage in verbal abuse of staff than were the boys. While the male staff members could respond directly with force to recalcitrant boys, the female staff members at Lancaster could not physically coerce the girls themselves and had to rely instead on security personnel from outside the cottage.

The inmate leaders in the treatment-oriented cottages operated in a substantially different normative context and under different constraints. The basic cottage norms, especially those regarding violence and informing, were significantly different. The process of formal collaboration between inmates and staff reduced the leaders' opportunities to maintain covert control of the inmate group, and obviated the need for staff to resort to informal collaboration. As the questionnaire responses suggest, the inmates who emerged as leaders in the treatment-oriented settings had a more positive orientation toward staff and other inmates than did their custody-oriented counterparts, and they played a more positive and institutionally supportive role in the subculture.

As part of the formal collaboration process, the inmate leaders often encouraged other inmates to speak up by assuring them that there would be no retaliation by other inmates. Similarly, on a number of occasions we observed inmate leaders either talking with other boys about their problems or encouraging boys to talk with each other. The leaders also aided the staff in community meetings by interpreting rules, rationalizing decisions, and explaining results to other inmates. For example, when an inmate did not get his levels of freedom raised, with the accompanying increase in privileges, because he was not "responsible," it was an inmate leader who was called upon by staff to explain to the group what being responsible meant. Similarly, when two boys committed a violation, and only one suffered a loss of privileges, it was a leader who explained the inconsistency, concluding with the observation that "besides, you goofed off all last week, and he did the work." They also helped to minimize conflict between lower ranking boys in the subculture. When boys picked on other boys, or harassed them, the leaders frequently intervened to prevent it.

This is not to suggest that the leaders never resorted to violence for their own advantage. A number of inmates raised complaints about the role of the leaders similar to those of inmates in the custody-oriented settings. On the basis of our observations, however, although leaders occasionally took advantage of other inmates or physically intimidated them, it was to a considerable lesser degree than their counterparts in the custody-oriented settings. Thus, to the extent that the staff people were successful in controlling violence within the subculture through formal collaboration, they created a situation in which inmates who were not actively committed to anti-institutional values could emerge as leaders.

Even if the leaders were not pro-social, the demands of formal collaboration at least required that they play that role. And even though they might intimidate other inmates to prevent them from informing against the leaders, they reinforced the more positive aspects of the culture by limiting the covert aggression or deviance of others. In short, formal collaboration changed the behavioral demands sufficiently to require the inmate leadership to at least appear to adopt a cooperative relationship with staff. While they may have tried to insulate their own behavior from such control, in the process of collaboration they enabled many other inmates to participate more positively with inmates and staff.

The leaders in treatment-oriented settings had certain advantages as well. Social control entailed formal collaboration between staff and inmates, and there was always the possibility of differential rule enforcement. For example, when one leader was reported for violating a cottage rule, the cottage community voted only to warn him but did not reduce privileges, prompting one staff member to complain about the uneven enforcement of the rules. He observed that "the kids bend the rules to fit the individual kid. It depends on who the person is, what you do with the rule. If that kid had been a soft touch, he would have got a level drop, and not just a warning." Several other boys then added, "Someone who's got a little weight around the place, he'll get off."

Leaders also enjoyed a privileged status in other respects. Eligibility for weekend home furloughs was determined by a recommendation from the small therapy groups to the cottage community. Since leaders were generally more highly regarded within their small groups, they were able to obtain weekend leaves with somewhat greater frequency than other inmates.

Leader vs. Leader. In the custody-oriented settings, the tougher, more fearless inmates were willing to initiate violence to achieve their ends, and they had no compunction about responding with force to threats to their position. Because of these characteristics, inmate leaders interacted carefully with other high-status inmates. While they were reluctant to force an issue because of the probable response of the other, they could not back down if the issue was forced on them. They treated each other gingerly, neither conceding the other's superiority nor attempting to force such a concession. Their relationship was similar to that of scorpions in a bottle; either could sting the other to death, but only while being fatally stung in the process. The occasional confrontations between leaders seldom brought the ultimate resolution by force. Here is a typical leadership encounter:

> Two inmate leaders, one white and one black, were ranking on each other. There has been some tension between these two in the past, and they were verbally getting on each other today. Finally, they squared off in the middle of the room, kicking over some chairs in the process. They were only a few steps apart, yet neither moved forward. Instead, they kept saying to each other, "Come on, sucker," until one of the staff members stepped between them and forced them to sit down at their respective tables. The staff intervention saved face for each of them and they retired to their

tables and continued their verbal abuse, saying "Come on sucker," "Why didn't you fight when you had the chance," "You can't fight," and the like. After this had continued for some time, one said to the other, "I don't say I can beat your ass. But you can't make me a punk."

The scene illustrates the limits to which leaders could force each other. Through ranking and threats of aggression, each attempted to intimidate the other into a subordinate position. When these failed, both were faced with the alternative of resorting to violence against a powerful adversary or losing face and corresponding status. The intervention by the staff "saved" each boy. They could avoid a fight without losing face, thereby maintaining equality. These leadership confrontations occurred in every cottage except "I Belong," the least violent setting in our sample. In Shirley cottage, two leaders were standing in line to get food. One bumped against the other, who took offense, and they both squared off. One threatened the other saying, "Come on man, I'll off you right here," but the other stood up to him, inviting him to fight. Finally, a lieutenant of one of the leaders intervened and persuaded his friend to conclude the encounter by warning of adverse staff action.

Significantly, virtually every leadership confrontation occurred between black and white inmate leaders. While their high status was safely established within their respective racial groupings, challenges to their position came from outside their group. In these critical encounters neither could concede the dominance of the other. Since these confrontations were almost never pushed to an ultimate resolution, within their groups leaders reigned supreme and unchallenged, while an uneasy accommodation prevailed between groups.

Other Inmate Roles

In addition to identifying the cottage inmate leaders, we asked inmates to identify other role types such as "finks," "punks," "conmen," "straight kids," and the like. We included a number of sociometric items with which we cross-validated our interview questions. Finally, by observation, we were able to identify relationships between inmates by noting those who hung around together, those who ate together, and the like. On the basis of these various measures we were able to develop a dynamic picture of the role relationships and subculture social structure within each cottage.

Apart from leaders, we were able to identify several other inmate roles and patterns of social relations. As a boy in a custodial setting once told us, survival in the institutions depended upon a person's ability to "out-talk, out-think, or out-fight" other boys. Many roles were allocated on the basis of these skills, with a residual category of boys who could not succeed on any dimension. Many of the roles were common to all the settings, although there was substantial cottage variation both in the prevalence of particular roles and especially in the patterns of interaction between various role incumbents.

Con-men. The leaders usually had several lieutenants. If not tough themselves, these somewhat lower ranking boys relied primarily on verbal skills and their ability to con other inmates to support their position [12]. Those who occupied top positions but could not out-fight maintained their position by means of their ability to out-think or out-talk others. The con-men were prevalent in all the cottage settings, perhaps because conning—verbally manipulating another person for one's own advantage—was so much a part of the lives of these boys and girls both within the institution and outside it [13].

An ability to out-talk and out-smart another for personal benefit was a valued skill in all the settings. In all of the cottages verbal manipulation served the same function as physical aggression, that is, getting another person to do what one wanted—giving up a cigarette, running an errand, trading personal property, relinquishing a place in line, and the like. In the more custodial settings, such as Cottages 8 and 9 and in the Lancaster cottages, there was a strong relationship between being identified as a tough leader and also being described as a con-man. The inmates in these cottages identified as leaders also received the bulk of nominations as con-men. Additionally, several other boys who closely associated with these leaders also received nominations as con-men. In these more custodial settings, where a lower ranking person's refusal to accede to verbal manipulation could be followed by violence, it is easy to understand the relationship between tough leadership and conning.

Even in the more treatment-oriented settings, however, this type of verbal manipulation was still practiced. To some extent the treatment settings, because of their emphasis on participation and interaction, placed a premium on the verbal skills that distinguished con-men. As one boy responded when asked if any of the boys in the cottage tried to con other boys, "Everybody in here is throwing a con to get out of here. You do everything you can to get out of this place, say what you do to get the group to go along." In several of the treatment-oriented cottages the verbally adroit inmates sometimes played a lawyer role, speaking at group meetings as a representative or advocate for another inmate, either presenting his case for him or cross-examining those who were presenting a case against his "client."

This pattern was probably a response to the group treatment process, since the demands of treatment were quite threatening to the many boys who strongly disliked revealing information about themselves or participating in the therapeutic program. In addition, many lacked the verbal skills that individual or group therapy required. In this situation the advocate-inmate served as the "mouthpiece" for a close friend and handled his representation in the community meetings. Black inmates appeared to be somewhat more verbally skillful and socially adept than their white counterparts, and thus were overrepresented in the con-man or lawyer roles in the custody and treatment-oriented settings.

Straight Kids. "Straight" inmates did not involve themselves extensively in the inmate culture and tried to associate with other "straight" boys, or to isolate themselves from the subculture altogether [14]. These boys, the juvenile equivalents of "Square Johns" [15], tried to blend into the background and avoid trouble or involvement with the more delinquent inmates. In the custody-oriented cottages this was achieved primarily through self-isolation or association with inmates of similar inclinations. In sociometric diagrams of the custody cottage social systems, they usually appear as isolates or in small clusters outside of the main groupings in the subculture. They tried to avoid the more aggressive or violent inmates. Although they might and occasionally would fight back to defend themselves against predators if pressed, they were much more likely to capitulate to the more delinquent boys in an effort to buy a measure of peace. They responded favorably and positively to staff, but within the normative constraints set by the inmate group. They followed rules and cooperated with staff, but not to such an extent that it would jeopardize their relations with other inmates. In short, these boys were *in* the culture, but not *of* it; they were minimizing their involvement, avoiding implication in deviance, doing their time, and trying to make the best of a bad situation.

In the treatment-oriented settings, self-isolation was a less suitable adaptation because the group treatment process required greater involvement. These boys were somewhat more outgoing and associated more freely with each other. The relative neutralization of violence in these settings effectively freed them to cooperate with staff. Although they could not act contrary to the inmate leadership, the more positive qualities of the inmate leaders and the overall reduction in violence and delinquency permitted these "straight boys" to take a more active and visible part in the cottage. In "I Belong," the cottage which unquestionably had the most positive inmate culture, the boys who were named as leaders also received the most designations as "straight," and they identified themselves as such, indicating the high degree of acceptance and legitimation of this type of behavior. We had the general impression from observations and conversations that "straight boys" in all the cottages were somewhat more conventional and less oriented to delinquent values than other boys.

Bush-boys. We also observed what Polsky called "bush-boys"— lower status inmates who were "a pale imitation of the tough boys farther up the hierarchy" [16]. These boys aspired to hang around and be identified with the higher status inmates, but lacked the necessary physical or verbal skills to successfully occupy those roles. In the custody-oriented cottages, they were flunkies for the leaders— running errands, relinquishing cigarettes, candy, and soda, and generally contributing to the material well-being of the more exploitative inmates higher in the status hierarchy. They, in turn, tried to exploit other inmates who were lower ranking than they were, but without a great deal of success. Boys who occupied this role also tended to be involved in the more self-destructive types of subcultural deviance such as sniffing glue to get high. Similarly, to demonstrate their toughness they would carve crude tatoos in their skin or burn themselves with cigarettes to prove that they could take it. Although they were actively involved in the delinquent subculture, their relationships with other boys were brittle and lacked substance. Because of their insecure status, they tended to overreact to slights and were sensitive to the least provocation.

In the treatment-oriented cottages the participation of bush boys in the program vacillated. On some occasions they were actively involved in the program, informing staff about the activities of other inmates, warning of impending runaways, and trying to support the positive culture. They occasionally "reverted to type," however, engaging in delinquent or proscribed activities, such as glue sniffing, petty thievery, encouraging other boys to run away, and the like. When they were confronted by the staff and inmates in these situations, they often reacted in a self-pitying or "pseudo-hard-guy" fashion, complaining about the program or the inequity of picking on them. They were ambivalent: not competent enough to be "successful" delinquents but not fully able to make a commitment to a more conventional orientation. Their role in the treatment cottage subcultures fluctuated between the two.

Punks. At the bottom of the cottage social structure lay the "punks" or scapegoats, boys who allowed themselves to be bullied and bossed around and who acquiesced in the role of victim [17]. Because they were reluctant or unable to defend themselves, in the custody-oriented settings these scapegoats literally existed at the sufferance of other inmates. They were perpetual punching bags, the victims of merciless taunting and pummeling. To some extent they brought some of their misery upon themselves. Scapegoats often had whining, grating personalities that almost provoked aggression. As an Elms cottage boy said of one of the punks in that cottage, "He can't fight back, he can't defend himself. But he talks big. He'll talk so much stuff, he'll get hit and he'll keep on talking, but he won't defend himself." They had no property of value since whatever they might have possessed initially was promptly expropriated by other boys.

For inmates at the bottom of the social system, especially in the custody-oriented cottages, the combined impact of aggression, threats of aggression, and ranking was devastating. The first rule of survival in the violence-based subcultures was that one must fight to defend one's integrity; those unable or unwilling to fight were at the mercy of those who would. A boy who was unable to defend himself was chronically victimized, physically and psychologically. In the custodial settings the strong norm against informing prevented either the victim or other boys who observed a violent encounter from telling the staff what really occurred. Even when staff suspected the truth, they were reluctant to pursue it since it forced them to deal with a situation they preferred to ignore. The following incident illustrates both the violence within the delinquent subculture and the inability of either the inmate-victim or the staff to counter these forces.

> A chronic victim of the cottage was seated at the table when one of the leaders who was returning to his seat hit him in the face, popping a boil that he had on his cheek. It was very painful and bled profusely. The victim went out to the kitchen to wash off the blood and cry in peace. One of the staff members asked another boy who was sitting at the table what had happened. The boy answered that the victim was picking his boil and that's why it was bleeding. When the victim came back in and sat down, the leader who had hit him initially came over and feigning a great interest in boils, said "Let me see that." When the boy uncovered the wound, he said, "Oh, that's ugly, does it hurt?" the very picture of innocence. The victim neither remonstrated the aggressor nor told the staff what had happened.

The ultimate physical aggression against punks by cottage leaders took the form of homosexual attacks. This violence was more than exploitative sexual satisfaction. It entailed conquest, domination, and humiliation, totally subjecting the victim to the will of the aggressor [18]. Every incident of homosexual assault of which we were aware can be analyzed in terms of leader-punk role relationships. So far as we were able to document, incidents of homosexual aggression took place only in the custody-oriented cottages. The staff's inability to control the violence in the subculture prevented inmates from revealing the extent of victimization within the culture, and left the victims at the mercy of their exploiters.

In the custody-oriented cottages ranking was one of the few forms of aggression in which low-status inmates could participate—if only with each other. They had nothing to lose; they knew that their targets would not fight back, just as they would not fight back. Even if they were "out-ranked" they would suffer very little loss of face, since they had none to lose. While they knew that they were safe denigrating each other, their ranking tended to be less creative, their attributions less colorful, and ranking sessions continued longer because threatening gestures were not forthcoming. Their exchanges did not alter the social order, since nobody else in the cottage took them seriously. As a consequence, to the limited extent that they participated in the inmate social system, even the victims reinforced the violent culture which gave rise to their victimization.

In sum the lives of the low-status inmates in the custody-oriented cottages were miserable. The deviant interaction processes constantly reemphasized their inferiority. The direct physical assaults and abuse were substantial and real. The attendant psychological trauma was equally apparent. These victims of terrorization were afraid of other inmates. Their fear emboldened others who, by their aggression, reinforced their fear. The punks adopted a variety of self-defensive strategies to protect themselves from violence. They sat near the staff for physical protection to avoid being beaten by the other boys. When the residents moved from place to place, the punks walked at the back of the lines to stay close to staff and to prevent inmates from getting behind them. One consequence was that in lines for food or desserts they received what was left, but that was a small price to pay for security. In Cottage 9 they asked to be locked in the isolation rooms to sleep, in order to avoid being beaten or raped in the dormitory. Because of the alienation between inmates and staff, however, cottage personnel provided them with little comfort or reassurance beyond the scant protection afforded by their physical presence.

In the treatment-oriented settings, punks did not suffer as much direct physical abuse, although they were still looked down upon and scorned as weak, immature, and lacking self-respect. They still performed services for other inmates, or relinquished their goods to more powerful inmates, but they were less likely to suffer the constant physical and psychological abuse their counterparts received in the more custodial cottages. As far as we know, there were no incidents of homosexual-aggression in the treatment-oriented cottages corresponding to those we reported in the custody-oriented settings. The types of aggression and violence that high-status inmates directed against the punks in the custody-oriented settings appeared to be effectively curbed by formal collaboration in the treatment cottages.

Similarly, the threatening gestures and warnings of physical retaliation were considerably diminished. The transformation of the norms governing informing—from opposition to support of informing—supported the constraints on physical aggression. Although some physical intimidation remained, formal collaboration in the small groups and community meetings provided a substantial check on the extent to which it could be used successfully.

Inmates were encouraged to talk with other inmates, but they were supposed to do so "responsibly," and ranking was proscribed. When one boy made a derogatory comment about another at a community meeting, another objected, "You're not supposed to cut nobody down. Calling him that, that's cutting him down." Even in more informal situations there were comparable constraints on verbal aggression. The little ranking that occurred did not involve the kinds of negative imputations or denigration that occurred in the custody-oriented settings, and tended to be more good-natured and nonmalicious. Moreover, unlike the custody-oriented cottages, where the flow of power and abuse was unidirectional and low-status inmates did not challenge leaders, inmates in the treatment-oriented cottages could respond to leaders. Such "true" ranking as there was in the treatment-oriented cottages occurred principally between lower status inmates, although there was still less of it than between inmates of comparable status in the custody-oriented cottages.

In contrast to the lives of the punks in the custody-oriented settings, low-status inmates in the treatment-oriented cottages enjoyed a comparatively benign incarceration experience. They were unlikely to be physically beaten or molested or even subjected to verbal abuse. Although they were not particularly liked or esteemed by other inmates, the adverse consequences that followed from that in custody-oriented settings did not occur in the treatment cottages. While their general behavior might be held to a somewhat higher standard of conduct than were higher status inmates, the concomitant psychological stresses or losses of privileges that this entailed paled in comparison with the physical and psychological trauma that low-status inmates suffered in more custodial settings.

Female Roles

Female role patterns at Lancaster were similar to those in the male custody-oriented cottages. Tough female leaders played the same aggressive role in controlling and exploiting other inmates as did the leaders in Cottages 8 and 9. Their lieutenants and con-men supported their power. The straight inmates, of whom there appeared to be proportionately more—probably as a result of the larger number of status offenders in female settings—adjusted to the situation much like their male counterparts, cooperating with the staff and avoiding involvement with other girls. The lower status girls who joined the inmate subculture participated in it as best they could. At the bottom of this structure was the punk role—that of a chronic victim, almost identical to the role observed in the male custody-oriented settings.

The patterns of deviant interaction between leaders and subordinates in the female settings were similar to those in the male individual custody cottages. The female leaders directed a considerable amount of verbal abuse against lower status girls for trivial reasons, such as giving them the wrong brand of cigarette, accidentally splashing water while swimming, and the like. Like their male counterparts, female leaders beat lower status inmates to reinforce their own position, regardless of the provocation.

The fear their beatings inspired were beneficial for the leaders in a number of respects. Meals were prepared in the cottages, and entailed considerable amounts of drudgery work, fixing meals, clearing tables, and washing dishes. Lower ranking inmates accepted the more unpleasant jobs that the leaders preferred to avoid. Leaders also used threats to control the behavior of subordinates. When a low-status girl offended her, a leader warned, "One more time, and I'll punch you in the mouth." Similarly, the leaders' positions were reinforced by their lieutenants who might warn a girl, "If [the leader] gets in trouble, you're gonna get it." Comparatively, the high-status inmates appeared to do somewhat more threatening than their male counterparts, frequently warning that "I'm going to do a number on that girl" or "I'm going to beat that girl up." If anything, aggressiveness and boldness appeared to be an even more effective unequalizer among the females than among the males.

Ranking between girls was as prevalent at Lancaster and served the same social-control functions as in the male cottages. Interestingly, the girls used negative imputations of homosexuality in much the same fashion as the boys did, ranking on girls for being "lessies" or lesbians, just as the boys derided others as "faggots."

On the other hand, we did not find any of the elaborate female homosexual roles reported in the literature, such as "butches," or "fems"; nor did we observe the elaborate family structures and kinship networks with corresponding mother, father, daughter, sister, and cousin roles that others had reported [19]. Our observer had extremely good rapport with the residents of the cottages that she studied. She lived on the grounds of the institution continuously for almost three months and spent a great deal of time talking with girls away from staff observation. Although a study of this same institution conducted several years earlier reported both homosexual courtship patterns and extended family networks, we found neither [20]. Their presence prior to our study was confirmed, however, by several girls who had been incarcerated at Lancaster earlier. One girl told our observer, "You're lucky that you weren't around last year, because then everyone was going together. This year, there's much less. There's no kissing." Other recidivists also confirmed that "there's less 'going together' this year than last." Other girls also noted that there were almost no pen-letters being sent, which is a frequently reported manifestation of the courtship process in other studies of female subcultures.

If these homosexual roles and kinship networks generally occur among female inmates in juvenile institutions, the processes that led to their development were probably attenuated by a variety of changes that had taken place at Lancaster—especially the brevity of periods of incarceration. Typically, the girls spent four months or less in the institution and enjoyed weekend home furloughs after the second month. Since the evolution of institutional homosexual alliances is normally attributed to emotional isolation, this impetus was substantially reduced at Lancaster.

THE INMATE SUBCULTURES: DISCUSSION AND CONCLUSIONS

Differences in organizational structure, particularly as these influenced the types of relationships that staff people established with inmates, had a major impact on the informal inmate social systems. Strongly consistent internally, the respective cottage cultures differed in a number of crucial respects: in inmates' perceptions of staff and of other inmates; in the types of institutional adaptations they pursued; in the prevailing norms and values; and in the ways inmates interacted with each other. The striking differences in subcultural organization reflect the relative success of staff in containing, controlling, and neutralizing the levels of inmate violence, thereby freeing inmates to respond positively to staff.

Our continuum of cottages, from the oppressive brutality of the group custody setting, Cottage 9, to the supportiveness of group treatment programs like "I Belong," provides a graduated transition in the social organization of both the staff and inmates that enables us to analyze the ways in which organizational structure affects the inmate subculture. Although each cottage subculture was unique, reflecting its constituent members, some general, organizationally related characteristics suggest the ways in which structure modifies subculture processes.

There is a striking parallel between the structure and operation of the staff social system and the inmate social system. In the oppressive custody-oriented settings—Cottage 8 and 9—staff roles were structured in an authoritarian, hierarchial fashion. Staff members were strictly custodial, enforcing the rules they were given, minimizing their contacts with inmates, attempting to maintain a high level of surveillance and control. The institutional settings were highly depriving situations, perceived by inmates as punitive and providing them with a variety of incentives to engage in covert deviance.

Staff social-control practices were authoritarian, severe, and brutal, although somewhat inconsistent. They were concerned with overt obedience and conformity and surpressing direct challenges to staff authority. The absence of programming and the lack of involvement of inmates in cooperative efforts with the staff precluded the development of individualized relationships with staff people and perpetuated the negative stereotypes each held of the other. As a consequence, inmates were extremely alienated from staff. Because of the staffs' negative views of inmate associations, they attempted to neutralize the operation of the inmate group by disruption, atomization, and the encouragement of self-isolation. Their efforts to disrupt the inmate group also rendered it more difficult for inmates to cooperate with each other to resolve the various institutionally created problems of adjustment, including exploitative violence.

In this context tough inmates emerged who developed covert deviant solutions to the institutional problems of adjustment that also made their own incarceration more bearable. They engaged in covert activities to obtain contraband, and they also exploited weaker inmates, expropriating their legitimate or illegitimate possessions. They used violence to reinforce their own status and to obtain the gratification of respect, safety and invulnerability that it provided.

Because of their deviant and violent behavior, they discouraged inmate contact with staff and punished inmates who informed.

Inmate informing was strongly condemned. The dominance of the more hostile inmates also tended to reinforce the staffs' efforts to atomize the inmates culture by making inmates distrustful and fearful of each other. The pattern was reflected in the inmates' negative perceptions of other inmates and in the lower levels of inmate solidarity. These custodial settings generated inmate cultures in which the law of the jungle prevailed. The extensive use of violence prevented the staff from gaining control over the inmate group. Tough leaders were able to minimize the contacts with and flow of information to staff that would make control possible. Inmates in these settings had fewer contacts with staff, and their contacts were insubstantial. Moreover, no program rationale existed that could justify either extensive staff-inmate contacts or information exchanges.

The use of violence by inmates, paralleling staff practices, resulted in a rigidly structured, authoritarian subculture in which the social distance between high- and low-status inmates was comparable to the gulf between inmates and staff. The ability to use violence determined the various roles in the inmate group. The prevalence of violence reinforced the negativism within the culture by preventing the emergence of pro-social inmate behavior. This was reflected in the support for negative inmate behavior and the rejection of cooperative inmate roles. In short, the absence of staff support for informing or for controlling violence forced the inmates to seek accommodation with the primary power source—the aggressive, oppositional leaders. This in turn reinforced inmates' alienation from other inmates. Their attempts at self-isolation and noninvolvement with other inmates precluded any collective response to aggression and left each individual inmate at the mercy of the leaders.

Even in the more intermediate custody-oriented cottages—Elms and Westview—violence remained the great unequalizer, and powerful inmates dominated the inmate group. But changes in organizational structure and staff relations with inmates provided the staff with somewhat greater control over the inmate group. Program individualization and the need to engage inmates in productive work resulted in considerably greater staff contact with inmates than was the case in the group-custody settings, Cottage 9, or even Cottage 8, where institutional programming was essentially nonexistent. The increased inmate contact with staff in programs and their involvement in joint tasks provided staff and inmates with some basis on which to relate with each other.

One consequence was that the stereotypes that staff and inmates held of each other were correspondingly more moderate and less antagonistic than those held by staff and inmates in settings where effective, cooperative contact was absent. Individualized programming also entailed less punitive social-control practices, and the increased use of a privilege system provided staff with a more flexible response to inmates than did the use of force and isolation cells. The less authoritarian control practices reduced the degree of inmate alienation from staff and alleviated some of their institutional deprivations. As the levels of deprivation declined, the need to engage in covert deviance to find alternatives declined accordingly. With less covert deviance there was less to hide, and hence less need to restrict inmate contact with staff. While inmates still disapproved of informing, it was not as ruthlessly suppressed.

Within this context, staff successfully co-opted the potentially aggressive inmate leadership. Through informal collaboration they enlisted the inmate leaders to maintain order and control within the subculture. In the course of protecting the privileges that were more readily available in these settings, the leaders informally maintained control for staff, suppressed some forms of anti-institutional activities, and reduced the overall levels of violence within the inmate group. The leaders, of course, enjoyed a privileged status for their efforts. The inmates recognized and to some degree accepted this role for inmate leadership. The success of the inmate leaders in restraining their own aggressive activities, and those of other inmates, tended to reduce the levels of alienation among inmates as reflected in their more favorable perceptions of other inmates and in greater levels of solidarity. The reduction in brutality and aggression by inmates resulted in a less rigidly structured, authoritarian subculture. Inmates were freer to interact with other inmates under nonthreatening circumstances.

The female subcultures in Lancaster contained a mixture of the characteristics of the two types of male custody-oriented cottages. Many of the organizational features of Lancaster were similar to those in the more benign of the individual custody cottages. The institution was very heavily programmed, most of the programs were individualized, and inmates had extensive contacts with staff. This was reflected in the inmates' more favorable perceptions of staff. Although the Lancaster staff used similar techniques of social control, such as granting or withholding privileges, they did not appear to be as successful as the staff in Elms and Westview in co-opting the inmate leadership to support staff goals. To some extent the heavily structured, individualized programs may have reduced the scope of the inmate leaders' role.

More important, the fact that the inmates were female affected the types of control responses from the staff. Lancaster staff people were not as able to directly confront inmate violence as were staff in the male settings. The female staff members relied on outside assistance when a girl became violent or was out of control, and the male custodial personnel who responded were more restrained in handling female inmates than male staff were in comparable male settings. As a result the more belligerent, aggressive female leaders were not under as effective control as their Elms and Westview male counterparts, and the violence in the subcultures was somewhat more similar to Cottages 8 and 9.

Since most of the female inmates were status offenders, they presumably had neither the criminal sophistication nor the experience with violence and aggression that their male criminal-delinquent counterparts had. Although they were probably initially more inclined to orient themselves toward staff than their male counterparts, in the face of aggressive, oppositional inmates they could be intimidated into keeping to themselves. This is reflected in the striking differences from males in their pattern of institutional adjustment: reduced involvement with other inmates in favor of cooperation with staff, or self-isolation. In the Lancaster cottages the female leaders were under less control than the corresponding male leaders, and they appeared to use violence and intimidation more extensively. While the organizational structure and female sex-role socialization generated tendencies toward moderation within the inmate culture, the reduced control over violent inmates pressed in the opposite direction, and the result was an inmate culture with characteristics of both types of male settings.

A substantial positive transformation in the character of the inmate cultures occurred in both the individual and group treatment settings. This success is largely attributable to the introduction of formal collaboration between staff and inmates as part of their programmatic practices. Formal collaboration, by which inmates and staff participated collectively in making decisions about the administration of the cottage, had a number of consequences that were reflected in subcultural processes as well.

Unlike the authoritarian bureaucracy found in custody cottages, formal collaboration introduced a much greater degree of equality among various staff members, between staff and inmates, and among inmates. It also provided a context in which staff and inmates could deal with each other more honestly in a variety of different roles. Collaborative participation reduced the degree of alienation inmates experienced from staff and from other inmates. In the most structured group treatment settings, Shirley cottage and "I Belong," the strengths of programmatic individualization achieved in Elms and Westview were reinforced by another range of relationships in the cottage community meetings and small-group treatment settings. It increased the opportunities for staff and inmates to work together, to gain an understanding of and insight into the problems of the other. This is reflected in the favorable views that inmates had of staff and other inmates.

Formal collaboration also made the workings of the inmate subculture more visible, providing the staff and inmates with a mechanism for coping with inmate violence. The staff succeeded in transforming the norm regarding informing from a negative one in the custody cottages to a more positive one in the treatment cottages. In part this transition reflected the staffs' ability to provide a rehabilitative rationale for informing. Equally important, however, the staff transformed their program itself, reducing the levels of deprivation to such a degree that the inmates themselves perceived the settings as committed to treatment rather than punishment, and experienced it as such. The availability of amenities further reduced the need for covert exploitation.

The increased flow of information enabled the staff to gain insight into and control over the levels of inmate violence. Control of violence reinforced the flow of information, thereby providing more collective control over violence. To the extent that formal collaboration enabled them to reduce inmate violence, inmates were then free to relate more positively with each other and with staff. This was reflected in their more positive perceptions of both. Freeing inmates from violence also diminished the authoritarian rigidity of subculture structure. Paralleling the changes in staff organization, inmates were able to enter into relationships with other inmates on the basis of friendship, rather than of necessity or through coercion. This was reflected in the higher levels of solidarity, and the reduction, if not elimination, of "deviant interaction processes," such as threats, exploitation, and ranking.

This is not to suggest that the staff people in treatment-oriented settings were able, by means of formal collaboration, to eliminate completely the violence within the inmate culture. The aggressive leaders did use violence and intimidation, although to a considerably lesser extent than in either of the custody-oriented contexts. The combined impact of an organizational rationale for informing coupled with formal collaboration made violence a less effective means of informal social control than it was in the custody-oriented cottages. The fact that violence was present at all, however, still had a potentially inhibiting effect on the willingness of nonviolent inmates to openly confront aggressive leaders.

To some extent the leaders were able to insulate themselves from some of the treatment pressures to which other inmates were subjected by implied threat. By occasionally "playing the role," they were able to do relatively easy time. Essentially, the process of formal collaboration made everyone's activities more visible and placed greater pressure on people to change their patterns of behavior. Leaders were sometimes able to divert the pressures on them to change by intimidating lower status inmates. Having freed themselves, however, they were still under some compulsion to at least appear to support the program by seeming to play a positive role. In the course of playing a positive role, they allowed other inmates to do so, at least as long as it did not jeopardize the leaders.

The success of formal collaboration, however, was always contingent and conditional. If inmate complaints of violence and intimidation were not responded to or if aggressive inmates were not sanctioned and controlled, a positive inmate culture could be dissipated quickly, and the more negative inmates could prevent further cooperation with staff.

✻ Chapter 5

The Presenting Culture: The Influence of Sex and Race on Subculture Adaptation

In our evaluation of functional explanations of subculture formation we started with the proposition that organizational differences affect the character of a subculture. We have attempted to show the linkages between staff ideology, intervention strategies, social-control practices, and the character of the inmate group. We now turn to an assessment of the importation explanations of subculture, to explore differences in inmate responses to similar organizational environments as these differences relate to the identifiable individual characteristics of inmates.

There are several potentially relevant background characteristics, but we will focus here only on sex-linked differences and race-linked differences to explore the extent to which young women and black youths perceive and react differently from white male inmates to what appear to be comparable social settings. We anticipate that variations in socialization experiences and prior roles associated with an inmate's sex or race will color their perceptions of and adaptations to the same organization.

That individuals with different social characteristics and backgrounds should respond differently to similar social situations seems intuitively obvious; backgrounds ought to influence both one's perceptions of a social situation and the range of response alternatives. An emerging literature on sex-linked inmate responses to organizational structure suggests that, to some degree, women respond to the experiences associated with incarceration differently from the way men do [1]. While the literature is not as extensive, there is a similar suggestion that black inmates respond differently from white inmates to the same incarceration experience [2]. Drawing upon these findings of sex- and race-linked adaptive differences, we examine in this chapter the extent to which importation explanations require the modification of functional explanations of subcultural characteristics.

SEX-LINKED DIFFERENCES

In several studies that have examined the impact of sex-role socialization on prison adaptations, the analysis has proceeded on the assumption that the organizational structure of female institutions was comparable to that of male settings. Observers then explained female subcultural differences in terms of differences associated with prior "female" socialization [3]. Although acknowledging, in the absence of comparative organizational data, that male and female institutions cannot be considered strictly comparable, such studies ignore the qualitative differences in settings, proceed *as if* they were roughly comparable, and then attribute the substantial subcultural differences to sex-linked socialization experiences.

Ward and Kassebaum, for example, proposed that the pains of imprisonment described by Sykes in male maximum-security institutions were approximately comparable in female settings with the additional deprivations of the "dispossession of the familial roles of wife and mother and the separation from family." They then asked "whether the reactions to the pains of imprisonment are similar for female and male prisoners" [4]. Giallombardo did not even try to establish organizational comparability but proceeded directly from the proposition that differences in cultural expectations surrounding male and female social roles lead to differences in subcultural organization. "If we find," she wrote, "the members of two social subsystems in an organization facing *similar conditions* for survival in the social environment, but the structure of social relationships and the sentiments attached to them exhibit significant differences in each system, then the reason may be found in the cultural definitions ascribed to the roles held by the members in the society from which they were drawn" [emphasis added] [5].

Unfortunately, in her analysis of the Federal Reformatory for Women in Alderson, West Virginia, Giallombardo did not provide any comparative data to support the inference that the women she studied faced conditions similar to those that confronted, for example, the male inmates of the New Jersey maximum-security facility that Sykes had analyzed. In her more recent comparative study of female juvenile correctional facilities Giallombardo categorically rejected any influence of organizational structure and attributed the total subculture character to imported sex-role socialization. There, she contended, "Irrespective of the goals of the formal organization, the structural form of the informal social system evolved by female juvenile offenders will be marriage, kinship, and family groups" [6]. But her descriptions of the comparative organizational structures in which she found similar subcultural social systems were not sufficiently detailed to allow for an assessment of formal organizational variations.

Despite the appeal of assuming organizational structural comparability and then attributing subcultural differences to sex-role socialization, those who have examined male and female subcultures in comparable organizational settings have reported much more limited differences. For example, Tittle's examination of subcultural organization among male and female inmates incarcerated in the same setting provided only limited support for the importation thesis [7]. While the character of homosexual relationships among female inmates were different from those among male inmates, they did not appear to be any more extensive and did not entail extended family kinship networks, courting rituals, and the like. Although Tittle found some sex-related differences in primary-group affiliations among male and female inmates, the similarities were as striking as the differences. Tittle's conclusions about sex-linked differences are consistent with the results of our study, in which we found less support for the importation thesis based on sexual differences than other reports have suggested. Tittle concluded:

> Differences in inmate organizational structure by sex have been examined in an institution where men and women are incarcerated under similar conditions. The data indicate small but consistent differences between the sexes with respect to form of inmate organization. The females show greater propensity to affiliate in primary groups while the men display greater tendencies toward integration into an overall symbiotic organization. This is consistent with previous research, but *the magnitude of the differences suggests that in this context at least, the influence of sex-linked factors is much less pervasive than might have been expected.* The two types of inmate structure were found to be somewhat parallel for both sexes rather than mutually exclusive. For both males and females in the institution studied, primary group organization and symbiotic organization appear to exist side by side, with one form slightly predominating in each context.
>
> Synthetic cohort variations and partial panel data tend to *confirm the theory of inmate organization as an institutional product*. . . . In general the data seem to justify the conclusion that *inmate organization is largely a response to institutional conditions* [8].

Our comparisons of the female inmate subcultures at Lancaster and the male subcultures in organizationally comparable cottages such as Westview or Elms indicate that substantial subcultural similarities exist along with some differences that may be attributed to sex-linked factors.

Our comparative research design used questionnaire, interview, and observation formats that enabled us to establish organizational and subcultural comparability to a much greater extent than was the case for most previous tests of the importation thesis. Moreover, like Tittle we also were able to study a coeducational facility—Topsfield—which provided even greater control over the organizational variables.

On the basis of comparative data on organizational structure, intervention strategies, social-control practices, and staff-inmate relations, we found the Lancaster girls' cottages to be closest in structure to Elms and Westview. The staff at Lancaster had somewhat more moderate perceptions of the "dangerousness" or trustworthiness of the inmates. They also felt somewhat more able to enter into positive relationships with their inmates than did the male cottage staff. They were somewhat less authoritarian and punitive. These differences are readily explicable in terms of differences in the nature of the offenses for which delinquent males and females were committed to the institution.

Despite these relatively minor ideological differences, staff in the male and female settings pursued virtually identical goals using similar intervention strategies. The programmatic emphasis was on containment, obedience and respect, and vocational training. Both settings relied extensively on inmate labor for institutional maintenance and the concomitant work experience as the intervention program. Lancaster's formal structure was that of a traditional industrial training school with a multiple-department structure. Despite cottage decentralization, Elms and Westview were organized on a similar basis.

There were some differences in social-control strategies between the male settings and the female settings that appeared to be reflected in the subculture organization as well. The male cottage staff relied on a system of privileges to induce conformity and informal collaboration between staff and the inmate elite. The Lancaster cottage staff also utilized a privilege system reinforced by more extensive use of room lock-ups to maintain order. Since outside security personnel provided physical controls, Lancaster staff people were less reliant on a system of informal collaboration, and the more aggressive or violent female inmates were under somewhat less effective control than their male counterparts. As a consequence of similarities in structure, intervention programs, and social-control practices, staff-inmate relations in the various settings were also similar, tending to be formal and somewhat distance. Staff related to inmates as authoritative adults who expected prompt inmate obedience and informal relations were exceptional. On the basis of our comparative analysis we can assert with much greater confidence than most other studies of female subcultures that the organizational structures of our settings were comparable.

The two preceding chapters revealed differences between the male and female subcultures in these comparable settings, as well as striking similarities. The Lancaster inmates were as likely as their male counterparts in Elms and Westview to regard the purposes of the institution as punitive. They were about as likely to see the staff as expecting behavioral conformity rather than gaining insight. The female inmates described their problems of adjusting to the institution in ways similar to the males on virtually every dimension. Male and female residents were also similar to the extent that all inmates had to cooperate with staff or other inmates in order to resolve their problems of adjustment.

Female perceptions of staff were almost identical with those of the Elms and Westview males, with negative perceptions somewhat predominating in all of the settings. These similarities were also reflected in the quality of contacts between inmates and staff. Although Lancaster staff emphasized individual counseling to a greater extent than did male staff, and, accordingly, female inmates were more likely to discuss personal problems with their counselors, their contacts with and perceptions of other staff members were comparable. Inmate perceptions of other inmates in the male and female settings were also similar, although the Lancaster inmates were somewhat more disposed to negative perceptions of other inmates than were their male counterparts.

Our discussion of inmate adaptations pointed to marked similarities. In terms of individual adaptations, the female inmates of this essentially custodial setting were as likely to emphasize obedience and conformity, following staff orders, and "doing time" as were the males. Perhaps the most significant sex-linked adaptive differences occurred in the context of primary group integration and inmate involvement with other inmates. (See Table 3−7). Female inmates were considerably less likely to become as extensively integrated into the inmate subculture. They were much more likely to limit their friendships to one or two other inmates rather than engage in the more extensive involvements reported by the boys in Elms and Westview.

This difference is also reflected in the sociometric choices that inmates made, with sociograms of the female settings revealing smaller groupings, dyads and triads with reciprocated choices, whereas in the male settings the clusters tended to be somewhat larger and looser, containing four or five inmates with proportionately fewer reciprocated choices. This is consistent with other reports on inmate subcultures that indicate women tend to enter into smaller, more stable relationships than do men [9].

The female differences in patterns of relationships were not, however, elaborated into homosexual family structures with extended kinship networks. The female inmates themselves commented on the extent to which these patterns were absent compared with prior incarcerations. To the extent that stable, affectional homosexual relationships are more likely to develop in female settings than in male, their absence at Lancaster can probably be attributed to the reduction in the period of incarceration. If affectional relationships are an adaptation to the loss of external relationships and supports, the four-month average period of incarceration with the great availability of weekend furloughs and home visits presumably reduced the female inmates' sense of isolation and their incentive to enter into short-term homosexual relationships. Thus, our data is consistent with Tittle's findings that women tend to enter into smaller, stable primary groups, but without the homosexual and extended family characteristics typically reported.

The more limited involvement of female inmates with each other was reflected in other minor subcultural variations. The reported levels of solidarity were somewhat higher among females than among the males. Lancaster residents indicated that they were more likely to share and "stick together" than male inmates, presumably reflecting a response to their smaller primary group. The Lancaster residents were about twice as likely to approve of informing as their counterpart male residents. Again, this may reflect their lessened involvement in the subculture as a whole, hence their more limited loyalty to inmates beyond their primary reference group. As status offenders, the female populations were presumably less criminally sophisticated than the male inmates, and this may also be reflected in their lower commitment to a criminal value system. Despite the greater normative approval of informing among the women, the prevalence of violence in the female cultures appeared comparable to that in the male settings, and Lancaster residents were as likely to be physically discouraged from "dime-dropping" as were their male counterparts.

Most measures of subcultural norms have suggested general similarities between male and female settings. Lancaster residents were proportionately as likely to approve of positive and negative inmate role behaviors as the males in comparable settings. Given these normative similarities, it is not surprising that the overall social structure of the respective subcultures—the patterns of roles and interaction between roles—were also similar.

The leaders in the female settings were described by other inmates as occupying a basically negative role within the subculture, fighting, doing time, and isolating themselves from staff people. On the basis of interviews and observation data, female leaders seemed as likely to be as violent, aggressive, and exploitative of other inmates as their male counterparts. If anything, the female leadership was under somewhat less staff control than their male counterparts in Elms and Westview because of the differences in staff social-control practices and elite co-optation. As a consequence the prevalence of violence within the female subcultures influenced the other roles that emerged, the underlying basis of interaction between them, and the overall hierarchical, authoritarian structure of the subculture. On the basis of our analysis of relatively comparable male and female settings, the similarities are more impressive than the differences, providing some support for functional explanations of subculture formation.

To further assess the importation theory of subculture formation, we compared the adaptations and reactions of male and female residents within the same treatment organization. Topsfield, a mixed individual-group treatment setting, was a coeducational facility with a resident population of seven boys and nine girls. Although the numbers involved were too small for statistical manipulation or inferences, they nonetheless provided a limited basis for comparing male and female responses to the same organizational setting. Since we found only slight differences between the boys and the girls in Topsfield, the results provide some additional corroboration for the Lancaster-Elms/Westview comparison.

The differences we obtained were consistent with those findings. The boys and girls at Topsfield were virtually identical in their perceptions of the cottage's treatment goals, and there was near unanimity that the purpose of their incarceration was to aid them in gaining psychological insight. They also described similar problems of adjustment. The bulk of inmates, both boys and girls, pointed to the therapeutic process itself as one of the most critical problems confronting them: "Trying to be honest, relating honestly with other people, trying to understand what people are saying, the way they feel." On the basis of their interview responses boys and girls appeared to find this experience equally stressful.

Our model of subculture formation proposes that resolving institutional problems of adjustment requires cooperation between inmates and staff or other inmates. Equal proportions of male and female residents regarded staff members as trustworthy and committed to helping them. Both male and female inmates held staff in equally high esteem, presumably reflecting extensive contacts and warm relationships. There were no appreciable differences by sex in the quantity of contacts or in the substantive quality of contacts.

Inmate perceptions of other residents were also overwhelmingly positive, with no discernible differences between boys and girls. Since the perceptions of cottage goals, staff, and other inmates were similar, it is not surprising that the institutional adaptations made by the boys and girls were similar as well. Consistent with staffs' treatment expectations, virtually all the residents, boys and girls, rejected the prisonized adaptation of prompt obedience and self-isolation and almost equal proportions chose gaining insight over conformity.

In general agreement with the Lancaster-Elms/Westview comparison, proportionately more boys than girls chose involvement with other inmates over cooperation with staff as a mode of adjustment, although the differences were not statistically significant. Similarly and consistently, proportionately more female residents than male residents made reciprocated sociometric choices, suggesting smaller and tighter bonding between females than between males. The male-female normative differences we obtained between Lancaster and Elms/Westview on the issue of informing also appeared at Topsfield, with the female residents more likely to approve of informing than the males. They were also proportionately more likely to approve of cooperative inmate role behavior than the males, although on other normative measures they appeared to be similar.

As we suggested in our interpretation of the Lancaster results and in our initial population descriptions, a far larger proportion of females than males was committed to the institutions for status offenses rather than criminal delinquency. Females were about three times as likely as males to be institutionalized for noncriminal misconduct. This pattern of differential commitment on the basis of sex and offense is so pervasive that it tends to override other factors in assessing male/female subcultural differences. To the extent that female status offenders are correspondingly less criminally sophisticated, their greater cooperation with staff and slightly more positive normative orientation may reflect little more than the importation of inmates with less advanced delinquent careers. Unfortunately our sample lacks sufficient male status offenders in comparable settings to test this possibility. In sum, even those few sex-linked differences we found may reflect yet another sex-mediated variable—differential offense commitment rates—rather than anything directly associated with sex-role socialization.

Within the Topsfield subculture social structure, two boys and two girls emerged as inmate leaders. There was some propensity for other inmates to describe the female leaders more positively than the males, and our own observations indicated that the female leaders played a more supportive, therapeutic role than their male counterparts. This may reflect the somewhat greater female support for staff and the slight sex-linked normative differences we reported. Overall the relatively small inmate population and the favorable staff-inmate ratio produced a sexually integrated subculture in which few sex-linked role differences emerged. As in other treatment-oriented settings, staff members were able to minimize the levels of violence, and physical prowess, a potential sex-linked "unequalizer," did not appear to be a significant factor determining stratification or role differentiation.

In interpreting the Lancaster and Topsfield comparisons, we can conclude that *at least in relatively short-term* (three or four months) juvenile residential settings, sex-linked characteristics do not appear to appreciably determine the character of the subculture. On the basis of the two types of comparative analysis, females do appear to form smaller, tighter groups than do males. In addition to their stronger primary-group affiliation, they appear to be more supportive of staff and less inclined to become extensively involved in the sub culture beyond their immediate group. Their reduced commitment to the cottage population beyond their own reference group is reflected in somewhat higher levels of in-group solidarity, and substantially greater approval of informing and positive, cooperative behavior.

Even the last conclusion, however, must be tempered by the possibility that the differences may be a function of male-female differences in commitment rates by offense, which are then related to differences in criminal sophistication and the progression of their respective delinquent careers. At the very least we may conclude that the frequently described sex-related subcultural phenomena of stable homosexual liaisons, courtship rituals, and extended family kinship networks do not appear to be an inherent characteristic of female institutional subcultures.

RACE-LINKED DIFFERENCES

To further assess the impact of imported characteristics on subculture formation, we examined the influence of racial differences as race serves as an indicator of differences in prior socialization and preinstitutional experiences. Despite the wealth of studies of correctional institutions and the obvious importance of race as a variable for testing importation theories, there has been surprisingly little consideration of the extent to which inmates with different prior social experiences, as a result of racial background, perceive and respond differently to the same objective social situation. Although the black inmates in our study shared many demographic and social characteristics with the white inmates, for purposes of testing importation theories we assume that being a black American is a qualitatively different experience from being a white American [10].

In our description of inmate background characteristics in Chapter 1, we noted that there were approximately equal proportions of black inmates in all of the cottage units; about 26 percent of the custody-oriented cottage residents and 25 percent of the treatment-oriented cottage residents. The Lancaster findings indicate that a substantially smaller proportion of black females than black males were committed to the institutions of the Department of Youth services [11].

Although we found some significant differences between black and white inmates within the same cottage, we used several strategies to eliminate the possibility that the cottage subcultural variations were the product of racial differences. To ascertain racial comparability, we tested and found no significant relationship between an inmate's race and age of first contact with the juvenile court, or the type or seriousness of the offense for which commitment resulted.

Through the use of significance tests, sign tests to identify any interaction effects between race and cottage treatment program, and comparisons of the zero-order scores with the separate partial scores for black and white inmates, we were able to conclude that the subcultural differences we obtained between cottages did not result from racial differences within the cottages. This was not surprising since the relative proportions of black and white inmates were comparable across cottages, and the magnitudes of differences between races within a cottage on any particular attitudinal dimension usually were not very large. Thus, while there are subcultural racial differences that warrant further analysis as a test of the importation hypothesis, we may safely reassert our conclusion that the substantial subcultural differences obtained between the cottages are not the product of racial differences and can appropriately be attributed primarily to organizational variables.

Inmates tended to segregate themselves by race whenever a "critical mass" of about three or more members of a racial minority were housed in a particular cottage. Racial self-segregation extended to virtually all activities—eating, playing, idling. As the number of black inmates in a given cottage increased, there was a corresponding tendency for virtually separate parallel racial subcultures to emerge. This was most pronounced in Elms and Westview cottages, which had among the largest cottage populations and the greatest proportion of racial minorities in residence. The significance of these parallel subcultures is reflected in differences within each grouping according to race and, more significantly, in terms of the relationships between the inmate racial groupings. We will first describe the extent to which racial groupings within the same cottage setting differed, and then explore the process of interaction between the racial groupings and the implications of these differences for the social structure of the subculture.

With the exception of Elms cottage, there were approximately three to five black residents in each cottage. The relatively small numbers in any cottage precluded the use of statistical tests, and we used sign tests, comparing signs within cottage types, in lieu of significance tests to identify attitudinal differences by race. If the partial score of one racial group consistently exceeded that of the other within a cottage-type, then we felt confident in treating this as evidence of a race-linked difference. On most dimensions, black and white inmates within the same cottage setting responded similarly, and there were few racially consistent differences that cut across an entire cottage treatment-type.

Black and white inmates were in general agreement on the respective purposes of their cottage and expectations of staff. The white inmates of the custody-oriented cottages, however, displayed a consistent tendency to regard the setting as somewhat more punitive than did the black inmates in those settings. When asked, "What is this place trying to do for you?" a larger proportion of white male inmates in all of the custody-oriented cottages indicated that they believed that it was "a place to punish kids for the things that they did wrong," while the black male residents were somewhat more inclined to regard those settings as places that "help kids understand the things that got them in trouble."

In a related fashion, the white male residents of the custody-oriented cottages were somewhat more likely than blacks to denigrate staff efforts, and larger proportions agreed that the staff people were indifferent to inmates and did not do much to help them. However, these slightly more negative views by white inmates in the custody-oriented cottages were not reflected in differences in their overall perspectives of staff, where there were no consistent racial differences. Nor did race appear to influence inmate perspectives of other inmates.

In view of the overall similarities in inmate perceptions of their respective cottages, staff, and other inmates, we expected their institutional adaptations to be similar. Whether the institutional adaptive expectations were obedience and conformity, as in the custody-oriented settings, or gaining insight, as in the treatment-oriented settings, there were few adaptive differences by race.

There were important racially linked adaptive differences in terms of inmate involvement in primary groups. Within the custody-oriented cottages, black inmates were less likely to isolate themselves and withdraw from involvement with other inmates. This tendency for black inmates in custody-oriented settings to become involved with other inmates was also reflected in the sociograms of virtually all of the cottages, which showed black inmates more likely to be integrated into a racially homogeneous primary group, as contrasted with larger proportions of white inmates who remained unaffiliated. As we will suggest, because of self-segregation and the limited numbers of minority group members, black inmates in virtually all settings tended to be more close-knit and exhibit greater degrees of collective solidarity than their white counterparts. This racial solidarity, in turn, had important implications for the relationships between black and white inmates within the cottage subculture.

Another related and important racial difference was the marked tendency for a disproportionately large number of black residents to emerge as inmate leaders in every setting. The overrpresentation of black inmates as leaders was significant at a .001 level in the overall sample, and at a .05 level in every cottage. Since stratification within virtually every cottage setting was based on physical prowess alone or in combination with verbal skills, black inmates, by inference, tended disproportionately to possess these qualities. Although not readily susceptible to direct measurement, on the basis of our observations and interviews, black inmates as a group appeared to be somewhat more physically competent, verbally adroit, and criminally and institutionally sophisticated than their white counterparts. They appeared to be more physically well-developed and athletically inclined, and they were more likely to participate in athletic events, pick-up basketball games, and the like. Their physical capabilities were also relevant to the physical attributes on which the violence-based subcultures were stratified.

Black inmates appeared to be more verbally skillful as well. Many staff members, black and white, observed that "the black kids are more sophisticated for the age groups. They come from a tougher, more sophisticated background." Others also observed that "the black kids in this unit are smarter. I don't mean intelligent, they're more sophisticated, they're slicker." When we asked about "informal rules," blacks were more familiar with the maxims of an "inmate code" than were their white counterparts. Although we lack the data to explain why black inmates possessed these characteristics, it appeared that they were better prepared to succeed within the inmate subcultures when stratification was based on physical or verbal manipulation or aggression. Larger proportions of black residents also described inmate leaders more positively than did whites in virtually every cottage. Since minority group members were significantly overrepresented in leadership positions and, on the basis of racial solidarity, protected the interests of their colleagues, this consistently more favorable assessment is readily understandable.

While the attitudinal similarities between black and white inmates greatly exceeded the differences, self-segregation, which fostered greater solidarity among black inmates than whites, and the predominance of blacks in leadership roles had important implications for the functioning of the inmate subculture and the relationships between racial subgroups within a cottage. Through our structured interviews and observations, we gathered additional information on the role of race and race relations within the subculture.

It was immediately apparent to even a casual observer that inmates preferred to associate with inmates of the same race. At meals, in informal groups, and in recreational activities, the pattern reflected racial self-segregation. As one inmate suggested, "We just stick in our own groups. Like we don't bother with the other kids, especially the colored kids, and they don't want to have much to do with us. So they let us go our way, and we let them go theirs." This self-segregation cut across all cottages—custody and treatment—and suggests the degree of salience that race has for subculture formation.

Cottage staff members were also aware of the tendencies for inmates to group on the basis of race. When asked about the prevalence of informal groups within the cottage, many staff members observed that "sometimes they stick together in groups by color. Colored kids hang around with colored kids and whites with whites." Others also noted that the "blacks are closer knit than the whites." Similarly, another commented that "blacks will group together more than the whites and stay together more."

Staff members, overwhelmingly white, also indicated that staff-inmate racial differences and the tendency for black inmates to associate almost exclusively with other black inmates made it somewhat more difficult to work effectively with them. Regardless of the treatment mode, staff members agreed that for white staff members, "It's a little tougher to gain the confidence of a colored kid, a black kid, than it is for a white kid, for obvious reasons." Many candidly acknowledged, "I'd have to say I'd have more of a difficulty in dealing with the black kids because of their defensiveness and it would be much harder, I believe, for them to trust me as much." In our own research experience it was comparatively easier for white researchers to gain access to the white inmates than to the blacks, and the most serious challenges to our research presence were raised by black inmates.

Although the white inmates and predominantly white staff were aware of and somewhat apprehensive about the degree of self-segregation and solidarity that blacks exhibited, black inmates did not regard the situation as abnormal. To the extent that inmates were socialized into the inmate subculture through their contacts with other inmates from home or associated with other inmates on the basis of shared interests, one would expect that the patterns of racial isolation in the larger society would be replicated within the institution.

Because white inmates were less well-integrated or organized into the violence-based subcultures than the black inmates, they were also more vulnerable to exploitation. A constantly recurring theme in our interviews was the extent to which racial identity provided blacks with a basis on which to organize collectively to a greater extent than whites. "Blacks are close together so they'll stick together, but the whites don't. Blacks are tight, white kids are not." Despite the fact that white inmates in every cottage constituted a clear numerical majority, the manifestly greater solidarity among black inmates gave them an advantage in their relationships with individual white inmates for whom racial identity did not provide as much collective security. In varying degrees, individual white inmates tried to avoid contacts with blacks because of their apprehension about exploitation. As one Lancaster inmate said, "If I have something and don't give it up to a black kid, I get the shit kicked out of me. Any time you see a black group together, you don't go near them." Similar concerns were echoed by white inmates in many cottages.

White inmates complained about the extent to which black inmates dominated the subculture and exploited them materially. In our structured interviews we asked the inmates who did the "strong-arming" (exploitation through violence) within the subculture, and black inmates were disproportionately identified. In the earlier analysis of the cottage subcultures we noted the tendency for inmate leaders to be frequently identified as strong-arms, especially in the more custody-oriented cottages. Since black inmates were disproportionately leaders, it was not surprising that they were frequently described as exploiters.

The perception among white inmates that they were subject to exploitation by black inmates was widespread, and the relationship between black solidarity and white victimization was frequently noted. A "divide-and-conquer" situation was especially prominent: small groups of blacks dispossessed individual whites who were unable to draw as readily upon similar group supports. Black dominance was also manifest in the music played in the cottages, control of television program selections, and the like. Certain areas of the cottages, the ping-pong tables, and other facilities were also the preserves of black inmates, and whites were present only by sufferance. Just as the potential for violence was the unequalizer among inmates within the overall subculture, it was also the basis for inequality between black and white inmates.

Just as blacks were disproportionately overrepresented in the tougher leadership positions by virtue of collective solidarity and personal characteristics, they were correspondingly underrepresented in the lowest status roles. None of the lowest status punks or scapegoats were black. Even a black inmate who occupied a lower status position within the black subculture could still expect to prevail in his encounters with similarly situated low-status white inmates. As a consequence of their prior social experiences blacks presumably acquired the physical and verbal skills that resulted in their being overrepresented in the upper stratification roles, and collective racial solidarity assured that even the lower status black inmates were not as vulnerable to exploitation as their white counterparts.

Racial solidarity among black inmates was also manifest in the more treatment-oriented cottages that had managed to curb somewhat the more direct forms of physical aggression through formal collaboration. One inmate role we observed in the treatment-oriented settings was that of a "lawyer," who acted as a representative of and advocate for another inmate at community meetings or small-group meetings. To a considerable degree black inmates were more verbally skilled and adept than white inmates, and they typically occupied this role. As one treatment staff member suggested, "Most of the black kids come from the city where a premium is placed on hustling and quick talking." Another added, "Blacks are much better with language, they're more skilled in that type of interpersonal relationship."

As a consequence of their greater verbal facility, black inmates were more active and effective participants in the group process. As a crude indicator of participation, we coded the number of times that inmates spoke during the community meetings. Proportionately, black inmates spoke much more frequently than did the white inmates. Several treatment staff members confirmed this observation, noting, for example, "At community meetings, the black kids speak out more."

The lawyer role, as a reflection of racial solidarity, was both defensive and offensive. Black inmates would rally to the defense of other blacks when they were being challenged in a community meeting. An inmate in one of the treatment settings observed, "As soon as one of the blacks get put on the spot, there's a little segregation. The other black person is there to help him." We observed numerous instances of "advocates" intervening on behalf of their "clients," defending them and presenting their case.

Similarly, black inmates were also more likely to participate in and lead the interrogation of white inmates who were the subject of a community inquiry. To some extent many of the inmates in the treatment-oriented settings availed themselves of community meetings and the formal collaboration process as a means of social control in lieu of direct physical action. Black inmates were active participants in this process, especially when the target of their contributions was a white inmate. The greater participation by black inmates in the group discussions stemmed not only from their verbal facility, but also from their greater sense of collective security that enabled them to "dime drop" on white inmates without fear of retaliation. Because their participation was less subject to physical intimidation, black residents were active contributors to the treatment process.

Although our findings suggest that the effects of sex-role socialization appear to be somewhat more moderate than others have reported, race appears to be an important variable for distinguishing inmates by presenting culture. The reduced influence of sex-linked characteristics may stem from the relatively short period of incarceration involved. Even assuming that females have different affectional needs than males, it may be that in institutions with an average period of incarceration of only about three months, and with visiting access to the community after only six to eight weeks, that the degree of isolation necessary to trigger the sex-linked subcultural processes may not become manifest. In short, the particular problem of adjustment—isolation and removal of affectional supports—may not be sufficiently critical under these circumstances to produce the type of subcultural forms reported by others that distinguish females from males.

Race-linked characteristics appeared to have greater salience for subcultural articulation. The street experiences of black inmates prior to institutionalization had given them opportunities to develop physical prowess and verbal skills that their white counterparts had not developed to the same degree. To the extent that subculture stratification was based on these qualities, black inmates may have been disproportionately more likely to succeed within the inmate subculture. Moreover, the greater collective solidarity that blacks exhibited clearly reinforced their relative position within the subculture. As a consequence of these two processes—initial qualities plus collective solidarity—the relative overall position of black inmates within the subculture was superior to that of the white inmates.

Although these race-linked differences did not appear to significantly affect inmate attitudes or questionnaire responses, our observations and interviews clearly provide support for the significance of race as a variable of the presenting culture that modifies the functional explanation of subculture formation.

❋   Chapter 6

Outcome and Conclusions: Institutional Treatment and the Differences It Makes

In light of the extensive literature suggesting the absence of a relationship between the mode of treatment and the correctional outcome, we must question whether the differences we observed in cottage programs and subcultures were also reflected in attitudinal or behavioral differences among inmates. A second and related issue concerns whether cottage structural differences have any long-term implications for the reintegration of inmates into their communities after release.

To assess the immediate effects of program differences, we administered several attitudinal measures of deviant and conventional orientations. We also included some items measuring inmate self-perception and self-concept on the assumption that inmates who were victimized less or who participated in their own "rehabilitation" might feel less negatively about themselves. To assess the longer range effects of program differences, we analyzed six-month and one-year recidivism data.

Table 6-1 contains several scales that provide indicators of a "deviant" or "conventional" orientation. The scale "wrong people jailed" assesses perceptions of the legitimacy of the legal order by asking inmates whether they agreed that "many of the people in prisons are actually innocent of the crimes for which they were convicted" and "the biggest criminals are protected by society and rarely get to prison." We assume that those who accept the fairness and legitimacy of the system are more likely to be law-abiding than those who do not. As their responses indicate, residents in the custody-oriented settings were almost twice as likely as inmates in the treatment-oriented

Table 6–1. Deviant and Conventional Orientation (percentages)

Scale	Custody-Oriented Cottages					Treatment-Oriented Cottages			
	Group	Individual				Individual	Group		
	Cottage 9	Cottage 8	Elms	Westview	Lancaster (female)	Topsfield (co-ed)	Sunset	Shirley	"I Belong"
1. Wrong people jailed	43%	44%	48% [50]	62%	32%	20%	20%	38% [28]	25%
2. Manipulative exploitative orientation	48	47 [47]	56	35	51	20	33	44 [33]	13
3. Conventional orientation	22	13 [25]	28	28	11	33	40 [33]	25	38

settings to believe that the criminal justice system operates unfairly. The scale "manipulative-exploitative orientation" contains items such as " 'might is right' and 'everyman for himself' are the main rules for living," and "there are basically just two kinds of people in the world —those in the know and those who are suckers." Positive responses to these items suggest a cynical, exploitative, isolated individual willing to take advantage of others. We assume that the values implicit in these items are inconsistent with positive relationships with others and facilitate deviant behavior. The inmates in the custody-oriented settings were more likely to subscribe to these values than were the residents of the treatment-oriented settings.

While the second scale provides an indicator of "deviant" attitudes, the third scale identifies a "conventional orientation." Inmate agreements with such statements as "for the most part, justice gets done by the police and the courts" and "most people try to be honest and law-abiding" reflect a more conventional orientation that accepts the legitimacy of the criminal justice process and the efforts of citizens to conform. Consistent with the previous indicators, the residents of the treatment-oriented cottages were somewhat more likely to express a conventional orientation than were their custody-oriented counterparts.

In considering the three scales together, it appears that some short-term attitudinal differences may be related to the treatment modalities. Inmates in the custody-oriented settings manifested somewhat more deviant attitudes, expressing greater cynicism and manipulativeness and denying the legitimacy of the legal system. These inmates were housed in settings where exploitation and violence prevailed, and their adaptive strategies included physical withdrawal and isolation from their fellow inmates as well as covert deviance. Their physical and psychological isolation, coupled with their exploitative manipulativeness, may well reflect the anomic "war of all against all" in which they lived. Inmates in the treatment-oriented settings tended to be more well-integrated and involved with their fellows. Their enhanced contacts with staff and more positive perceptions of the institutions may be related to their somewhat greater likelihood to reject deviant or manipulative items and to respond favorably to more conventional ones. Although the differences by programs are small and the causal relationship between program and attitudes may be tenuous, some marginal differences among inmates may be associated with variations in the character of the subcultures.

We also presented the inmates with several items measuring self-perception and self-concept. These are reported in Table 6−2. The first item asked inmates to choose among a variety of statements

Table 6–2. Inmate Self-Concepts (percentages)

	Custody-Oriented Cottages				Treatment-Oriented Cottages			
	Group	Individual			Individual	Group		
	Cottage 9	Cottage 8	Elms	Westview	Lancaster (female)	Topsfield (co-ed)	Sunset	Shirley	"I Belong"
Boys who are here think different things about themselves. Check the statement that comes the closest to describing what you think about yourself:									
Someone who got a raw deal; someone who knows what the score is and how to play it cool; someone who doesn't let anyone push him around	48%	60%	45% [48]	45%	26%	7%	47%	38% [39]	29%
Someone with personal problems	26	7	13 [10]	7	13	27	20	13 [18]	29
Someone who is trying to straighten out	26	33	42 [43]	48	62	67	33	50 [42]	43
Scale: Negative Self-Concept	30%	33%	18% [23]	24%	25%	13%	13%	6% [13]	29%

that indicated differing self-images. The largest group in all the settings described themselves as people who were "trying to straighten out," and there were virtually no differences by treatment types. There were important differences, however, among the other self-descriptions. Inmates in the custody-oriented cottages were about 10 percent more likely than inmates in the treatment-oriented cottages to describe themselves as people who could not be pushed around, or who knew the score and played it cool. This variation may be related to the more extensive violence in the custodial subcultures where inmate concerns with exploitation predominated. Conversely, the inmates in the treatment-oriented settings, consistent with the nature of the programs, were more likely to describe themselves as people with personal problems.

We also presented inmates with several self-concept items, and constructed a scale of "negative self-concept" containing items such as "I sort of only half-believe in myself," and "I don't try to be friendly with people because I think they won't like me." The programs in the treatment-oriented settings appear to have been somewhat more successful in reducing negative self-images than were those in the custody-oriented settings. A plausible interpretation is that reduced victimization increases self-esteem. To the extent that a positive self-concept provides an insulator against deviance, we would expect the residents of treatment-oriented settings to experience a more successful readjustment to the community.

The inmates in the treatment-oriented settings were experiencing, then, if not more beneficial programs, at least less harmful ones. They were somewhat more likely to trust people and less likely to subscribe to deviant orientations than the inmates of the custody settings. They also had somewhat better perceptions of themselves. Although the overall differences among the several treatment programs were not great, they appear to be consistent with an interpretation that humane living experiences with reduced violence and exploitation engender more positive feelings about one's self and others.

An obvious question is whether these short-terms treatment differences are also reflected in long-term differences in adjustment in the community. We used recidivism data to assess the long-term effectiveness of a particular treatment program: does the offender get into trouble again following parole, and to what extent? Using recidivism data as an indicator of treatment outcome, however, poses several problems. It measures a program's effectiveness only indirectly, and may ultimately reflect factors such as changes in police practices or the exercise of prosecutorial discretion, over which a rehabilitation program has relatively little control. If, as the literature on "hidden delinquency" suggests, much delinquency goes undetected and unreported, and little if any initial difference exists between "official" delinquents and "hidden" delinquents, then recidivism rates may often reflect only the official responses to a known pool of suspects and the results of differential surveillance. Nonetheless, since recidivism continues to the primary indicator of the long-term effectiveness of penal measures, we report the results of our follow-up study as well.

Massachusetts has a centralized criminal record system administered by the Department of Probation. A single record indicates both juvenile and adult court appearances and dispositions. Access to such a centralized system is a great asset to evaluation research, but like most official record systems in constant daily use for making individual case decisions, it also poses special problems for research. It depends on the recording of essential data by each of seventy-two juvenile courts in the state, and is subject to any errors arising from lack of uniformity or completeness in court reporting to the central file. In addition, the centralized system is not yet computerized, and the sheer volume of records processed makes human error likely. Even with these reservations, the centralized system still yields the best estimates of criminal history available to us.

We used two criteria of recidivism: (1) any court appearance during a six-month period and also during a twelve-month period following release from a program; and (2) any court appearance within six months or twelve months after release that results in probation or recommitment disposition. The former criterion defines as a recidivist any youth who reappears in juvenile or adult court on any charges other than traffic offenses, with the most serious delinquent or criminal offense charged used for their classification. The latter criterion focuses on the disposition by the court, classifying as recidivists those youths whose dispositions entail restrictions on or losses of liberty—probation or recommitment to the Department of Youth Services or to an adult institution. The latter is a somewhat more conservative measure of recidivism since it emphasizes the extent to which a youth's repeated involvement in unlawful behavior requires at least some restriction on his or her liberty.

The results of these six-month and twelve-month follow-ups are contained in Table 6-3. As the cottage totals indicate, with the exception of a half-dozen missing cases, complete records were available. Unfortunately, those few inmates for whom no information could be obtained were residents of treatment-oriented cottages and their absence slightly distorts our results. Our analysis is based on the

Table 6–3. Percentage of Inmates Recidivating (percentages)

	Custody-Oriented Cottages					Treatment-Oriented Cottages			
	Group	Individual				Individual	Group		
Recidivism Criteria	Cottage 9	Cottage 8	Elms	Westview	Lancaster (female)	Topsfield (co-ed)	Sunset	Shirley	"I Belong"
1. Reappearance in court within:									
(a) 6 months	54%	53%	70% ⎤ [63]	59% ⎤	18%	8%	67% ⎤	50% ⎤ [50]	0%
(b) 12 months	58	67	75 ⎦ [72]	70 ⎦	27	25	84 ⎦	57 ⎦ [67]	33
2. Restriction on liberty disposition. Of those reappearing, percent receiving probation or recommitment:									
(a) 6 months	50	62	38	25	10	10	22	18	0
(b) 12 months	65	69	59	54	18	10	44	36	0
$N =$	26	15	40	27	49	12	15	14	6

available cases. Even if we assume that all the missing cases were recidivists, some substantial differences in inmate recidivism rates by treatment program still remain.

Using our first measure of inmate recidivism—a court reappearance within six months following parole—it appears that inmates released from custody-oriented programs were somewhat more likely to recidivate than those released from treatment-oriented programs. When inmates did recidivate, moreover, the former residents of custody-oriented settings were considerably more likely to reappear in court for more serious types of offenses—that is, those committed against the person—while the recidivists from the treatment-oriented programs were more likely to have been reinvolved in comparatively less serious property offenses. One further recidivistic difference is reflected in the reappearance rates of females as contrasted with males. Former residents of Lancaster and Topsfield had markedly lower reappearance rates, probably related to the initial status-offender bases for their institutional commitment. As a final observation, the overall recidivism rates for males and females using the criterion of court reappearance were similar to an earlier sample taken from the Department of Youth Services before 1968.

Twelve months after parole an even larger proportion of inmates had reappeared in court. While former residents of custody-oriented programs were still more likely to recidivate than were the residents of treatment-oriented settings, the differences were not as great as at six months, suggesting that the treatment-oriented programs retarded, but did not prevent, subsequent reinvolvement in delinquent or criminal activity. Significantly, however, the seriousness of the offense, as we observed earlier, was again greater for the former inmates of the custody-oriented settings. While the overall proportions of former residents of custody and treatment programs who reappeared in court were roughly similar, the inmates of custody-oriented programs were far more likely to be charged with serious offenses against the person than were those from the treatment-oriented programs. The sex-related differences also prevailed, with the female residents of Lancaster and Topsfield much less likely than males to make a court reappearance within one year. These one-year recidivism-reappearance rates were not dissimilar to the rates reported for a sample of inmates released in 1968, prior to Miller's arrival in Massachusetts.

When we examine our second, more conservative, measure of recidivism—court dispositions entailing some degree of restriction on liberty, either probation or recommitment to a juvenile or adult institution—the differences between the former residents of custody and treatment programs emerge more clearly. Within six months after release from the institutions, more than twice as many of the former residents of custody programs as treatment programs had experienced some subsequent court-imposed restriction on liberty. This same pattern prevailed after one year, although the magnitude of difference was not as great.

One explanation for the substantial program-recidivism differences relates to the seriousness of the offenses for which the inmates reappeared in court. Recidivating inmates who commit more serious offenses are correspondingly more likely to suffer greater restrictions on their liberty. To the extent that former residents of custody-oriented programs were more likely to have reappeared in court for more serious types of offenses, the greater restrictions on their liberty appear to follow. When these results are compared with those from the 1968 recidivism study, the residents of the treatment-oriented program appear to have experienced a somewhat lower rate of restrictions than did their 1968 counterparts, while the former residents of the custody-oriented programs experienced a somewhat higher rate. The female patterns of restrictions were similar in both samples.

In view of the generally negative findings on the outcomes of institutional treatment programs on subsequent recidivism, discretion counsels caution in interpreting these results. Our data and research design do not permit the attribution of a causal relationship between program type and recidivism. However, there does appear to be an association between the degree of custody and security to which an inmate was subjected and subsequent recidivism. The residents of the more custodial, secure programs also had greater and more serious reinvolvement in the juvenile and criminal justice systems than their counterparts in the more therapeutic, less-secure programs. Even after controlling for differences in inmate background characteristics and cottage population selection, the variations in inmate recidivism remain. This result is also consistent with findings from the other components of the Harvard study of the Massachusetts Department of Youth Services. These, too, suggest a relationship between the degree of security to which an inmate is subjected and his or her subsequent community readjustment.

CONCLUSIONS

Despite the experiment of the Massachusetts Department of Youth Services with deinstitutionalization and community-based treatment of most youthful offenders, it is likely that for the foreseeable future substantial numbers of young people and adults convicted of criminal behavior will be incarcerated in institutional settings. This study has examined alternative methods of handling youthful offenders in institutions. We believe the findings are instructive for a variety of juvenile and adult correctional policy issues.

When a society incarcerates people, whether for benevolent rehabilitation or any other purpose, it assumes a responsibility to do so under the least harmful and destructive circumstances, simply because they are human beings. Virtually every incarcerated juvenile will eventually return to the community, and it is imperative for both the community and the individual that the period of separation not be a source of harm, injury, or irreconcilable estrangement. We are legally and morally obliged to avoid inflicting additional pain and suffering on those whom we already punish through imprisonment.

This study has focused on institutional violence and the organizational features that exacerbate or mitigate it. Many inmates in the institutions came from cultural backgrounds where norms of exploitation, toughness, and aggression prevailed. Often their institutionalization was a cumulative result of these focal concerns, and acting in accordance with these norms placed them in conflict with societal interests. Institutionalization in custodial violence-based settings may actually reinforce these negative values rather than modify them. Failure to confront inmate violence may actually amplify the success of tough and exploitative behavior and lead to further maladjustment when inmates are released into the community.

A primary goal of correctional programs must be the maintenance of an organizational structure that minimizes physical and psychological brutalization and victimization. Predatory exploitation is antithetical to the lesson that institutions in a democratic society must teach, and the reduction in prison violence should be sought as an end in itself.

More fundamentally, violence degrades those who use it and destroys the potential of those who suffer it. Aggressors deny their victim's humanity and ultimately their own through their inability to empathize. Compassion and concern for others are, or certainly should be, social virtues; if so, "successful" inmates in violent settings will find themselves virtually disqualified from social participation by their institutional experiences.

Much has been written of the functional quality of the "inmate code," how it provides inmates with a normative basis for recouping lost status, self-respect, and material possessions by uniting in solidary opposition to staff. But one must ask, "Functional for whom?" The inmate code serves only the interests of the exploitative elite by sheltering their predation from staff scrutiny. It provides an ideological justification for the unrestrained exploitation of the bulk of inmates. While the victims derive nothing, their oppressors enjoy only limited relief from their own incarceration experiences, and then only at the cost of their own human qualities.

For the victim, institutional violence has more devastating consequences. Having one's property and personal possessions subject to expropriation is a considerable inconvenience if it only happens occasionally. The chronically victimized suffers even greater pains of imprisonment than others by virtue of relative deprivation. But for those inmates who become the targets of assaults and rapes, the loss of physical integrity is the ultimate victimization. These victims, apart from the physical pain, are without recourse or remedy, and the ensuing feelings of helplessness and futility can only have damaging consequences. Victims can either resist and become involved in an escalating cycle of violence, or they can acquiesce and thereby further assure their exploitation and the internalizing of their "loser" status.

The reduction of institutional violence should be sought as an end in itself because it is so destructive. As our research has indicated, the alleviation of violence may also have beneficial ancillary effects: the residents of the less violent programs had less negative self-concepts and somewhat better readjustment to the community. While we cannot ascribe a causal connection between the reduction of violence and the self-concept/recidivism findings, that they are somehow related is certainly plausible. Regardless of the ultimate impact on recidivism, however, constraining inmate violence for its own sake should be a priority of correctional programs.

To a greater extent than prior subculture studies, our findings suggest the institutional correlates of inmate violence. There clearly appears to be a relationship between the correctional organization and its programs and the inmate subculture that emerges. For better or worse, the social structure of the inmate subculture tends to parallel the structure and interaction processes of the formal organization. In the custodial settings, staff are situated within hierarchical bureaucracies, mere cogs within these authoritarian, antidemocratic settings. They deal with inmates impersonally, and are attuned to superficial aspects of external behavior such as conformity, deference, and demeanor. They use violence to control inmates, either themselves directly, as in the group custody settings, or indirectly through the informal co-optation of the aggressive inmate elite. The inmate subcultures are correspondingly violent, stratified on a hierarchical basis, and organized around exploitation and aggression. Institutional features give inmates incentives to exploit each other.

Inmate alienation from staff reduces staff knowledge about the workings of the inmate culture and precludes their effective control of inmate deviance and violence. In the face of chronic predatory behavior, an inmate emphasis on toughness and resisting manipulation reinforces the violent basis of subculture organization. The prevalence of violence within the subculture leads to authoritarian inmate relationships in which high-status inmates physically and psychologically dominate their inferiors, just as staff do inmates. A clear lesson to be drawn from the more custodial settings is the truism that "violence begets violence." All of the people in these settings—staff and inmates—were brutalized by their experience.

In treatment organizations, and especially in group treatment settings, the transition from authoritarian bureaucracies to more democratic treatment communities is reflected in a corresponding transformation of the subcultures. The staff-team model engenders far greater equality among staff members who participate in the change process. The problem-solving method carries over into their relationships with inmates, as reflected in efforts at persuasion rather than coercion.

The elimination of staff-inflicted violence reduces inmate alienation, and the problem-solving model provides an alternative basis for interaction among inmates. The point is not that group treatment is necessarily an optimal form of correctional therapy, but that a number of ancillary characteristics of group-treatment intervention promote organizational features with a salutary impact on subculture development. The subculture reflects the greater organizational democracy, with a substantial reduction in the levels of inmate violence, more positive inmate norms, and greater opportunities for more pro-social inmate roles to emerge.

Many of the correctional policy recommendations that follow from the structure-subculture relationships we have described have been made before. Prisons have been subjected to closer scrutiny than virtually any other organizational setting. Hopefully, however, the observations we make will receive greater credence by virtue of our theoretical explication of the organizational processes involved and the comparative data that supports our interpretation.

Correctional programs must be designed to pursue humane goals by humane means. A reduction in the institutional and staff brutalization of inmates is a necessary but not sufficient prerequisite. The wanton infliction of harm and injury has no place in a just and decent society. Our social institutions—including penal—must pursue the values of a democratic society. They may not succeed, but they will be less inevitably doomed to failure than authoritarian institutions that do not make a pretense of compassion or concern.

If organizations pursue humane goals, then staff recruitment and selection becomes problematical. As our analysis of staff ideology indicated, not all people are equally compatible with all types of programs. Custodial staff who hold essentially authoritarian beliefs are less likely to respond successfully within threatment-oriented organizations. The organizational demand that they deal with inmates in an open, tolerant manner is simply inconsistent with their basic world-view and personality orientation. During the Massachusetts experiment, we half-facetiously observed that we would not be able to rehabilitate the inmates until we had rehabilitated the more custodially oriented staff. Demographically, custodial staff were significantly older and less well educated than personnel in the treatment cottages. Maintaining a custodial program of supervision and perhaps some rudimentary vocational instruction does not place a premium on sophisticated, energetic staff.

At least as experienced in the Massachusetts Department of Youth Services, promoting inmate change through actively engaging staff and inmates in the same problem-solving group required better educated, highly committed and involved personnel. With training, many people who had previously served with the department and functioned in essentially custodial roles were able to restructure their prior roles and participate in a problem-solving setting. However, the use of such personnel in treatment settings was fraught with difficulties—there was always a danger of unconscious double messages emphasizing custodial over treatment concerns or even program subversion.

Analyzing staff ideology raises the issue of the extent to which people with a particular set of beliefs can realistically change their orientations, even with a major training effort. The correctional ideologies we described are part of a basic personality constellation that is also reflected in the way staff relate to their spouses, their own children, and others. It may be impractical, without a greater training investment than seems warranted, to expect staff with a heavy commitment to authoritarian beliefs to adapt readily to a democractic orientation and practice. There are too many inconsistencies and conflicts about fundamental assumptions of human nature and the process of change. Without deciding whether custodial or treatment beliefs are the better description of human nature, it is probably unrealistic and unproductive to attempt to retrain a person from one such orientation to another in order to work in a treatment-oriented setting. The magnitude of personal change is comparable to that of converting a juvenile who is well advanced in a delinquent career into a person committed to a more conventional orientation.

While it is important to select democratic personnel committed to pursuasion rather than coercion, it is critical that they be strong, limit-setting individuals. The discontinuation of the Topsfield program was partly the result of a lack of structure and limits set by staff. Just as inmates are able to manipulate other inmates verbally and by intimidation, many middle-class college-educated people are unprepared to confront and control inmates coming from a more aggressive lower-class background. Inmates in treatment programs often "ranked" and threatened staff in an effort to intimidate them and reduce staff controls. It takes a realistic and self-assured staff, secure in its own identity and purpose, committed to democratic values and the protection of inmates to simultaneously foster a democratic setting while maintaining adequate structure and security to cope with the more antisocial members of the program.

We have described two sets of potentially inconsistent orientations for personnel: "democratic humanism" and "structured realism." Yet from our observations, the programs that established and maintained positive inmate cultures contained both elements. They are an extraordinarily difficult set of demands to place on a staff and raise the danger of reviving the custody-treatment divisions often described in multiple-goal institutions. Structuring both acceptance and limits requires enormous energy. Eliciting and sustaining the balance between democracy and control requires a strong team leader, almost a charismatic figure, who can inspire the degree of staff commitment and investment that is required. It would be disingenuous to underemphasize the difficulties encountered in developing structured, democratic treatment programs. But it is also clear that there are compensatory returns on the investment in terms of inmate security and performance.

A wide range of program alternatives existed in the cottages we studied. Those that housed the more positive subcultures were also those that utilized the greatest diversity and richness of programs. As one moved across the cottage treatment continuum, there was a gradual increase in the variety of programs. The absence of programs in Cottage 9 was implicated in the levels of inmate deviance and violence in that setting. The focus solely on vocational education in the individual custody settings detracted from the potential effectiveness of such programs. Institutional maintenance and life support does not necessarily make a "program." The exploitation of inmate labor with little or no pretense for instruction does not foster the types of staff-inmate relations that might facilitate inmate change.

The treatment-oriented programs placed primary emphasis on group therapy strategies and cottage community meetings, which were supplemented by academic instruction or vocational training programs. The programs were useful for whatever skills might be acquired, and more importantly as a means to structure and vary the daily routine and establish more extensive interchanges between inmates and staff. The significance of institutional programs is probably determined less by the specific skills imparted than by the types of opportunities they afford for staff and inmate relationships. The substantive content of a program may be less important than the content of the exchanges between staff and inmates that mutual participation encourages.

To the extent that human change occurs in the context of structured relationships, it is the quality of the relationship rather than where it takes place that is crucial. Accordingly, staff-inmate ratios are important. The custodial settings had substantially larger inmate populations and poorer staff-inmate ratios than the treatment settings. Once the number of residents in a program rises above fifteen or twenty, problems of management, supervision, and security begin to take precedence. The most positive inmate culture we studied only had eight boys in residence. Favorable ratios and small populations are important for a variety of reasons: they maximize the inmates' opportunity for positive contacts with adults; they provide sufficient staff to support and reinforce the subculture without being overwhelmed by it; they limit the potential allies of oppositional inmates; and they provide a staff presence that assures the physical security of residents. Maintaining a favorable staff-inmate ratio is somewhat difficult, however, when joined with the suggestion that inmate populations be kept relatively low. It becomes increasingly difficult to maintain an adequate variety of programs and evening and weekend staff coverage for security once the number of inmates and staff drops below about a dozen.

The introduction of several different programs poses potential problems of conflict, coordination, and consistency. When developing programs, it should be clear what the goals of the setting are and how particular programs contribute to the attainment of these goals. While there may be several separate programs, they must be administered according to the same criteria to accomplish the same basic ends. Program consistency may be lost in multiple-departmental structures where disjointed activities take place in unconnected fashion.

The staff-team model is one mechanism for maintaining coordination and consistency. Regular staff meetings provide an obvious vehicle for coordination. The problems of administering and coordinating a diversity of programs create strains and conflicts that can be resolved by bringing the parties together. Moreover, in order to coordinate programs to serve the cottage's treatment goals, personnel in every program who have contact with an inmate should have the opportunity to make a contribution about the inmate's progress in their program. In addition to facilitating program coordination and the consistent monitoring of inmate change, staff meetings also assure staff accountability by allowing staff members to confront each other on their relationships with inmates and staff. Confrontation provides staff with the opportunity to resolve interpersonal grievances by using the same problem-solving techniques staff are teaching inmates. Moreover, confrontation and the ensuing clarification help to maintain a unified staff front in dealing with inmates. This consistency avoids the danger of "double messages" by different personnel and denies inmates the opportunity to play various staff groups off against each other to the detriment of program consistency.

Perhaps the most important single organizational feature distinguishing those settings with more positive cultures from those with less cooperative subcultures was the introduction of formal collaboration—the problem-solving model. Formal collaboration occasions a major shift in staff-inmate relations, with both participating as equal members of the same cottage community. We have noted the importance of collaboration for encouraging positive relationships between inmates and staff, facilitating the flow of information, and providing staff with greater access to and control over the activities of the inmate culture. Collaboration is the essential mechanism that allows staff to learn about and control inmate violence. Small-group therapy and formal collaboration in the community meeting contribute to a positive culture, not necessarily by "rehabilitating" inmates, but because as a by-product of these processes staff know more about the dynamics of the inmate group.

That inmates can successfully maintain pressure on other inmates to change in desirable directions is an underlying rationale of group treatment. This places a major burden on staff to support the positive aspects of the inmate culture. A favorable staff-inmate ratio, a high level of interaction, and knowledge of the group gained through formal collaboration enable staff to support the inmate group by insuring a continuous staff presence and awareness. Staff must be available to confront inmate deviance whenever it occurs and to reinforce inmate efforts at self-help.

Consistency in responding to every troublesome incident is an important aspect of a well-structured program. When an incident occurs and the staff people are informed, their failure to act in response implicitly tells inmates either that this type of behavior is condoned or that the inmates cannot rely upon staff to support them in combating it. Either message can destroy a positive subculture. The fundamental responsibility of staff is to provide every inmate with the security—physical and psychological—that he or she can safely participate in a positive manner. A cardinal rule of the more successful treatment cottages was "no physical violence." In the absence of adequate supervision and control, a subculture will quickly reorganize around the contrary proposition that "might makes right." To counter this, staff must respond to every situation in which an inmate is threatened, and thus create a structure within which the inmate can safely confront an attacker without fearing further retaliation.

Correctional institutions using formal collaboration in a democratic, egalitarian structure have a great additional virtue over more authoritarian custodial programs. To the extent that our society is based on values of a participatory democracy, correctional institutions that prepare inmates to return to their communities offer them an opportunity for democratic participation. The values of participation in the shaping of one's life, responsibility for one's own conduct and the conduct of other people, and internalization of controls are unlikely to be learned in authoritarian institutions that deny individuals responsibility for their actions.

Appendix

COTTAGE POPULATION COMPARABILITY

In selecting our cottage sample, we tried to match cottages on the basis of inmate background characteristics. In Chapter 1 we described the cottage population background characteristics. Here we describe the analyses that led us to relate subcultural variations to differences in the cottages' social structure rather than to variations in the characteristics of the inmate population itself.

This analysis of the influence of background variables on inmate attitudes is necessary because we cannot formally establish statistical comparability without a fully controlled random assignment of populations to the various cottage treatments. To the extent that differences in population are present in a nonrandomized design, our thesis that subcultural variation is a product of social structural variation is weakened. While matching groups on the basis of background characteristics may not conclusively establish cottage population similarity, it is the only means available for establishing comparability between groups already in existence. Despite the fact that matching can only establish weak comparability, an effort to maximize population similarities guided our initial selections of cottages.

We gathered information on a number of inmate background characteristics and used a variety of techniques to ascertain the degree of comparability among the various cottage groups. In addition to the direct comparison of cottage population characteristics described in Chapter 1, we also controlled for the effect of the background characteristic within cottage units and between cottage units and allowed for interaction effects between the background characteristics and the cottage treatment-type. We used these techniques to determine whether a particular background characteristic was associated with systematic differences within the population of a particular cottage or cottages and whether the differences between cottages appear to be a product of these population differences.

Previous studies indicate that the population characteristics that may influence the character of the inmate subculture include inmate age; race; the type of offenses committed; the initial age of involvement in criminal activity; and previous institutionalization. Since the relatively small sizes of our cottage populations only permitted us to control for the effects of one variable at a time, it was initially necessary to determine whether any relationships existed between the several background characteristics. We performed chi-square tests between inmates' present age, race, present criminal offense, and age of first contact with the juvenile court to determine whether there were any relationships between these variables. While there was an obvious and unsurprising association between an inmates' present age and age of first contact with the juvenile court ($p < .05$), there did not appear to be any relationship between an inmate's age and the type of crime for which he or she was committed ($p < .30$), or between the age of first contact with the juvenile court and the seriousness of the present offense for which the juvenile was committed ($p < .30$), or between an inmate's race and age of first contact with juvenile court ($p < .20$). Among the boys there was no relationship between race and the crime for which the inmate was presently committed ($p < .50$); but black females were underrepresented as "status offenders," suggesting a possible relationship between race and the offense for which the female inmates were committed ($p < .10$). (See Chapter 5, note 11, for a possible explanation of these disparities).

In light of the relative independence among the various background characteristics, we concluded that it would not weaken our statistical or theoretical arguments to be able to control for the effects of only one background variable at a time. The following analyses represent our efforts to identify or eliminate differences in population characteristics as plausible alternative explanations of the differences in subculture we are attributing to cottage treatment effects.

The primary characteristics we considered were inmate age, race, age of first contact with juvenile court, criminal offense patterns, and prior incarceration. By selecting the cottages as we did, we obtained a reasonably close approximation among the various cottage units on most of these dimensions. This also reinforces our observations regarding the nonselective basis of inmate cottage assignments.

In addition to comparing the cottages on these dimensions (see Chapter 1), we attempted to discover whether there was any relationship between a background factor and inmate attitudes or values. To test for any such relationships, we selected a number of questionnaire items and scales that discriminated between custody- and treatment-oriented cottages [1]. To ascertain the effects of background variables on attitudes, we analyzed the scores of inmates within a cottage on the various scales, comparing, for example, older and younger inmates, black and white inmates, and the like. We ran chi-square tests on each of the cottage subtables [2], hypothesizing that there were no differences within cottage populations due to background factors and employing a .10 significance criterion to minimize the possibility of Type II errors—failing to reject the hypothesis when it was actually false [3].

By using a .10 significance criterion rather than the more common .05 or .01, we deliberately "stacked the deck" against ourselves so as to avoid the possibility of mistakenly finding no background effects if some were actually present [4]. The small sample size in several of the cottages required that we take this additional precaution. Moreover, we combined theoretically related rows or columns whenever possible to increase the expected frequency of cells, and used a Fisher's exact test whenever appropriate.

Employing a .10 criterion, we expected significant results 10 percent of the time by chance alone. If there were any important relationships between background variables and inmate attitudes, we expected substantially more than 10 percent of the tests to be significant. Through this analysis, we felt confident in accepting our null-hypothesis that there was no relationship between inmate attitudes within the cottages and inmate age, age of first contact with juvenile court, criminal offense for which committed, or prior incarceration.

The hypothesis of no relationship between race and attitudes was rejected, since nearly 12 percent of the tables revealed a statistically significant association between race and attitudes. Because we found some differences between the races within the cottages, we analyzed further to ascertain whether the "treatment" differences that we found between custody and treatment cottages might be the result of racial composition within cottages rather than cottage structure influences.

For purposes of comparability, the racial make-up within the custody-oriented cottages and the treatment-oriented cottages was very similar, with 25.7 percent of the custody-oriented inmate population being black as compared with 25.0 percent of the treatment-oriented inmate populations (see Chapter 1, Table 1-2). We compared our overall cottage scores, or zero-order results, with the partial scores for blacks and whites across cottages, comparing the response patterns between the cottages for white and black inmates with the aggregate differences between the cottages. The results of this comparison allowed us to conclude that the differences we found between the cottages were not the result of differences in attitudes by race. This result was not surprising, since (1) the relative proportions of black and white inmates were fairly similar across cottages; (2) on the vast majority of variables, there were no significant differences between races; and (3) even where significant differences obtained, the magnitude of differences was usually not very large and clearly insufficient to account for the substantial custody/treatment differences. Thus, while the impact of race on subculture formation requires separate consideration (see Chapter 5), we may safely conclude that the differences obtained between the cottages are not the product of these racial differences.

In addition to testing for a relationship between background variable and attitude within each cottage, we also employed a sign test that allowed for interaction effects between these factors and the individual cottage treatment strategy. We assumed that if there were any interaction effect between a background variable and the cottage treatment technique that this relationship would be apparent in the patterns of signs among the cottages. We counted the number of instances when the same signs occurred within the custody or treatment cottages. Since the number of instances where similar signs across cottage treatment types obtained were less than the probability by chance alone, we felt safe in concluding that there was no interaction effect between cottage treatment strategy and the background variables.

As noted at the beginning of this appendix, in the absence of randomization it is difficult to establish statistically the equivalence of experimental groups already in existence. In this analysis we examined the possible influences of a number of background variables that might provide plausible alternative explanations for the cottage subculture variation we obtained. We tried to eliminate these explanations by examining differences within the groups on these dimensions. In virtually every instance we found that while there were substantial differences between the cottages, they could not be attributed to variations in the composition of inmate populations within the respective cottages. This reinforces our conclusions that the subcultural variations we obtained are properly attributed to the cottages' social structures rather than to differences in inmate characteristics.

SCALE CONSTRUCTION

We followed the protocols suggested by Edwards and others in constructing our summated scales [5]. We first established item discrimination by cross-tabulating cottages by the questionnaire items, and by selecting appropriate cutting points, we were able to determine if an item discriminated between the cottage types. We ran a chi-square test on this table for the limited purposes of establishing whether there were any differences between populations on a particular item. We were concerned only with whether an association was present and not with its nature or strength [6]. We also employed F-tests on the individual items as an additional strategy to identify differences between the cottages [7].

Having established item discrimination, we correlated the various discriminating items to identify interitem relationships. Although we did not use a factor-analysis program in scale construction, conceptually that was the process we employed. On the basis of the interitem correlations and the face content of the items, we constructed unidimensional scales. The interitem correlations of items summated into scales were all significant at a .05 level at least, and most were at .01 or .001 levels. The r^2 ranged between 0.25 and 0.8, with most scales made up of individual items which correlated in the 0.4 to 0.7 range.

Illustrative of this process is the scale "respect for authority" (Chapter 2, Table 2-1). The items included in this scale are: "Understanding may be important in helping delinquents but what is really needed is strictness and firmness"; "The trouble with delinquents is that they haven't learned to treat adults with respect and obedience"; "Obedience and respect for authority are the most important virtues children should learn"; and "Society is going to have to be a lot tougher than it has been if it is going to cut down on delinquency." The correlation matrix for the scale "respect for authority" is shown in Table A-1. This scale is typical of the face content relationship of items as well as their intercorrelation.

Table A-1. Correlation Matrix: Respect for Authority

	Item Number			
	1	2	3	4
1. Strictness and Firmness	—			
2. Don't Respect Adults	0.581[a]	—		
3. Obedience and Respect	0.678[a]	0.731[a]	—	
4. Society Get Tougher	0.672[a]	0.624[a]	0.727[a]	—

[a] Interitem correlation significant at .001.

Notes

NOTES TO CHAPTER 1

1. Gresham Sykes and Sheldon Messinger, "The Inmate Social System," *Theoretical Studies in Social Organization of the Prison* (New York: Social Science Research Council, 1960), n. 1; Sheldon Messinger, "Issues in the Study of the Social System of Prison Inmates," *Issues in Criminology* 4 (1970): n. 9; George Grosser, "The Role of Informal Inmate Groups in Change of Values," *Children* 5 (January–February 1958): 25; David Street, Robert Vinter, and Charles Perrow, *Organization for Treatment* (Glencoe, Ill.: Free Press, 1960), p. 223; George C. Homans, *The Human Group* (New York: Harcourt, Brace & World, 1950); Albert K. Cohen, *Delinquent Boys* (Glencoe, Ill.: Free Press, 1955); Bernard Berk, "Organizational Goals and Inmate Organization," *American Journal of Sociology* 71 (March 1966): 522–34; Howard Polsky, *Cottage Six* (New York: Wiley, 1962); Gresham Sykes, *Society of Captives* (Princeton, N.J.: Princeton University Press, 1958); Stanton Wheeler, "Socialization in Correctional Communities," *American Sociological Review* 26 (October 1961): 706–11.

2. John Irwin and Donald Cressey, "Thieves, Convicts, and the Inmate Subculture," *Social Problems* 10 (1962): 142; Rose Giallombardo, *The Social World of Imprisoned Girls* (New York: Wiley, 1974); Howard S. Becker and Blanche Geer, "Latent Culture: A Note on the Theory of Latent Social Roles," *Administrative Science Quarterly* 5 (September 1960): 305.

3. Clemens Bartollas, Stuart J. Miller, and Simon Dinitz, *Juvenile Victimization: The Institutional Paradox* (New York: Wiley, 1976); Polsky, *Cottage Six*; Albert K. Cohen, George F. Cole, and Robert G. Bailey, eds., *Prison Violence* (Lexington, Mass.: Lexington Books, 1976); Hans Toch, *Peacekeeping: Police, Prisons, and Violence* (Lexington, Mass.: Lexington Books, 1976).

4. Marvin Wolfgang and Franco Ferracuti, *The Subculture of Violence* (London: Methuen, 1967); Walter B. Miller, "The Lower Class Culture as a Generating Milieu of Gang Delinquency," *Social Issues* 14 (1958): 5.

5. Polsky, *Cottage Six*; George Grosser, "The Role of Informal Inmate Groups in Change of Values," *Children* 5 (January–February 1958): 25–29; Lloyd Ohlin and William Lawrence, "Social Interaction among Clients as a Treatment Problem," *Social Work* 4 (1959): 3.

6. We standardized the measurement instruments and observation techniques to facilitate cross-cottage comparisons. We also "triangulated" the data-gathering process, obtaining information from different sources bearing on the same issue, in order to enhance reliability. Norman K. Denzin, *The Research Act* (Chicago: Aldine, 1970). The Appendix includes a description of the methodology.

7. Edwin Powers, *The Basic Structure of the Administration of Criminal Justice in Massachusetts* (Boston: Massachusetts Correctional Association, 1968).

8. This progression of political crises and organizational change is described in greater detail by Lloyd Ohlin, Robert Coates, and Alden Miller, "Radical Correctional Reform: A Case Study of the Massachusetts Youth Correctional System," *Harvard Educational Review* 44 (1974): 74. See also Andrew Rutherford, *The Dissolution of the Training Schools in Massachusetts* (Columbus, Ohio: Academy for Contemporary Problems, 1974).

9. See, e.g., Maxwell Jones, *Beyond the Therapeutic Community: Social Learning and Social Psychiatry* (New Haven: Yale University Press, 1968); *Social Psychiatry in Practice: The Idea of the Therapeutic Communities* (London: Tavistock Publishing Co., 1952). Miller was exposed to Jones's work while developing treatment programs in England and distributed excerpts from his works to the staff. Jones was also brought in as a consultant to discuss his research and its programmatic implications.

10. The process of organizational change at Lancaster is described in greater detail by Frederick Thatcher, "Effecting Changes in a Training School for Girls," in Yitzhak Bakal, ed., *Closing Correctional Institutions* (Lexington, Mass.: Lexington Books, 1973).

11. In March 1971 Miller closed the John Augustus Hall facility at Oakdale, Massachusetts, a residence for boys from seven to twelve years of age who were committed to DYS as delinquents. Miller was strongly opposed to institutionalizing boys this young, and he pursued a number of alternatives. He began closing Oakdale at about the same time he began closing the Industrial School at Shirley. He sought foster homes and other noninstitutional placements for as many youngsters as possible. The group of younger boys for whom placements could not be arranged took up residence in one of the vacant cottages on the grounds of Lancaster. Their presence generated a number of program alternatives for the girls in the institution. Several girls became involved with them as child-care workers or helping with food preparation and the like. One honor cottage was opened for girls who could handle additional freedom, and they provided services for these boys, working with them part of the day as well as participating in a cottage treatment program.

12. Donald T. Campbell and Julian C. Stanley, *Experimental and Quasi-Experimental Designs for Research* (Chicago: Rand McNally, 1963), p. 12.

13. Ibid., p. 14. Campbell and Stanley note that the static-group comparison is:

> [a] correlational design of very weak form, implying as it does the comparison of but two natural units, differing not only in the presence and absence of X [the experimental treatment], but also in innumerable other attributes. Each of these other attributes could create differences in the Os [outcomes], and each therefore provide a plausible rival hypothesis to the hypothesis that X had an effect. We are left with a general rule that the differences between two natural objects are uninterpretable. Consider now this comparison expanded so that we have numerous independent natural instances of X and numerous ones of no-X, and concomitant differences in O. Insofar as the natural instances of X vary among each other in their other attributes, these other attributes become less plausible as rival hypotheses.

14. Campbell and Stanley (ibid., pp. 70–71) note that one serious problem of this approach is the possibility that the determinants of exposure to the experimental treatment may also be the determinants of the outcome even without the experimental treatment; that is, that the matching variables are correlated in the same direction with both the experimental treatment and the outcome. Thus, as will be seen, there are somewhat more criminally sophisticated inmates in custody cottages than in treatment cottages. It is therefore necessary to determine whether the same bias that consigns some inmates to custodial cottages is also the same variable that determines the cottage treatment effect outcome. A second weakness of matching is that self-selection for exposure or nonexposure to a treatment is also a product of numerous antecedents, including many other determinants besides the background variables we consider. There is the possibility that these factors will have an effect on outcome independent of the experimental treatment. (For a general discussion of the problems of "undermatching," see ibid., pp. 70–71). However, one saving feature of this design is that with a sufficiently large number of units it is possible to reduce the plausibility of rival alternative hypotheses.

15. With the exception of Cottage 9, a boy's assignment to a cottage was considered permanent and, particularly after institutional decentralization, there was considerable reluctance to change cottage placements. The most common type of dropping out occurred when a boy ran away from the institution. Obviously, differential runaway rates create some potential sources of population bias within the cottages. Although running away was a relatively frequent occurrence, it was not a major source of population bias. Although the number of boys who at some point run away from an institution exceeds 50 percent, the number of successful runaways is low, even when as crude a measure of "success" as one week of freedom before recapture is employed. Most boys are apprehended within hours of their flight.

With the exception of "I Belong," which excluded runaways from the cottage, and Cottage 9, which was the primary repository for Industrial School runaways, in all of the other institutions and cottages runaways were almost invariably returned to the cottages from which they ran, usually after a brief period of incarceration in a disciplinary cottage. Moreover, when boys ran away they generally did so fairly soon after their arrival at the cottage. Our normal practice was to wait about a week before interviewing new inmates. Thus, several runaways simply eliminated themselves from our prospective sample at one point, only to reenter it at a later time.

16. Raymond L. Gold, "Roles in Sociological Field Observation," *Social Forces* 36 (March 1958): 219.

17. To give one example of this "testing," three days after our arrival in one cottage, a boy told us that he had had sexual relations with a girl from a nearby cottage. The encounter was described in considerable detail. Needless to say, if true it would constitute a violation of several school rules. Several weeks later the same boy told us that he had not been involved as he had previously claimed, but that he was testing us to see whether or not we would tell the staff of the incident.

18. In most of our analyses of the effects of race we found it necessary for statistical purposes to combine the scores of black inmates and Spanish-surnamed inmates. There were only six Spanish-surnamed inmates in our sample, and Elms was the only cottage that contained more than one. We believed that as a minority group, their previous social experiences were closer to those of black inmates than to those of whites. Based on our observations, we found that inmates tended to segregate themselves on the basis of race, with Spanish-surnamed inmates more likely to associate with black inmates than with whites. We have therefore included the Spanish-surnamed group in the black category.

19. The property-related offenses for males and the juvenile status offenses for females are characteristic bases of institutional commitment. In addition to comparing the current offenses for which the inmates were committed, we also checked the institutional records to obtain a measure of the range of offenses they committed, recording the number and types of offenses of which each was charged or convicted. In the course of a delinquent career a juvenile may commit a number of different offenses, and there is considerable similarity between the patterns of violations by inmates in the treatment cottages and in the custody cottages. Property-related offenses dominate the boys' records, and juvenile status offenses mark the girls'. While the boys in the treatment cottages also had a greater number of juvenile status offenses than their custody-oriented counterparts, this may be somewhat misleading since prosecutors and courts sometimes use admissions or pleas to these offenses to mask more serious charges.

Another strategy we used to compare the criminal characteristics of the populations we studied was a self-reported measure of offenses. Self-reports have been found to give a very different picture of offense patterns than those based on official reports. See Lamar Empey and Maynard Erickson, "Hidden Delinquency and Social Status," *Social Forces* 44 (1966): 45; Jay Williams and Martin Gold, "From Delinquent Behavior to Official Delinquency," *Social Problems* 20 (1972): 209; Ivan Nye, James Short, Jr. and V.J. Olson, "Socioeconomic Status and Delinquent Behavior," *American Journal of Sociology* 63 (1958): 381.

We asked the inmates the types of behavior in which they normally engaged that could get them into trouble with the law, rather than behavior for which they had necessarily been arrested or adjudicated delinquent. This dramatically changed their patterns of offenses. Drug usage is much more widespread than either the official offense history or the offense of current commitment would suggest. There is also substantially less "serious" criminality as "normal" activity. One expects serious offenders to be overrepresented in an inmate sample because, while one may only occasionally commit a serious crime, the likelihood of apprehension may be greater and commitment following adjudication more common than is the case for minor offenses. See Jay Williams and Martin Gold, "From Delinquent Behavior to Official Delinquency," *Social Problems* 20 (1972): 209. There is a marked presence of "serious" offenders in Elms Cottage and some skewing of serious offenders in the custody-oriented cottages. Despite these tendencies, property and automobile offenses remain the male pattern, augmented by "hidden" drug usage. Drug usage also augments the status offense as the "hidden" female delinquent pattern.

A different pattern of offenses emerged from the institutional records for the female residents, with girls committed almost exclusively for juvenile status offenses and further implicated in "hidden" drug offenses. These differences in offense patterns probably reflect sex-linked cultural and socialization experiences as well as the sexist paternalism present in the administration of juvenile justice and the application of a double standard of sexual conduct to "girls who act like women."

In summary, while there are some differences between the custody cottage inmates and the treatment cottage inmates in terms of the offenses for which they are presently committed, when their overall criminal histories and self-reported offense patterns are considered, many of the differences become less important. As a minimum, when considering all of the offense measures we employed—offenses for which currently committed, all offenses contained in official institutional records, and self-reported offenses—one is struck by the extent to which the inmates' criminal histories and offense patterns overlap.

20. In this study we found that on the average, more than half the residents ran away from the institution at some point. This finding is consistent with the results of a 1970 survey conducted by the Harvard Center for Criminal Justice, which found that at one time or another nearly 60 percent of the inmates had run away from the institutions. Moreover, studies of absenting suggest that absconders are no different from other residents, and that running away is more likely a product of institutional factors than of individual differences.

In a major study of institutional runaways, R.V.G. Clarke and D.N. Martin, *Absconding from Approved Schools* (London: Her Majesty's Stationary Office, 1971), p. 16, found that training school runaways were more likely to have also run from other institutions, and the more often they have run before, the more likely they are to do so again. The background factor most powerfully related to running away appeared to be the number of previous runs. Clarke and Martin also report:

> contrary to expectation, a view of absconding which emphasized the nature of the school environment was better supported by the findings than one which stressed individual differences. Many associations between environmental variables and absconding were demonstrated, but absconders

appear to differ little from other boys in home background and personal history, in personality, and in attitudes. Further, there appeared to be a learned habitual element in persistent abscondings.

NOTES TO CHAPTER 2

1. See David Street, Robert Vinter, and Charles Perrow, *Organization for Treatment* (New York: Free Press, 1966); Oscar Grusky, "Organizational Goals and Behavior of Informal Leaders," *American Journal of Sociology* 56 (1959): 59; Bernard Berk, "Organizational Goals and Inmate Organization," *American Journal of Sociology* 71 (1966): 522; Donald R. Cressey, "Prison Organization," in J. March, ed., *Handbook of Organizations* (Chicago: Rand McNally, 1965).

2. Elliot Studt, Sheldon L. Messinger, and Thomas P. Wilson, *C—Unit: Search for Community in Prison* (New York: Russell Sage Foundation, 1968).

3. Street, Vinter, and Perrow, *Organization for Treatment.*

4. Lloyd E. Ohlin, "Organizational Reform in Correctional Agencies," in Daniel Glaser, ed., *Handbook of Criminology* (Chicago: Rand McNally, 1974).

5. See David J. Rothman, *The Discovery of the Asylum* (Boston: Little, Brown, 1971); Sanford Fox, "Juvenile Justice Reform: An Historical Perspective," *Stanford Law Review* 22 (June 1970): 1187; Robert S. Pickett, *The New York House of Refuge: 1825—1857* (1969). Although the assumptions of delinquency etiology varied, including both free will and environmental corruption, the correctional response of incarceration within structured, authoritarian total institutions was the same. Also see Anthony Platt, *The Childsavers* (Chicago: University of Chicago Press, 1969); Seymour L. Halleck, *Psychiatry and the Dilemmas of Crime: A Study of Causes, Punishment and Treatment* (New York: Harper & Row, 1967); Roy Lubove, *The Professional Altruist: The Emergence of Social Work as a Career 1880—1930* (Cambridge, Mass.: Harvard University Press, 1971); Dorwin Cartwright, "Achieving Change in People: Some Applications of Group Dynamics Theory," *Human Relations* 4 (1951): 381; Donald Cressey, "Changing Criminals: The Application of the Theory of Differential Association," *American Journal of Sociology* 61 (1955): 116; James F. Short, Jr. and Fred L. Strodtbeck, *Group Process and Gang Delinquency* (Chicago: University of Chicago Press, 1965).

6. The protocols we followed in constructing the summated scales are described in the Appendix.

7. Erving Goffman, "On the Characteristics of Total Institutions," in *Asylums*, p. 78; Street, Vinter, and Perrow, *Organization for Treatment*, p. 18. Such occupational ideologies have a variety of organizational functions. An ideology may guide organizational behavior by providing a short-hand device for decision-making and for communicating the bases of decisions to others. V. Thompson, *Bureaucracy and Innovation* (University of Alabama Press, 1969), p. 7; Aaron Cicourel, *The Social Organization of Juvenile Justice* (New York: Wiley, 1968). It may also furnish standards for evaluating the activities of the organization. By rationalizing and explaining the appropriate kinds of organizational behavior, it may provide a tool for boosting internal morale. By providing a common outlook and vocabulary for dealing with recurrent organizational problems, it may

enhance organizational effectiveness through a shared understanding of the organization's objectives. Not only may shared understanding reduce the level of intraorganizational conflict, but it may also allow the organization to recruit and socialize individuals whose beliefs will be consistent with the objectives of the organization. Ideology may also reduce the levels of conflict between participants at difference levels within the organization. Such consensus allows supervisors to delegate greater discretion to subordinates because of the common perspectives governing the manner in which such discretion will be organized. J. Price, *Organizational Effectiveness*, p. 104. D. Katz and R. Kahn, *The Social Psychology of Organizations* (New York: Wiley, 1966), p. 55, summarizing the functions of an organizational ideology, note that it has the general function of tying people into the system so that they remain within it and carry out their role assignments. The more specific functions are twofold: (1) system norms and ideology furnish cognitive maps for members, which facilitate their work in the system and their adjustment to it; and (2) norms and ideology provide the moral or social justifications for systems activities both for members and for people formally outside the system.

8. A. Strauss, L. Schatzman, R. Bucher, D. Erlich, and M. Sabshin, *Psychiatric Ideologies and Institutions* (New York: Free Press, 1964), p. 8; Amitai Etzioni, *Comparative Analysis of Complex Organizations*, p. 72. Over a period of time, the relationship between staff ideology and organizational goals results in a relatively homogenous belief system. This relationship arises because one requisite of a stable and effective organization is that its members subscribe to an ideology about the organization that supports the organization's policies. Also see Street, Vinter, and Perrow, *Organization for Treatment*. A number of factors operate to generate relatively consistent and homogenous beliefs among staff, including: the basic role definitions of the task; organizational indoctrination; socialization experiences associated with the work; the self-recruitment of individuals who are compatible with the preexisting organizational ideology; and selective turnover of personnel. Self-selection and selective recruitment of personnel whose beliefs are consistent with the organization's goals will increase ideological and goal consensus. Once personnel are within the system, an indoctrination program or socialization experience will increase ideological homogeneity.

9. Amitai Etzioni, *Comparative Analysis of Complex Organizations*. His definition of compliance as "a relation in which an actor behaves in accordance with a directive supported by another actor's power, and to the orientation of the subordinated actor to the power applied" (p. 3) highlights the relationships between control techniques and the subject's reactions to them. Etzioni described three mechanisms for obtaining organizational compliance—coercive, remunerative, and normative power. All three types of control are used in correctional settings, although coercive and normative-coercive controls predominate. The types of compliance mechanisms used relate to the goals that the organization pursues; where order goals are pursued, coercive controls are employed; where cultural goals are pursued, normative or normative-coercive controls are employed (pp. 72–73). Organizations pursuing order or cultural goals correspond to our distinctions between custody and treatment goals, permitting us to

compare social-control strategies in different settings. Coercive power is exercised in organizations with order as a major goal. Coercive power, which rests on physical control, should be distinguished from normative power, which "rests on the allocation and manipulation of symbolic rewards and deprivations through employment of leaders, manipulation of mass media, allocation of esteem and prestige symbols, administration of ritual, and influence over the distribution of 'acceptance' and 'positive response'" (p. 5). Even though normative organizations prefer to rely upon internalization and commitment by participants, some secondary coercive control such as transfer to a secure setting or a loss of privileges are often necessary. The responses of those subjected to coercive or normative controls differ, with the former tending to produce alienation and the latter tending to generate commitment.

10. Erving Goffman, "On the Characteristics of Total Institutions," in *Asylums*, pp. 48—50, notes:

> The inmate begins to receive formal and informal instruction in what will here be called the privilege system.... First, there are the "house rules," a relatively explicit and formal set of prescriptions and proscriptions that lays out the main requirements of inmate conduct.... Secondly, against this stark background a small number of clearly defined rewards or privileges are held out in exchange for obedience to staff in action and spirit. ... The third element in the privilege system is punishments; these are designated as the consequences of breaking the rules. One set of these punishments consists of the temporary or permanent withdrawal of privileges....

11. Richard Cloward, "Social Control in the Prison," in *Theoretical Studies in Social Organization of the Prison* (New York: Social Science Research Council, 1960). Cloward describes one way in which this process occurs. He notes that the two primary groups in the prison—custodians and inmates—seek, respectively, social order and escape from deprivations. The custodian employs coercion and inducement, force and incentive to secure order from the inmates, but "in the absence of absolute force, the prisoner must be led to share in the process of social control." He suggests that disruptive behavior is ameliorated by guards by providing access to illegitimate means whereby the prisoners can reduce their deprivations. "The official system accommodates to the inmate system in ways that have the consequence of creating illegitimate opportunity structures." To some extent the guards can determine which prisoners will have access to these opportunities, and in turn these prisoners maintain order for the guards as a means of protecting their own privileged positions. This occurs, Cloward reasons, because "certain prisoners, as they become upwardly mobile in these structures, tend to become progressively conservative.... Seeking to entrench their relative advantage over other inmates, they are anxious to suppress any behavior that might disturb the present arrangements."

This process described by Cloward is also consistent with the suggestions of Richard McCleery, in his "Communication Patterns as Bases of Systems of Authority and Power," in *Theoretical Studies in Social Organization of the Prison*; as well as with Gresham Sykes, *Society of Captives* (Princeton, N.J.: Princeton University Press, 1958), p. 61. Sykes writes that the guards must rely on the inmates to maintain order because of the "lack of a sense of duty among those who are held captive, the obvious fallacies of coercion, the pathetic collection of rewards and punishments to induce compliance, the strong pressures toward the corruption of the guard in the form of friendship, reciprocity, and the transfer of duties into the hands of trusted inmates—all are structural defects in the prison's system of power rather than individual inadequacies." See also, Sykes, "The Corruption of Authority and Rehabilitation," *Social Forces* 34 (1955): 257-62.

12. See, e.g., Don Gibbons, *Changing the Lawbreaker: The Treatment of Delinquents and Criminals* (Englewood Cliffs, N.J.: Prentice-Hall, 1965), p. 150, for the distinctions between individual therapy in a group setting and "true" group therapy designed to change the character of the group rather than the individual.

13. Charles Perrow, "Reality Adjustment: A Young Institution Settles for Humane Care," *Social Problems* 13 (1966): 69-79.

NOTES TO CHAPTER 3

1. Gresham Sykes and Sheldon Messinger, "The Inmate Social System," in *Theoretical Studies in Social Organization of the Prison* (New York: Social Science Research Council, 1960), n. 1; Sheldon Messinger, "Issues in the Study of the Social System of Prison Inmates," in *Issues of Criminology* 4 (1970): n. 9; George Grosser, "The Role of Informal Inmate Groups in Change of Values," *Children* 5 (January-February 1958): David Street, Robert Vinter, and Charles Perrow, *Organization for Treatment* (New York: Free Press, 1960), p. 223; George C. Homans, *The Human Group* (New York: Harcourt, Brace & World, 1960); Albert K. Cohen, *Delinquent Boys* (New York: Free Press, 1955); Bernard Berk, "Organizational Goals and Inmate Organization," *American Journal of Sociology* 71 (March 1966): 522-34.

2. Sykes and Messinger, "The Inmate Social System"; Lloyd Ohlin, *Sociology and the Field of Corrections* (New York: Russell Sage Foundation, 1956); Gresham Sykes, *Society of Captives* (Princeton, N.J.: Princeton University Press, 1958); Richard Cloward, "Social Control in the Prison," in *Theoretical Studies in Social Organization of the Prison*.

3. Sykes and Messinger, "The Inmate Social System"; Richard McCleery, "The Governmental Process and Informal Social Control," in *The Prison*, Donald Cressey, ed., (New York: Holt, Rinehart, & Winston, 1961); Gresham Sykes, "The Corruption of Authority and Rehabilitation," *Social Forces* 34 (1956); 257-62; Cloward, "Social Control in the Prison"; Lloyd McCorkle and Richard Korn, "Resocialization Within Walls," *The Annals* 293 (1956): 88; Norman Hayner and Ellis Ash, "The Prisoner Community as a Social Group," *American Sociological Review* 4 (1939): 362.

4. Gresham Sykes, "The Corruption of Authority and Rehabilitation"; Hayner and Ash, "The Prisoner Community as a Social Group"; Cloward, "Social Control in the Prison"; McCorkle and Korn, "Resocialization Within Walls."

5. Hayner and Ash, "The Prisoner Community as a Social Group," p. 362; Donald Clemmer, *The Prison Community* (New York: Holt, Rinehart & Winston, 1958), p. 299.

6. Stanton Wheeler, "Socialization in Correctional Communities," *American Sociological Review* 26 (October 1961): 706–11; Peter Garabedian, "Social Roles and Processes of Socialization in the Prison Community," *Social Problems* 11 (Fall 1963): 139–52; Daniel Glaser, *The Effectiveness of a Prison and Parole System* (Indianapolis: Bobbs-Merrill, 1964).

7. Street, Vinter, and Perrow, *Organization for Treatment*; Oscar Grusky, "Organizational Goals and Behavior of Informal Leaders," *American Journal of Sociology* 65 (1959): 59; Bernard Berk, "Organizational Goals and Inmate Organization," *American Journal of Sociology* 71 (1966): 522.

8. Street, Vinter, and Perrow, *Organization for Treatment*; and see, e.g., Rose Giallombardo, *The Social World of Imprisoned Girls* (1974), p. 9.

9. Arnold M. Rose and George H. Weber, "Changes in Attitudes Among Delinquent Boys Committed to Open and Closed Institutions," *Journal of Criminal Law, Criminology & Police Science* 62 (July 1961): 166–77; Howard Polsky, *Cottage Six* (New York: Wiley, 1958); George Grosser, "The Role of Informal Inmate Groups in Change of Values," *Children* 5 (1958): 28; Gordon Barker and W. Thomas Adams, "Social Structure of a Correctional Institution," *Journal of Criminal Law, Criminology & Police Science* 49 (1959): 417. All lend support to the solidary opposition model of inmate cultures in juvenile correctional settings.

10. Howard S. Becker and Blanche Geer, "Latent Culture: A Note on the Theory of Latent Social Roles," *Administrative Science Quarterly* 5 (September 1960): 305.

11. In studies of women's prisons, the latent culture is that of the sex roles defined by the larger society. See, e.g., David A. Ward and Gene G. Kassebaum, *Women's Prison: Sex and Social Structure* (Chicago: Aldine, 1965); Rose Giallombardo, *Society of Women* (New York: Wiley, 1966); Rose Giallombardo, *The Social World of Imprisoned Girls*.

12. John Irwin and Donald Cressey, "Thieves, Convicts and the Inmate Subculture," *Social Problems* 10 (1962): 142.

13. Julian Roebuck, "A Critique of 'Thieves, Convicts and the Inmate Subculture,'" *Social Problems* 11 (1963): 193.

NOTES TO CHAPTER 4

1. Howard Polsky, *Cottage Six* (New York: Wiley, 1962), p. 57.

2. Marvin Wolfgang and Franco Ferracuti, *The Subculture of Violence* (London: Methuen, 1967); Franco Ferracuti and Graeme Newman, "Assaultive Offenses," in D. Glaser, ed., *Handbook of Criminology* (Chicago: Rand McNally, 1974); Walter Miller, "The Lower Class Culture as a Generating Milieu of Gang Delinquency," *Journal of Social Issues* 14 (1958): 5.

3. Polsky, *Cottage Six*, p. 59.

4. Gresham Sykes and David Matza, "Techniques of Neutralization: A Theory of Delinquency," *American Journal of Sociology* 22 (1957): 664.

5. Polsky, *Cottage Six*, p. 62. David Matza, *Delinquency and Drift* (New York: Wiley, 1964), p. 43, describes the same process as "sounding," which entails an "imputation of negative characteristics . . . [wherein the recipient] concurs with the perpetrator in the negative evaluation of the substance of the remark." This process of verbal denigration is prevalent in female inmate interactions as well. See, e.g., Giallombardo, *Society of Women* (New York: Wiley, 1966).

6. See, e.g., Lloyd Ohlin, *Sociology and the Field of Corrections* (New York: Russell Sage Foundation, 1956); Gresham Sykes and Sheldon Messinger, "The Inmate Social System," in *Theoretical Studies in Social Organization of the Prison* (New York: Social Science Research Council, 1960).

7. Richard McCleery, "Communication Patterns as Bases of Systems of Authority and Power," in *Theoretical Studies in Social Organization of the Prison*; "The Governmental Process and Informal Social Control," in D. Cressey, ed., *The Prison* (New York: Holt, Rinehart, & Winston, 1961).

8. Arnold M. Rose, *Sociology: The Study of Human Relations*, 2nd ed. (New York: Alfred A. Knopf, 1965), p. 730.

9. A number of scholars have studied inmate roles in the subcultures of prisons. They conclude that "conformity to, or deviation from, the inmate code is the major basis for classifying and describing the social relations of prisoners." Gresham Sykes and Sheldon Messinger, "The Inmate Social System," in *Theoretical Studies in Social Organization of the Prison*, p. 3. See also Ohlin, *Sociology and the Field of Corrections*; and Gresham Sykes, *Society of Captives* (Princeton, N.J.: Princeton University Press, 1958).

10. Polsky, *Cottage Six*, pp. 75–84.

11. To determine to what extent the inmate leaders set the tone of the cultures, we compared their responses with the responses of nonleaders in a cottage. See, e.g., Oscar Grusky, "Organizational Goals and Behavior of Informal Leaders," *American Journal of Sociology* 65 (1959): 59; Bernard Berk, "Organizational Goals and Inmate Organization," *American Journal of Sociology* 71 (1966): 522. There was some tendency for inmate leaders to be more negative and oppositional than nonleaders in the custody-oriented settings, while they tended to be somewhat more positive than nonleaders in the treatment-oriented settings. However, very few of the intracottage differences between leaders and nonleaders were significant, although they were generally in the predicted directions. The small sample sizes influenced these results as well.

12. Polsky, *Cottage Six*, p. 79, provides the best description of this role within the subcultures of juvenile institutions.

13. Miller, "The Lower Class Culture as a Generating Milieu of Gang Delinquency," p. 5, also notes the emphasis on verbal skills as one of the focal concerns characteristic of the lower class communities he observed.

14. Polsky, *Cottage Six*, p. 31.

15. John Irwin and Donald Cressey, "Thieves, Convicts, and the Inmate Culture," *Social Problems* 10 (1962): 142.

16. Polsky, *Cottage Six*, pp. 81–82.

17. Ibid., pp. 82–84.

18. Susan Brownmiller, *Against Our Will: Men, Women, and Rape* (New York: Simon & Shuster, 1975), pp. 285−97. Her analysis of rape, heterosexual or homosexual, not as an act of lust but of power, violence, and subjugation is consistent with our own observations within the violence-based inmate cultures. Ms. Brownmiller's analysis of prison rape corroborates our own interpretation that it is "an acting out of power roles within an all-male authoritarian environment in which the younger, weaker inmate . . . is forced to play the role that in the outside world is assigned to women." She further argues, at 296, that prison rapes are not a response to deprivations of heterosexual contacts, but reflect "the need of some men to prove their mastery through physical and sexual assault, and to establish, most strikingly within the special crucible of the male-violent, a coercive hierarchy of the strong on top of the weak." Every incident of sexual exploitation involved high status inmates intimidating and coercing the lowest status residents of their cottages. Since an inmate's race was associated with status and black inmates tended to predominate within the subculture, the homosexual encounters we documented disproportionately involved black inmates exploiting low status white inmates. This observation is also corroborated by Ms. Brownmiller at 294, where she notes that "It is 'safer' for a member of a powerful majority group, in this case the prison blacks, to aggress against a weak minority group, in this case the prison whites."

19. See, e.g., David Ward and Gene Kassebaum, *Women's Prison* (Chicago: Aldine, 1965); Rose Giallombardo, *Society of Women* (New York: Wiley, 1966), and *Social World of Imprisoned Girls* (New York: Wiley, 1974); Esther Heffernan, *Making It in Prison: The Square, The Cool, and The Life* (New York: Wiley, 1972); Thomas W. Foster, "Make Believe Families: A Response of Women and Girls to the Deprivations of Imprisonment," *International Journal of Criminology and Penology* 3 (1975): 71.

20. Barbara Carter, "Reform School Families," *Society* 11 (November−December 1973): 36.

NOTES TO CHAPTER 5

1. See, e.g., David Ward and Gene Kassebaum, *Women's Prison* (Chicago: Aldine, 1965); Rose Giallombardo, *Society of Women* (New York: Wiley, 1966), and *Social World of Imprisoned Girls* (New York: Wiley, 1974); Esther Heffernan, *Making It in Prison: The Square, The Cool, and The Life* (New York: Wiley, 1972); Charles R. Tittle, "Inmate Organization: Sex Differentiation, and the Influence of Criminal Subcultures," *American Sociological Review* 34 (1968): 492.

2. Leo Carroll, *Hacks, Blacks, and Cons* (Lexington, Mass.: D.C. Heath, 1974); James B. Jacobs, "Stratification and Conflict among Prison Inmates," *Journal of Criminal Law and Criminology* 66 (1976): 476; Clemens Bartollas, Stuart J. Miller, and Simon Dinitz, *Juvenile Victimization: The Institutional Paradox* (New York: Wiley, 1976).

3. Ward and Kassebaum, *Women's Prison*; Giallombardo, *Society of Women*; Heffernan, *Making it in Prison*.

4. Ward and Kassebaum, *Women's Prison*, pp. 28−29.

5. Giallombardo, *Society of Women*, p. 17.
6. Giallombardo, *Social World of Imprisoned Girls*, p. 12.
7. Tittle, "Inmate Organization: Sex Differentiation and the Influence of Criminal Subcultures," p. 492.
8. Ibid., p. 503 (emphasis added).
9. See, e.g., Ward and Kassebaum, *Women's Prison*; Giallombardo, *Social World of Imprisoned Girls*.
10. See, e.g., Carroll, *Hacks, Blacks, and Cons*, p. 92. Carroll notes that "while black culture has much in common with the lower class culture of poverty, nonetheless ... there exists a set of shared perspectives and modes of action that are the products of black experience and that may be viewed as a distinctive black-American culture."
11. Data contained in Table 1-2 indicate approximately equal proportions of black inmates in all of the cottage units, with the exception of Lancaster. There was a striking difference in the proportions of black males and black females committed to the Department of Youth Services Institutions; approximately two and a half times as many black males as black females were committed. Although we lack the data to explain this discrepancy, several factors may be involved. One difference may stem from the types of offenses committed by boys and girls. Girls are much more likely to be committed for juvenile status offenses, whereas boys are more likely to be committed for property-related offenses. Commitments for status offenses are typically initiated by the parents of the child who finally conclude that the child is "stubborn," or "ungovernable." *Commonwealth* v. *Brasher*, 270 N.W.2d 389 (1971). Property-related offenses are regarded as more serious indicators of criminality, and the juvenile justice process is more likely to be set in motion without any initiative on the part of the child's family.

A hypothesis for later testing would hold that the parents of white children tend to view the juvenile process more favorably than do the parents of black children for purposes of seeking court assistance in dealing with status offenses. A related hypothesis would be that there is more tolerance for status-type deviance within the black community than within the white, and that juvenile offenses such as running away from home, sexual misconduct, and the like, may not be regarded as seriously. See, e.g., Jane R. Mercer, "Social System Perspective and Clinical Perspective: Frames of Reference for Understanding Career Patterns of Persons Labelled as Mentally Retarded," *Social Problems* 13 (1965): 21. Mercer argues in the context of mental retardation that the lower-class retarded person is more likely to be released from a hospital to live at home than is one from the middle class, because there is more distance from the cultural core values and "official definitions," and that the lower-class social system is more likely to reject the social definition. A similar cultural distinction may be involved in the context of race and status offenses.

A third hypothesis may also explain proportional differences in commitment rates of males and females by race. Certain Massachusetts juvenile court judges were reputedly reluctant to commit youngsters to institutions for status offenses. They also presided over the larger, urban juvenile courts with which a large proportion of black children had contact. Their reluctance to commit on the basis of status offenses may also partly explain the differences in proportions of black and white residents in male and female settings.

These race-by-sex hypotheses are speculative and tentative and beyond the scope of our present data. However, any one of them, if true, could partly explain the differences in proportional representation by sex and race.

NOTES TO APPENDIX

1. We established item discrimination by cross-tabulating cottages by the item or scale, and by selecting appropriate cutting points we were able to determine if an item discriminated between cottage types. We normally ran a chi-square test on this table although we were less concerned with statistical significance than we were with substantive differences. We also employed F-tests on the individual items to further establish differences between the cottages. See generally, William L. Hays, *Statistics* (New York; Holt, Rinehart & Winston, 1963), chap. 11; David J. Armour and Arthur S. Couch, *The Data-Test Primer* (New York: Free Press, 1972), chaps. 10, 12.

2. We are familiar with the methodological differences concerning this approach. See, e.g., Hanan C. Selvin, "A Critique of Tests of Significance in Survey Research," *American Sociological Review* 22 (October 1957): 519–27; David Gold, "A Comment on 'A Critique of Tests of Significance,'" *American Sociological Review* 23 (February 1958): 85–86; Denton E. Morrison and Ramon E. Henkel, *The Significance Test Controversy* (Chicago: Aldine, 1970). Selvin argues that it is improper to use significance tests "where two [or more] groups are sampled without randomization, [since] there is no statistical procedure for assessing the possible effects of the uncontrolled variables." Thus, he concluded that except for the study whose sample is large enough to control for all uncontrolled variables simultaneously, significance tests are improper for nonrandomized, nonexperimental designs. There have been numerous critical responses to Selvin's argument, the essence of which have been that significance testing for the limited purposes of establishing whether there are differences between populations on a particular item is an acceptable technique for establishing whether an association is present, even though one would have to use other measures of association to establish the strength of the association or to make causal inferrences about the nature of the association. See, e.g., Gold, "A Comment"; Robert McGinnis, "Randomization and Inference in Sociological Research," *American Sociological Review* 23 (August 1958): 408–14.

3. See, e.g., Hubert M. Blalock, *Social Statistics* (New York: McGraw-Hill, 1960), pp. 93–96, 122–28; Sidney Siegel, *Nonparametric Statistics for the Behavioral Sciences* (New York: McGraw-Hill, 1956), pp. 9–11.

4. See, e.g., James K. Skipper, Anthony L. Guenther, and Gilbert Nass, "The Sacredness of .05: A Note Concerning the Uses of Statistical Levels of Significance in Social Science," *American Sociologist* 2 (February 1967): 16–18; Sanford Labovitz, "Criteria for Selecting a Significance Level: A Note on the Sacredness of .05," *American Sociologist* 3 (August 1968): 200–22.

5. Allen Edwards, *Techniques of Attitude Scale Construction* (New York: Appleton-Century-Crofts, 1957).

6. See, e.g., Hanan C. Selvin, "A Critique of Tests of Significance in Survey Research," *American Sociological Review* 22 (1957): 519; Gold, "A Comment," p. 85; McGinnis, "Randomization and Inference in Sociological Research, p. 408; Morrison and Henkel, *The Significance Test Controversy.*

7. See generally, Hayes, *Statistics*, chap. 11; Armour and Couch, *The Data-Test Primer*, chaps. 10, 12; Blalock, *Social Statistics*; Siegel, *Nonparametric Statistics for the Behavioral Sciences.*

Bibliography

Adorno, T., E. Frenkel Brunswick, D. Levinson, and R. Sanford. 1950. The Authoritarian Personality. New York: W.W. Norton.

Aichhorn, A. 1963. Wayward Youth. New York, Viking Press.

Akers, R., N. Hayner and W. Gruninger. 1974. "Homosexual and Drug Behavior in Prison." 21 Social Problems 410.

Arnold, D., ed. 1970. The Sociology of Subculture. Berkeley: Glendessary Press.

Atchley, R. and M. McCabe. 1967. "Socialization in Correctional Communities." 33 American Sociology Review 774.

Bakal, Y., ed. 1973. Closing Correctional Institutions. Lexington, Mass.: D.C. Heath & Co.

Barker, G., and W. Adams. 1959. "Social Structure of a Correctional Institution." 49 Journal of Criminal Law, Criminology, and Police Science 417.

Bartollas, C., J. Miller, and S. Dinitz. 1976. Juvenile Victimization: The Institutional Paradox. New York: Wiley.

Baum, M. 1967. "The Institutional Career of Delinquent Boys." Unpublished Ph.D. dissertation, Harvard University.

Becker, H., and B. Geer. 1960. "Latent Culture: A Note on the Theory of Latent Social Roles." 5 Administrative Science Quarterly 305.

Berk, B. 1965. "Organizational Goals and Inmate Organizations." 71 American Journal of Sociology 522.

Blalock, H. 1960. Social Statistics. New York: McGraw-Hill.

Brown, R. 1965. Social Psychology. New York: Free Press.

Brownmiller, S. 1975. Against Our Will: Men, Women, and Rape. New York: Simon & Schuster.

Campbell, E., and C. Stanley. 1963. Experimental and Quasi-Experimental Designs for Research. Chicago: Rand McNally.

Carroll, L. 1974. Hacks, Blacks and Cons. Lexington, Mass.: D.C. Heath & Co.

Carter, B. 1973. "Reform School Families." 11 Society 36.

Cartwright, D. 1951. "Achieving Change in People: Some Applications of Group Dynamics Theory." 4 Human Relations 381.

Cicourel, A. 1968. Social Organization of Juvenile Justice. New York: Wiley.

Clark, R., and D. Martin. 1971. Absconding from Approved Schools. London: Her Majesty's Stationary Office.

Clemmer, D. 1958. The Prison Community. New York. Holt, Rinehart, and Winston.

Cline H., and S. Wheeler. 1963. "The Determinants of Normative Patterns in Correctional Institutions." 2 Scandinavian Studies in Sociology 173.

Cloward, R. 1960. "Social Control in the Prison." In Theoretical Studies in Social Organization of the Prison. New York: Social Science Research Council.

Coates, R., A. Miller, and L. Ohlin. 1975. Exploratory Analysis of Recidivism and Cohort Data on the Massachusetts Youth Correctional System. Cambridge: Harvard Law School Center for Criminal Justice.

Cohen, A. 1955. Delinquent Boys: The Culture of the Gang. New York: Free Press.

Cohen, A., G. Cole, and R. Bailey, eds., 1976. Prison Violence. Lexington, Mass.: Lexington Books.

Cressey, D. 1965. "Prison Organization." In J. March, ed., Handbook of Organizations. Chicago: Rand McNally.

_____. 1960. "Limitations on Organization of Treatment in the Modern Prison." In Theoretical Studies in Social Organization of the Prison. New York: Social Science Research Council.

_____. 1959. "Contradictory Directives in Complex Organizations." 4 Administrative Science Quarterly 5.

_____. 1958a. "Achievement of an Unstated Organizational Goal." 1 Pacific Sociological Review 43.

_____. 1958b. "The Nature and Effectiveness of Correctional Techniques." 23 Law and Contemporary Problems 754.

_____. 1955. "Changing Criminals: The Application of the Theory of Differential Association." 61 American Journal of Sociology 116.

Denzin, N. 1970a. The Research Act. Chicago: Aldine.

_____. 1970b. Sociological Methods. Chicago: Aldine.

Deutsch, M., and M. Collins. 1965. "The Effect of Public Policy in Housing Projects upon Interracial Attitudes." In H. Proshansky and B. Seidenberg, eds., Basic Studies in Social Psychology. New York: Holt, Rinehart & Winston.

Downs, A. 1967. Inside Bureaucracy. Boston: Little, Brown.

Edwards, A. 1957. Techniques of Attitude Scale Construction. New York: Appleton, Century, Crofts.

Empey, L., and M. Erickson. 1966. "Hidden Delinquency and Social Status." 44 Social Forces 45.

Empey, L., and S. Lubeck. 1972. The Silverlake Experiment. Chicago: Aldine.

Empey, L., and J. Rabow. 1961. "The Provo Experiment in Delinquency Rehabilitation." 26 American Sociological Review 679.

Etzioni, A. 1961. A Comparative Analysis of Complex Organizations. New York: Free Press.

Feld, B. 1972. Subcultures of Selected Boys' Cottages in Massachusetts Department Youth Services Institutions in 1971. Harvard Law School, Center for Criminal Justice.

Ferracuti, F., and G. Newman. 1974. "Assaultive Offenses." In D. Glasser, ed., Handbook of Criminology. Chicago: Rand McNally.

Foster, T. 1975. "Make Believe Families: A Response of Women and Girls to the Deprivations of Imprisonment." 3 International Journal of Criminology and Penology 71.

Fox, S. 1970. "Juvenile Justice Reform: An Historical Perspective." 22 Stanford Law Review 1187.

Gabennesch, H. 1972. "Authoritarianism as World-View." 77 American Journal of Sociology 857.

Galtung, J. 1958. "The Social Functions of a Prison." 6 Social Problems 140.

Garabedian, P. 1963. "Social Roles and Processes of Socialization in the Prison Community." 11 Social Problems 139.

Giallombardo, R. 1974. The Social World of Imprisoned Girls. New York: Wiley.

_____. 1966. Society of Women. New York: Wiley.

Gibbons, D. 1965. Changing the Law Breaker: The Treatment of Delinquents and Criminals. Englewood Cliffs, N.J.: Prentice-Hall.

Gilbert, D., and D. Levinson. 1957. " 'Custodialism' and 'Humanism' in Mental Hospital Structure and Staff Ideology." In M. Greenblatt, et al., eds., The Patient and the Mental Hospital. Glencoe: Free Press.

Glaser, D. 1964. The Effectiveness of a Prison and Parole System. Indianapolis: Bobbs-Merrill.

Goffman, E. 1961. "On the Characteristics of a Total Institution." In Asylums. New York: Anchor Books.

Gold, M. 1966. "Undetected Delinquent Behavior." 3 Journal of Research in Crime and Delinquency 27.

Gold, R. 1958. "Roles in Sociological Field Observation." 36 Social Forces 219.

Greenblatt, M., D. Levinson, and R. Williams. 1957. The Patient and the Mental Hospital. Glencoe: Free Press.

Grosser, G. 1960. "External Settings and Internal Relations of the Prison." In Theoretical Studies in the Organization of the Prison. New York: Social Sciences Research Council.

_____. 1958. "The Role of Informal Inmate Groups in Change of Values." 5 Children 25.

Grusky, O. 1959a. "Organizational Goals and Behavior of Informal Leaders." 65 American Journal of Sociology.

_____. 1959b. "Role Conflict in Organization: A Study of Prison Camp Officials." 3 Administrative Science Quarterly 453.

Hall, J., M. Williams, and L. Tomaino. 1966. "The Challenge of Correctional Change: The Interface of Conformity and Commitment." 57 Journal of Criminal Law, Criminology, and Police Science 493.

Halleck, S. 1967. Psychiatry and the Dilemmas of Crime: A Study of Causes, Punishment and Treatment. New York: Harper & Row.

Hasenfeld, Y. 1972. "People Processing Organizations: An Exchange Approach." 37 American Sociological Review 256.

Hayner, N., and E. Ash. 1939. "The Prison Community as a Social Group." 4 American Sociological Review 362.

Heffernan, E. 1972. Making It in Prison: The Square, The Cool, and The Life. New York: Wiley.

Homans, G. 1950. The Human Group. New York: Harcourt, Brace & World.

Irwin, J., and D. Cressey. 1962. "Thieves, Convicts, and the Inmate Culture." 10 Social Problems 142.

Jacobs, J. 1976. "Stratification and Conflict among Prison Inmates." 66 Journal of Criminal Law and Criminology 476.

Jones, M. 1968a. Beyond the Therapeutic Community: Social Learning and Social Psychiatry. New Haven: Yale University Press.

———. 1968b. Social Psychiatry in Practice: The Idea of the Therapeutic Community. Baltimore: Penguin Books.

———. 1952. Social Psychiatry: A Study of Therapeutic Communities. London: Tavistock.

Kassebaum, G., D. Ward, and D. Wilner. 1971. Prison Treatment and Parole Survival. New York: Wiley.

Katz, D., and R. Kahn. 1966. The Social Psychiatry of Organizations. New York: Wiley.

Knight, D. 1971. The Impact of Living Unit Size In Youth Training Schools. Sacramento: California Youth Training Authority.

Lipton, D., R. Martinson, and J. Wilks. 1975. The Effectiveness of Correctional Treatment: A Survey of Treatment Evaluation Studies. New York: Praeger.

Lubove, R. 1971. The Professional Altruist: The Emergence of Social Work as A Career 1880–1930. New York: Atheneum.

Martinson, R. 1974. "What Works? Questions and Answers about the Rehabilitation of Prisoners." 35 Public Interest 22.

Matza, D. 1964. Delinquency and Drift. New York: Wiley.

McCleery, R. 1961. "The Governmental Process and Informal Social Control." In D. Cressey, ed., The Prison. New York: Holt, Rinehart & Winston.

———. 1960. "Communication Patterns as Bases of Systems of Authority and Power." In Theoretical Studies in Social Organization of the Prison. New York: Social Science Research Council.

McCloskey, H. 1958. "Conservatism and Personality." 52 American Political Science Review 27.

McCorkle, L., A. Elias, and F. Bixby. 1958. The Highfields Story. New York: Holt, Rinehart & Winston.

Mercer, J. 1965. "Social System Perspective and Clinical Perspective: Frames of Reference for Understanding Career Patterns of People Labelled Mentally Retarded." 13 Social Problems 21.

Messinger, S. 1970. "Issues in the Study of the Social System of Prison Inmates." 4 Issues in Criminology 133.

Miller, W. 1958. "The Lower Class Culture as a Generating Milieu of Gang Delinquency." 14 Social Issues 5.

Morris, N. 1974. The Future of Imprisonment. Chicago: University of Chicago Press.

Nye, I., J. Short, Jr., and V. Olson. 1958. "Socioeconomic Status and Delinquent Behavior." 63 American Review of Sociology 381.

Ohlin, L. 1974. "Organizational Reform in Correctional Agencies." In D. Glaser, ed., Handbook on Criminology. Chicago: Rand McNally.

____. 1960a. "Conflicting Interests in Correctional Objectives." In Theoretical Studies in Social Organization of the Prison. New York: Social Sciences Research Council, Pamphlet #15.

____. 1960b. Delinquency and Opportunity: A Theory of Delinquent Gangs. New York: Free Press.

____. 1956. Sociology and the Field of Corrections. New York: Russell Sage Foundation.

____, R. Coates, and A. Miller. 1974. "Radical Correctional Reform: A Case Study of the Massachusetts Youth Correctional System." 44 Harvard Educational Review 74.

____, and W. Lawrence. 1959. "Social Interaction among Clients as a Treatment Problem." 4 Social Work 3.

O'Leary, V. 1971. "Correctional Policy: A Classification of Goals Designed for Change." 17 Crime and Delinquency 373.

Perrow, C. 1966. "Reality Adjustment: A Young Institution Settles for Humane Care." 13 Social Problems 69.

____. 1964. "Hospitals: Technology, Structure, and Goals." in J. March, ed., Handbook of Organization. Chicago: Rand McNally.

____. 1961. "The Analysis of Goals in Complex Organizations." 26 American Sociological Review 855.

Pickett, R. 1969. The New York House of Refuge: Origins of Juvenile Reform in New York State, 1815–1857. Syracuse, N.Y.: Syracuse University Press.

Pilliavin, I., and S. Briar. 1964. "Police Encounters With Juveniles." 70 American Journal of Sociology 206.

Platt, A. 1969. The Childsavers. Chicago: University of Chicago Press.

Polsky, H. 1962. Cottage Six. New York: Wiley.

____. 1959. "Changing Delinquent Subcultures: A Social Psychological Approach." 3 Social Work 15.

Powelson, H., and R. Bendix. 1951. "Psychiatry in Prison." 14 Psychiatry 72.

Powers, E. 1968. The Basic Structure of the Administration of Criminal Justice in Massachusetts. Boston: Massachusetts Correctional Association.

Price, J. 1968. Organizational Effectiveness. Homewood, Ill.: Richard D. Irwin.

Radzinowicz, L. 1966. Ideology and Crime. New York: Columbia University Press.

Reckless, W. 1961. "A New Theory of Delinquency and Crime." 25 Federal Probation 42.

____. S. Dinitz, and E. Murray. 1956. "Self-Concept as an Insulator against Delinquency." 21 American Sociological Review 745.

Robinson, J., and G. Smith. 1971. "The Effectiveness of Correctional Programs." 17 Crime and Delinquency 67.

Roebuck, J. 1963. "A Critique of 'Thieves, Convicts, and the Inmate Subculture.'" 11 Social Problems 193.

Rolde, E., J. Mack, D. Scherl, and L. Macht. 1970. "The Maximum Security Institution as a Treatment Facility for Juveniles." In J. Teele, ed., Juvenile Delinquency. Itasca, Ill.: Peacock Publishing Co.

Rose, A. 1965. Sociology: The Study of Human Relations. 2nd ed. New York: Alfred A. Knopf.

_____, and G. Weber. 1961. "Changes in Attitude among Delinquent Boys Committed to Open and Closed Institutions." 52 Journal of Criminal Law, Criminology and Police Science 166.

Rothman, D. 1971. The Discovery of the Asylum. Boston: Little, Brown.

Rutherford, A. 1974. The Dissolution of the Training Schools in Massachusetts. Columbus, Ohio: Academy for Contemporary Problems.

Schrag, C. 1960. "Some Foundations for a Theory of Corrections." In D. Cressey, ed., The Prison. New York: Holt, Rinehart, & Winston.

_____. 1954. "Leadership among Prison Inmates." 19 American Sociological Review 37.

Schur, E. 1973. Radical Non-Intervention. Englewood Cliffs, N.J.: Prentice-Hall.

_____. 1972. Labeling Deviant Behavior. New York: Harper & Row.

Schwartz, B. 1971. "Pre-Institutional vs. Situational Influence in a Correctional Community." 62 Journal of Criminal Law, Criminology and Police Science 532.

Schwartz, M. 1957. "What is a Therapeutic Milieu?" In M. Greenblatt et al. eds., The Patient and the Mental Hospital. Glencoe, Ill.: Free Press.

Scott, W.R. 1964. "Theory of Organizations." In R.E.L. Faris, ed., Handbook of Modern Sociology. Chicago: Rand McNally.

Selznick, P. 1957. Leadership in Administration. Evanston, Ill.: Row, Peterson.

_____. 1949a. T.V.A. and the Grassroots. Berkeley: University of California Press.

_____. 1949b. "Foundations of the Theory of Organizations." 13 American Sociological Review 32.

Short, J., and F. Nye. 1958. "Extent of Unrecorded Delinquency: Tenative Conclusions." 49 Journal of Criminal Law, Criminology and Police Science 296.

_____, and F. Strodtbeck. 1965. Group Process and Gang Delinquency. Chicago: University of Chicago Press.

Siegel, S. 1956. Nonparametric Statistics for the Behavioral Sciences. New York: McGraw-Hill.

Simon, H. 1957. Administrative Behavior. New York: Free Press.

Strauss, A., L. Schatzman, R. Bucher, D. Erlich, and M. Sashbin. 1964. Psychiatric Ideologies and Institutions. Glencoe, Ill.: Free Press.

Street, D. 1965. "The Inmate Group in Custodial and Treatment Settings." 30 American Sociological Review 44.

_____, R. Vinter, and C. Perrow. 1966. Organization for Treatment. New York: Free Press.

Studt, E., S. Messinger, and T. Wilson. 1968. C-Unit: Search for Community in Prison. New York: Russell Sage Foundation.

Sykes, G. 1958. Society of Captives. Princeton, N.J.: Princeton University Press.

———. 1956. "The Corruption of Authority and Rehabilitation." 34 Social Forces 257.

———, and D. Matza. 1957. "Techniques of Neutralization: A Theory of 'Delinquency.'" 22 American Journal of Sociology 664.

———, and S. Messinger. 1960. "The Inmate Social System." In Theoretical Studies in Social Organization of the Prison. New York: Social Science Research Council.

Tangri, S., and M. Schwartz. 1967. "Delinquency Research and the Self-Concept Variable." 58 Journal of Criminal Law, Criminology and Police Science 182.

Thatcher, F. 1973. "Effecting Changes in a Training School for Girls." In Y. Bakal, ed., Closing Correctional Institutions. Lexington, Mass.: D.C. Heath & Co.

Thompson, J., and W. McEwen. 1958. "Organization Goals and Environment." 23 American Sociological Review 23.

Thompson, V. 1969. Bureaucracy and Innovation. University of Alabama Press.

Tittle, C. 1974. "Prisons and Rehabilitation." 21 Social Problems 385.

———. 1968. "Inmate Organization: Sex Differentiation and The Influence of Criminal Subcultures." 34 American Sociological Review 492.

Vinter, R., and M. Janowitz. 1959. "Effective Institutions for Juvenile Delinquents: A Research Statement." 33 Social Service Review 118.

Ward, D., and G. Kassenbaum. 1965. Women's Prison: Sex and Social Structure. Chicago: Aldine.

Weber, G. 1961. "Emotional and Defensive Reactions of Cottage Parents." In D. Cressey, ed., The Prison. New York: Holt, Rinehart & Winston.

Weinberg, S. 1941. "Aspects of the Prison's Social Structure." 47 American Journal of Sociology 717.

Wheeler, S. 1969. "Socialization in Correctional Institutions." In D. Goslin, ed., Handbook of Socialization Theory and Research. New York: Rand McNally.

———. 1966. "The Structure of Formally Organized Socialization Settings." In O. Brim and S. Wheeler, ed., Socialization after Childhood. New York: Wiley.

———. 1961. "Socialization in Correctional Communities." 26 American Sociological Review 706.

———, L. Cottrell, and A. Romasco. 1967. "Juvenile Delinquency: Its Prevention and Control." In Task Force Report: Juvenile and Youth Crime. Washington, D.C.: Government Printing Office.

Wilkins, L. 1969. Evaluations of Penal Measures. New York: Random House.

Williams, J., and M. Gold. 1972. "From Delinquent Behavior to Official Delinquency." 20 Social Problems 209.

Wilson, J. 1975. Thinking About Crime. New York: Basic Books.

———. 1974. "Crime and the Criminologist." 58 Commentary 47.

Wilson, T. 1968. "Patterns of Management and Adaptation to Organizational Roles: A Study of Prison Inmates." 74 American Journal of Sociology 717.

Zald, M. 1963. "Comparative Analysis and Measurement of Organizational Goals." 4 Sociological Quarterly 212.

Zald, M. 1962a. "Organizational Control Structures in Five Correctional Institutions." 68 American Journal of Sociology 335.

_____ 1962b. "Power Balance and Staff Conflict in Organizational Goals." 6 Administrative Science Quarterly 22.

_____. 1960a. "The Correctional Institution for Juvenile Offenders: An Analysis of Organizational 'Character,' " 8 Social Problems 61.

_____. 1960b. "Multiple Goals and Staff Structure." Unpublished Ph.D. dissertation, University of Michigan.

Index

academic programs, 7, 13, 69, 79, 81, 82, 85; instructors, 65-66; and reforms 58, 76, 77
age: inmates, 19, 23-24, 180, 208; staff, 34, 66, 110-111
aggression: *see* fighting; ranking; violence
Alderson (W.Va.) Federal Reformatory for Women, 172
authoritarianism, 43

blacks, 24, 171-172, 180-187; commitment rates, 225; females, 24, 180, 208; leaders, 150, 182, 183, 185; proportion of inmates, 180; and roles, 147; self-segregation, 181, 183-184; and staff, 181-182, 183-184; verbal skills, 181-182
bogarting, 132
boredom, 62, 104, 106, 126; and work programs, 33, 68
Bridgewater Institute for Juvenile Guidance, 6-7
Brownmiller, Susan, 224
bush boys, 147, 158

Calhoun, John, xiii
Campbell, Donald T., 18-19, 215
Center for Criminal Justice, Harvard Law School, xi, xii
Children's Bureau (HEW), 6
cigarettes, 7, 65, 72, 73-74, 77, 79, 84, 105
civil rights for children, xii

Clara Barton cottage, 17, 64; *see also* Lancaster Industrial School for Girls
clothing, 7, 65, 73, 77, 79, 84, 105
Cloward, Richard A., xvi
Coates, Robert, xvi
coeducational facilities, 32, 174, 177-178
collaboration of inmates and staff, 59, 73, 87, 128, 167-168, 169, 204-205
con-men, 146-147, 156-157, 162
contraband, 63-64, 72
corporal punishment, 7, 72; *see also* physical coercion
Cottage 8, 8, 12; assignment to, 32; control, 71; individualization, 54, 55; leaders, 151; staff, 65-66, 108, 110, 111, 164
Cottage 9, 9, 12; adaptation of inmates, 119-120, 126-127; assignment to, 32, 215; control, 54, 55, 59-64, 88-89; inmate relations, 116, 123-124; leaders, 150, 151; material deprivation, 101; parole, 124; population, 36; roles, 160; staff, 47-48, 50, 51, 53-54, 111, 164; violence, 133-134, 202
cottages: assignment to, 30-33, 66; control in, 59-88; ideologies and goals, 42-58; meetings, 16, 67, 76, 85-86, 106, 186; reforms in structure, 7-8, 9-10, 12-14, 15-16; security, 60-61; *see also* custody-oriented cottages; treatment-oriented cottages

237

238 Index

counseling, xii, 55, 69-70, 76; family, 82
counselors, 16, 66, 69; trustworthiness, 113
court appearance, 19, 24-26, 180
Cressey, Donald R., xv, 93-94
custody-oriented cottages: adjustment, 102, 104-105, 106, 114-121; assignment of inmates, 32, 126-128; blacks, 182-185, 210; control, 59-75; criminal justice system, perceptions of, 189-191; and decentralization, 58; goals, 51-52, 96-98, 101-102; homosexuality, 160; informing, 139-141, 142, 165; inmate backgrounds, 24-26; inmate relations, 114; leaders, 148, 150-152, 223; offenses, 217; population, 36; recidivism, 30, 196-197; resistance to authority, 143-144; roles, 157, 160; self-perception, 191-193; staff, 33-36, 46-47, 48-49, 55, 106-107, 110-111, 113-114, 123-124, 136-137, 164; violence, 95, 132-134, 136-137

decentralization of juvenile institutions, 8, 10-11, 13, 15-16; and control, 73; and ideologies, 43, 57-58
Delinquency and Opportunity, xvi
Designing Correctional Organizations for Youths, xvi
dime-dropping: *see* informing
discipline, 59, 60, 72; and parole, 71; selective, 72-73; transfers, 72, 87
Diversity in a Youth Correctional System, xvii-xviii
drugs, 17, 217

escape: *see* runaways
Etzioni, Amitai, 59
extortion, 151

family, 48-49, 82, 104
Feld, Barry, xvi
female inmates, 171-179; adaptation, 128; black, 24, 180, 208; commitment rates, 225-226; counseling, 70; court contacts, 26; discipline, 16, 73-75; homosexuality, 163, 173, 176, 179; relations among inmates, 114, 124; roles, 162, 214; and staff, 47, 166-167; violence, 134; *see also* Lancaster Industrial School for Girls

fighting, 63, 86, 132-135
furloughs, 71, 83, 154, 163

Giallombardo, Rose, 172-173
Gold, Raymond L., 21-22
Guided Group Interaction, 83

homosexuality, 4, 50, 150, 159-160, 161, 224; female, 163, 173, 176, 179
humane care model, 80

"I Belong" cottage, 11, 12; age of inmates, 24; assignment to, 30, 215; control strategies, 54, 55, 83-86; leaders, 158; population, 36; and reforms, 58; staff, 54, 84-85
ideologies, 42-58, 200-201, 218-219; and subcultures, 92-93
importation model of subcultures, 2, 92, 171, 177, 180-181
indigenous origins model, 2, 92-93
individualization of treatment, 54-55, 77, 89; and inmate culture, 145, 146
industrial training school model, 40
informing, 176-177, 178; and violence, 132, 135, 136, 138, 142-143, 165
inmates: adjustment, 102-107, 116-123; age, 19, 23-24, 180, 208; and aggression, 63, 131-138; assignment to cottages, 30-33, 215; backgrounds, 33-34, 171-172, 207-212; codes, 2, 3, 5, 135, 198-199; control of, 49, 54-55, 59-68, 71, 73-75, 95, 174-175; cooperation, 107; court appearances, 24-26, 180; and criminal system, 189-191; freedoms, 67, 77; groups, 50-51, 123-124, 183-184; hierarchies, 142, 143, 147; and other inmates, 49-50, 114-116, 175-176, 178, 182, 204-205; isolation, 50, 116, 123, 126; literacy, 20-21; norms, 2, 143-146, 150; obedience, 43, 117-118; offenses, 26, 180, 216-217, 225-226; orientation, 67, 76, 79, 81; outside contacts, 62; possessions, 105, 150-151, 184, 199; and purposes of cottages, 95-102; and race, 19, 24, 180-187, 209-210; recidivism, 26-27, 193-197; and reforms, 8; and regulations, 104, 106; role differentiation, 146-163; self-perception, 191-193; socialization, 2; and staff, 4, 8, 59,

Index 239

88-91, 107-114, 124, 126, 128, 138, 166, 167-168, 178, 200, 202; subcultures, 2-3, 91-129; and violence, 3, 94-95, 131-138, 199
isolation units, 59, 60-61, 62, 63

Job Corps, 82
John Augustus Hall (Oakdale, Mass.), 214

Kasselbaum, Gene, 172
Klein, Arlette, xvi

Lancaster (Mass.) Industrial School for Girls, 14-17, 214; academic programs, 70; adjustment, 104, 105, 106, 128; age of inmates, 24; control, 54, 55, 73-75, 174-175; counseling, 70; facilities, 65, 152; goals, 52-53, 96, 101; informing, 142-143; 176-177; leaders, 148, 166-167; parole, 120; roles, 162-163; solidarity, 176; staff, 34, 46, 47, 48, 50, 66, 89, 108, 110, 113, 166, 174; violence, 134, 176-177; vocational training, 68-69
leaders, 146, 148-150, 169; black,150, 182, 183, 185; and con-men, 156; and discipline, 73, 151, 153; female, 162; and other leaders, 154-155; and staff, 70, 73, 150, 151, 153, 166; and violence, 134; *see also* collaboration of inmates and staff
Leavey, Joseph, xiii
Lyman School (Westboro, Mass.), 11, 12-14, 32; assignment to, 66; control, 68, 79, 81
Lyman, Theodore, 12

McEwen, Craig, xvi
Management Engineering Task Force, 6
Massachusetts: Attorney General's Advisory Committee on Juvenile Crime, 6; criminal record system, 194; Department of Youth Services, xi, 6, 17-18, 42, 80; Youth Service Board, 5
maximum security model, 40, 91-92, 93
Miller, Alden, xvi
Miller, Jerome G., xii; and physical coercion, 62-63; reform plans, 6-9, 10, 13, 15, 43, 214; and vocational program, 67-68
Mobilization for Youth, xvi

Neighborhood Youth Corps, 82

Ohlin, Lloyd E., 39-40
organizational factors: and adjustment, 102-107, 116-123; and cooperation, 107; and inmate relations, 114-116; models, 39-42; and perception of treatment, 95-102; and staff, 107-114; and subculture, 94-95, 163-164; and violence, 1-2, 4, 95, 164-165, 199

Pappenfort, Donnel M., xv
parole, 120-121; and discipline, 71, 74; and informing, 142; and privilege system, 77
participant-as-observer strategy, 21-22
Perrow, Charles, 39
physical coercion, 59, 62-63, 64, 89; and girls, 74, 174-175
Piven, Herman, xv
Polsky, Howard, 137, 146, 158
privilege system, 59, 69-72, 73-74, 86, 174; step system, 70-71, 77-78; and violence, 95
punks, 147, 159-162; and blacks, 185
Putnam cottage, 17, 64; *see also* Lancaster Industrial School for Girls

race, 19, 24, 180-187, 209-210
ranking, 3, 62, 137-138, 155, 160, 161, 162-163
recidivism, 26-27, 193-197; rates, xii
recreation, 61-62, 80, 105
Reforming Juvenile Corrections: The Massachusetts Experience, xvii
riots, 72, 150
runaways, 13-14, 215-216, 217-218; discipline, 32, 61, 71-72, 74

STEP: *see* Student Tutor Education Program
Sargent, Francis, xii
scapegoats: *see* punks
self-isolation, 50, 116, 123, 157
Shirley cottage, 11, 13, 14; assignment, 32; control, 54, 55, 80-83, 86, 87; leaders, 155; reforms, 58; staff, 54, 80, 81
Shirley (Mass.) Industrial School for Boys, 9-12, 13; assignment, 66
solidarity, 92, 93-94, 123-125; females, 176
sounding, 223
Spanish-surnamed inmates, 216

staff: age, 34, 66, 110-111; assaults on, 72; and assignment of inmates, 30-32; attitudes toward deviance, 46-48; and blacks, 181-182, 183-184; control methods, 49, 54-55, 59-88, 164; favoritism, 110; ideology and goals, 42-58, 96-102, 138-139, 201-202; and informing, 135; and inmate groups, 50-51, 123-124; and inmate ratios, 36, 88; and inmates, 4, 8, 59, 88-91, 107-114, 124, 126, 128, 138, 166, 167-168, 178, 200, 202; and leaders, 70, 73, 150, 151, 153, 166; and psychological techniques, 46; recruitment, 10, 34-36, 43, 201; resistance to reforms, 7, 10-11, 13-14, 43-46; and security, 61; shortages, 10, 55, 78, 79-80; and therapy, 11, 17-18, 84; trustworthiness, 108-109, 113; unions, 10, 11-12; and violence, 72, 135-137, 168-169, 200, 202
Stanley, Julian C., 18-19, 215
static-group comparison, 18-19
Stoltz, Barbara, xvi
straight kids, 147, 157-158
Street, David, 39, 92-93
strong arming, 132, 185
Student Tutor Education Program (STEP), 10, 12
Studt, Elliot, 39, 40
subculture: and organizational structure, 94-129, 163-164; and social structure, 131-169; theories, 91-95; and violence, 3, 4-5, 95, 105-106, 131-138, 164-165, 168, 199, 205
Sunset Cottage, 14; assignment to, 33, 66; control, 54, 55, 78-80, 86; material deprivation, 105; staff, 78-79

A Theory of Social Reform, xv, xvii
therapy, xii, 14, 55, 79; and control, 177-178; group, 76-77, 81-82, 129, 203; staff, 79-80; training, 11, 14, 17-18
third-person responsibility, 87-88
Tittle, Charles, 173
Topsfield (Mass.) Regional Training Center, 17-18; assignment to, 30; control, 55, 75-78; individualization, 54; informing, 178; leaders, 179; reforms, 58; staff, 54, 76, 111, 129; violence, 179
treatment-oriented cottages: adjustment, 102-103, 104, 105, 122-123; blacks, 185-186; control, 75-88, 203; and criminal system, 190-191; goals, 51, 52, 53, 96-98, 101; homosexuality, 161; informing, 135-136, 139, 141, 168; inmate relations, 114, 124; leaders, 148, 152-154; offenses, 217; population, 36; and race, 185-186; recidivism, 30, 196-197; roles, 157-158, 160-162; self-perception, 193; staff, 34, 36, 46, 47, 48-49, 53, 55, 80, 81, 83, 96-97, 106, 111, 113, 134-136, 146, 167-168; violence, 95, 134-136, 179

verbal aggression, 3, 137; *see also* ranking
Vintner, Robert, 39
violence, 198; and blacks, 185; and informing, 132, 135, 136; and material deprivation, 3-4; models, 2; and organizational factors, 1-2, 4-5, 94-95, 164-165, 199; and sexuality, 4, 159-160, 224; and staff, 72, 135-137, 168-169; and subcultures, 3, 4-5, 95, 105-106, 131-138, 164-165, 168, 199, 205
visiting privileges, 62, 71
vocational programs, 7, 67-68, 76, 78, 174; instructors, 54, 55, 65-66, 108-109; and parole, 120-122; and reforms, 9-10, 11, 12, 58

Ward, David, 172
Westview cottage, 14, 65, 176; assignment to, 32-33, 66; and blacks, 181; control, 71; counseling, 69-70; individualization, 54, 55; leaders, 151, 152, 166; material deprivation, 105; parole, 120; staff, 54, 108, 110, 128; violence, 165; work programs, 68
Wisconsin prison reform, xv, xvii
work experience, 32-33, 55, 68, 76, 82; and boredom, 68

About the Author

Barry C. Feld is Professor of Law at the University of Minnesota. He received his J.D. degree from the University of Minnesota and his Ph.D. in Sociology from Harvard University. His teaching and research interests are in criminal policy and criminal justice and juvenile justice administration. His previous publications include *Rights of Minors* (with Robert Levy), a volume in the Institute of Judicial Administration—American Bar Association—Juvenile Justice Standards Project.